The Size of Chesterton's Catholicism

The Size of Chesterton's Catholicism

DAVID W. FAGERBERG

University of Notre Dame Press

NOTRE DAME AND LONDON

Library of Congress Cataloging-in-Publication Data

Fagerberg, David W., 1952–
    The size of Chesterton's Catholicism / David W. Fagerberg.
      p. cm.
    Includes bibliographical references and index.
    ISBN 0-268-01764-6 (cloth : alk. paper). — ISBN 0-268-01765-4
(pbk. : alk. paper)
    1. Chesterton, G. K. (Gilbert Keith), 1874–1936—Contributions in
apologetic for the Catholic Church.   2. Catholic Church—Apologetic
works—History and criticism.   I. Title.
BX1752.F27   1998
230'.2'092—dc21   98-4938

∞ *The paper used in this publication meets the minimum requirements of the*
American National Standard for Information Sciences—Permanence of
Paper for Printed Library Materials, ANSI Z39.48-1984.

To Søren & Kaj

With thanks for being such help to your mother while I was
away writing this, and because as you grow up you will find
Uncle Gilbert a good man to know.

Contents

ONE

The Amplitude of Mr. Chesterton

In the tradition of Catholic apologetics, no one was as concurrently friendly and fervent as Mr. Gilbert Keith Chesterton. He countered his ideological opponents with tenacity, zeal, eagerness, enjoyment, conviction, an incisive wit, and a complete lack of personal animosity. As though his great physical girth was a materialized image of the amplitude of his intellect and heart, Chesterton accommodated both unshakable conviction and good humor, presenting his arguments categorically but without rancor. He combined the quality of serious debate about an argument with a good-natured attitude toward the debater, believing that "the principal objection to a quarrel is that it interrupts an argument."[1] The result of this rare coalescence is that Chesterton persuades by effusion, not traducement, and his apology for the Catholic Church and its faith feels like a romp, not a panicky bulwarking. By consequence, Chesterton presents a Catholicism of greater size and robustness than do depictions of the narrow and tremulous kind. He is apologetic, but not in the sense of being defensive or rueful. "As an apologist I am the reverse of apologetic," he writes, and "so far as a man may be proud of a religion rooted in humility, I am very proud of my religion."[2]

This study of Chesterton as Catholic apologist proposes to gather passages from his works and weave them around a series of issues which reveal the capaciousness of Catholic paradox which he was so fond of exploring and which he articulated with such esprit. Chesterton has a rhetorical style which makes him easily quotable, and I hope to exploit this for the reader's benefit. I would like the reader to encounter Chesterton's thought as directly as possible. Of course, one must be careful that excising a passage does not contort it, but what I have discovered is that certain illustrations are used reiteratively by Chesterton, and each use reveals a slightly different facet of the paradox he is delineating. Therefore, in contrast to a historical study where chronology and objective event would serve as the framework for conveying Chesterton's personality and elucidating his thought, I have organized this material around a framework of themes, seven in number, gathering up repeated illustrations and arguments from across his apolo-getical works as one would gather up glazed tiles with the intent of fashion-ing a mosaic. When these illustrations are constelled, I hope the mosaic recreates in sum the effect each particular paradox was intended to create. Chesterton's good friend Hilaire Belloc described the intended impact of these paradoxical parallelisms this way: "Now parallelism is a gift or method of vast effect in the conveyance of truth. . . . Whenever Chesterton begins a sentence with, 'It is as though' (in exploding a false bit of reason-ing), you may expect a stroke of parallelism as vivid as a lightning flash."[3]

Chesterton eludes easy classification, for while he does wish to con-serve truth, he states clearly that doctrine develops. He provides an overall impression of the Catholic Church as a living institution which has con-founded the premature obituaries written by its critics half a dozen times in history. The obedience to authority which he endorses is the opposite of obsequiousness. The Catholicism for which Chesterton makes apology embraces the world, the common person, ritual life, and pagan antiquity, giving the imagination ample material for its work, and he finds doctrine to structure thought, not stifle it. "To become a Catholic is not to leave off thinking, but to learn how to think. It is so in exactly the same sense in which to recover from palsy is not to leave off moving but to learn how to move."[4] Though Chesterton is sometimes interpreted as strait and narrow, I have found him straight and broad.

It is a mistake to take either his dogmatic confidence or his enthusiastic humanism in isolation from the other. This has sometimes been done, both in his lifetime and since, on the one hand by crabbed critics who failed to appreciate Chesterton's taste for the delicious pun, and on the other hand by purblind secularists who enjoyed his paradoxes and puns but could not believe he meant them to be taken seriously. The former were puzzled by his habit of taking every opportunity for paradox which presented itself—no, that he went out of his way to create such opportunities. One critic wrote, "Paradox ought to be used like onions to season the salad. Mr. Chesterton's salad is all onions. Paradox has been defined as 'truth standing on her head to attract attention.' Mr. Chesterton makes truth cut her throat to attract attention."[5] The latter type of person Chesterton recalls encountering at one particular dinner early in his career.

> I had just had a very pugnacious public argument with Mr. Blatchford, which, as I was then a comparatively young though relatively rising jour-nalist, was naturally a landmark in my life. But I remember that there was, sitting next to me at this dinner, one of those very refined and rather academic gentlemen from Cambridge. . . . [H]e said suddenly, with abrupt civility, "Excuse my asking, Mr. Chesterton, of course I shall quite understand if you prefer not to answer, and I shan't think any the worse of it, you know, even if it's true. But I suppose I'm right in thinking you don't really believe in those things you're defending against Blatchford?" I informed him with adamantine gravity that I did most definitely believe in those things I was defending against Blatchford. His cold and refined face did not move a visible muscle; and yet I knew in some fashion it had completely altered. "Oh, you do," he said, "I beg your pardon. Thank you. That's all I wanted to know." And he went on eating his (probably vegetarian) meal. But I was sure that for the rest of the evening, despite his calm, he felt as if he were sitting next to a fabulous griffin.[6]

A griffin's physical bicorporality may be just the image required to appre-ciate Chesterton's cognitive bipolarity when he begins applying paradox to a thought. To appreciate his fusion of incisiveness with mirth, the reader should know that these were personal, practical issues for him, not abstract, theoretical ones.

Chesterton was born in 1874 in Sheffield Terrace, Campden Hill, below the great tower of the Waterworks. Whereas he was accused of later adopting a religion which some say depends upon the credulousness of its subjects, and whereas his entrance into Catholic Christianity meandered through a resistant path of agnosticism, in the last book he wrote, *The Auto-biography of G. K. Chesterton* (in the year of his death, 1936) he makes light of both his supposed gullibility and the hydraulic feature in that place.

> Bowing down in blind credulity, as is my custom, before mere authority and the tradition of the elders, superstitiously swallowing a story I could not test at the time by experiment or private judgment, I am firmly of opin-

ion that I was born on the 29th of May, 1874, on Campden Hill, Kensington; and baptised according to the formularies of the Church of England
in the little church of St. George opposite the large Waterworks Tower
that dominated that ridge. I do not allege any significance to the relation of
the two buildings; and I indignantly deny that the church was chosen because it needed the whole water-power of West London to turn me into a
Christian.[7]

Gilbert's father, Edward Chesterton, and his mother, Marie Grosjean, belonged to the English middle-class, which Chesterton describes as still possessing the peculiarity of being really a class and really in the middle. He had
one brother, Cecil, five years younger, whose birth he welcomed with the
remark, "Now I shall always have an audience."[8] Chesterton describes his
childhood as a time of wonder, made all the more wonderful by his father
whose "versatility both as an experimentalist and a handy man . . . was
amazing. His den or study was piled high with the stratified layers of about
ten or twelve creative amusements; water-colour painting and modelling
and photography and stained glass and fretwork and magic lanterns and
medieval illumination. . . . He never dreamed of turning all of these plastic talents to any mercenary account, or of using them for anything but his
own private pleasure and ours."[9] And thus Gilbert must apologize to those
future psychological biographers who might wish to explain him by raking
the ashes of childhood.

> I am sorry if the landscape or the people appear disappointingly respectable
> and even reasonable, and deficient in all those unpleasant qualities that
> make a biography really popular. I regret that I have no gloomy and savage
> father to offer to the public gaze as the true cause of all my tragic heritage;
> no pale-faced and partially poisoned mother whose suicidal instincts have
> cursed me with the temptations of the artistic temperament. I regret that
> there was nothing in the range of our family much more racy than a remote
> and mildly impecunious uncle; and that I cannot do my duty as a true
> modern, by cursing everybody who made me whatever I am.[10]

Though having been baptized according to the formularies of the Anglican Church, Chesterton does not describe the religious presence in his

household as memorable. The day was awash in a liberal optimism which accompanied a myth of progressive evolution, promising to turn religion into an ideal which could survive without dogmas or rites. The English-man's house at this time, so far from being stiff with orthodox religion, "was almost the first irreligious home in all human history. Theirs was the first generation that ever asked its children to worship the hearth without the altar. This was equally true, whether they went to church at eleven o'clock . . . or were reverently agnostic or latitudinarian, as was much of my own circle. For the most part, it was family life stripped of its festivals and shrines and private cults, which had been its poetry in the past."[11] This shall help explain the connection we shall see later between sacred ritual and sacred hearthfire.

Chesterton attended St. Paul's School, but the prodigious mind he later displayed was, it seems, frugally shown during this period. Maisie Ward, his friend and early biographer, gathered the half-year reports from his form masters between the age of thirteen and eighteen.

> December 1887. Too much for me; means well by me, I believe, but has an inconceivable knack of forgetting at the shortest notice . . .
>
> July 1888. Wildly inaccurate about everything; never thinks for two consecutive moments to judge by his work: plenty of ability, perhaps in other directions than classics.
>
> July 1889. A great blunderer with much intelligence.
>
> July 1890. Can get up any work, but originates nothing.

And this last note:

> July 1892. Not on the same plane with the rest: composition quite futile, but will translate well and appreciate what he reads. Not a quick brain, but possessed by a slowly moving tortuous imagination. Conduct always admirable.[12]

This teacher was right on every score—admirable conduct, appreciative of what he reads, imaginative—but one: Chesterton will prove quite adept at composition. Though he trained at London's Slade School of Art, com-position became his livelihood. Chesterton consistently described himself simply as a journalist. He made his living from articles and essays and book reviews and books. In 1901, the year of his marriage to Frances Blogg, he settled into Fleet Street in London, home of the newspapers, and began his career of weekly columns. He admits himself to be "an accident in Fleet Street."

> The profound problem of how I ever managed to fall on my feet in Fleet Street is a mystery; at least it is still a mystery to me. . . . On the whole, I think I owe my success (as the millionaires say) to having listened re⁄ spectfully and rather bashfully to the very best advice, given by all the best journalists who had achieved the best sort of success in journalism; and then going away and doing the exact opposite. For what they all told me was that the secret of success in journalism was to study the particu⁄ lar journal and write what was suitable to it. And, partly by accident and ignorance and partly through the real rabid certainties of youth, I cannot remember that I ever wrote any article that was at all suitable to any paper. . . . I wrote on a Nonconformist organ like the old *Daily News* and told them all about French cafés and Catholic cathedrals; and they loved it because they had never heard of them before. I wrote on a robust Labor organ like the old *Clarion* and defended medieval theology and all the things their readers had never heard of; and their readers did not mind me a bit.[13]

Besides the columns in the *Daily News* that he began in 1901, in 1905 he accepted an offer from the *Illustrated London News* to write a weekly column titled "The Notebook." "Over the next thirty⁄one years, G.K.C. was to write almost 1,600 columns averaging 2,000 words a week. The essays were to arrive at the offices . . . every Monday by noon,"[14] a task which Chester⁄ ton describes as enjoyable but a process which does sometimes distract the serial essayist from more important business.

> Playing with children is a glorious thing: but the journalist in question has never understood why it was considered a soothing or idyllic one. It reminds him, not of watering little budding flowers, but of wrestling for hours with gigantic angels and devils. Moral problems of the most monstrous complexity besiege him incessantly. He has to decide before the awful eyes of innocence, whether, when a sister has knocked down a

brother's bricks, in revenge for the brother having taken two sweets out of his turn, it is endurable that the brother should retaliate by scribbling on the sister's picture-book. . . .

Just as he is solving this problem upon principles of the highest mo-rality, it occurs to him suddenly that he has not written his article; and that there is only about an hour to do it in. He wildly calls to somebody (prob-ably the gardener) to telephone somewhere for a messenger; he barricades himself in another room and tears his hair, wondering what on earth he shall write about. A drumming of fists on the door outside and a cheerful bellowing encourage and clarify his thoughts. . . . He sits down desper-ately, the messenger rings at the bell; the children drum on the door; the servants run up from time to time to say the messenger is getting bored; and the pencil staggers along, making the world a present of fifteen hundred unimportant words. . . . Then the journalist sends off his copy and turns his attention on the enigma of whether a brother should commandeer a sister's necklace because the sister pinched him at Littlehampton.[15]

Betwixt these articles (which will make up eleven of the projected thirty-five volumes of collected works), he produced books of poetry (*The Wild Knight, The Ballad of the White Horse, Collected Poems*), novels (*The Napoleon of Not-ting Hill, The Man Who Was Thursday, Manalive*) and plays (*Magic, The Judg-ment of Dr. Johnson*); he attained fame as the author of a series of detective stories (the *Father Brown Mysteries*) which some say rejuvenated the genre, and for his literary criticism (on Dickens, Stevenson, Chaucer); he spoke as a polemicist on the lecture circuit, wrote two profound religious biographies (*St. Francis of Assisi* and *St. Thomas Aquinas*), and worked out his corpus of theological works (*Orthodoxy, The Everlasting Man*) and Catholic apologeti-cal works (*The Thing: Why I Am a Catholic, Where All Roads Lead, The Well and the Shallows*).

There is a dispute about exactly when Chesterton became Catholic, even though the date of his baptism into the Roman Catholic Church is known (1922). One might say he became Catholic a few years before no-tifying Rome about it, having first notified the world about it in his writ-ings. In 1908, just after the publication of *Orthodoxy*, a book appeared by an anonymous author entitled *Gilbert K. Chesterton: A Criticism*, which contended that Chesterton's "assault on the moderns" and his "anti-liberalism" were in fact part of a "drift towards orthodoxy." The book further placed responsibility for this at the doorstep of Hilaire Belloc. "[W]hile Mr. Chesterton's views were still in process of formation, those of Mr. Belloc had already, so speak, solidified and solidified round the iron framework of Catholic dogma. . . . Now, it may be taken as an almost invariable rule that if two persons are closely associated, and one of them has unsettled opinions while the opinions of the other are fixed, the former will gravitate towards the philosophy of the latter as a meteor gravitates towards a planet. So, under the probably unconscious influence of Mr. Belloc, Mr. Chesterton was drawn towards the Catholic Faith."[16] The book suggested that Chesterton's dissatisfaction with his family's latitudinarianism, his resistance to the idea that religion can evolve beyond an institutional form into simple ideals, and his denunciation of various facets of modernism could, in fact, be interpreted as a religious journey and not merely a philosophical one. It was ultimately revealed that the author of this book was Gilbert's brother, Cecil.

Gilbert himself credits Frances, his wife, with embodying a more viable form of Christianity, as I shall note later. Father John O'Connor, who finally baptized Chesterton, confirms this in his memory of a conversation from the spring of 1912.

> He interrupted me . . . by telling me he had made up his mind to be received into the Church and was only waiting for Frances to come with him, as she had led him into the Anglican Church out of Unitarianism. . . . I was thrilled, naturally, but not surprised. The surprise always had been at his natural affinity for all those things for which Catholics are persecuted or brow-beaten. I found during those years of intercourse preceding that night that, whatever he believed, he had rejected before I knew him all the slanders, and had unravelled for himself all the misrepresentations.[17]

Chesterton said that he learned Christianity from its adversaries. Although his first book appears to be a series of philosophical, political, and anthropological essays, it was not a mistake for him to entitle it with a theological label: *Heretics.* He was in fact learning Christianity by a sort of *via negativa.* "I began to piece together the fragments of the old religious scheme; mainly by the various gaps that denoted its disappearance. And the more I saw of real human nature, the more I came to suspect that it was really rather bad for all these people that it had disappeared."[18]

Therefore we take Chesterton at his word that he is seriously arguing about what he believes are serious arguments, even when he is being droll. His pleasure in the pun should not be mistaken for frivolousness. When he makes his sermons and speeches amusing "it is for the very simple and even modest reason that we do not see why the audience should listen unless it is more or less amused. Our mode of speech is conditioned by the fact that it really is what some have fancifully supposed the function of speech to be; something addressed by somebody to somebody else."[19] The sort of flippan-cies to which Chesterton confesses "are only used by a very serious person."

Chesterton makes this clear even in his earliest pieces. The underlying complaint in *Heretics* is that today's heretics seem to be more concerned with being ten minutes ahead of the game than with any real questions of truth. They have thus turned the meaning of heresy on its head.

> [The modern heretic] says, with a conscious laugh, "I suppose I am very heretical," and looks round for applause. The word "heresy" not only means no longer being wrong; it practically means being clear-headed and courageous. The word "orthodoxy" not only no longer means being right; it practically means being wrong. All this can mean one thing, and one thing only. It means that people care less for whether they are philosophi-cally right. For obviously a man ought to confess himself crazy before he confesses himself heretical.[20]

He wrote *Orthodoxy* when critics complained that he had faulted other philosophies while not offering his own ("an incautious suggestion to make to a person only too ready to write books upon the feeblest provocation"), so he can hardly be accused of writing it in the same impertinent spirit of those he had already condemned. If he indulges in paradox and pun, it is not for vacuous rhetorical effect. "Mere light sophistry is the thing that I happen to despise most of all things, and it is perhaps a wholesome fact that this is the thing of which I am generally accused. I know nothing so contemptible as a mere paradox; a mere ingenious defence of the indefensible. . . . I never in my life said anything merely because I thought it funny; though of course, I have had ordinary human vainglory, and may have thought it funny be-cause I had said it."[21] *Orthodoxy* is offered with the utmost seriousness and "with the heartiest sentiments to all the jolly people who hate what I write, and regard it (very justly, for all I know) as a piece of poor clowning or a single tiresome joke." Chesterton may clown, but he drives his jests home with all the subtlety of a sharp stick, which is the sign of successful clowns, he says, while "it is only the unsuccessful clowns who comfort themselves with being subtle."[22] If his critics had understood his complaint in the first book, they would never have accused him of being flippant in the second.

Even with this protestation at the opening of his literary career, he still felt obliged at the end of his life to defend his lifelong practice of using play⁄ ful literary expression when making a serious point.

> I have never understood . . . why a solid argument is any less solid because you make the illustrations as entertaining as you can. . . . If you say that two sheep added to two sheep make four sheep, your audience will accept it patiently—like sheep. But if you say it of two monkeys, or two kanga⁄ roos, or two sea⁄green griffins, people will refuse to believe that two and two make four. They seem to imagine that you must have made up the arithmetic, just as you have made up the illustration of the arithmetic. And though they would actually know that what you say is sense, if they thought about it sensibly, they cannot believe that anything decorated by an incidental joke can be sensible. Perhaps it explains why so many suc⁄ cessful men are so dull—or why so many dull men are successful.[23]

Reflecting the same sentiment, he describes his paper, *G.K.'s Weekly,* by saying it is to contain both contrast and combination, and professes that he "cannot see why convictions should look dull or why jokes should be in⁄ sincere. I should like a man to pick up this paper for amusement and find himself involved in an argument. I should like him to pursue it purely for the sake of argument and find himself pulled up short by a joke. . . . I never can see why a thing should not be both popular and serious; that is, in the sense of being both popular and sincere."[24] I shall try to honor his desire, and read him as he requested: seriously and with great enjoyment.

Those who misunderstand may think him only to be playing, perhaps playing with them, in which case they are offended for not being treated with the gravity they think they deserve; or else playing with an idea, in which case they think Chesterton just to be playing make⁄believe, like a child. Now, in one way, this is an occupational hazard for an apologist,

since his or her avowed purpose is precisely to make belief. But it is a particular mistake to conclude on the basis of Chesterton's child-like jocularity
that he confuses make-believe and belief. In the child's make-believe there
may be more moral perspicuity than in the adult aesthete who speaks
solemnly about grave matters but treats them trivially.

> I am inclined to contradict much of the modern Cult of the Child at
> Play. . . . The worst heresy of this school is that a child is concerned only
> with make-believe. For this is interpreted in the sense, at once sentimental
> and sceptical, that there is not much difference between make-believe and
> belief. But the real child does not confuse fact and fiction. He simply likes
> fiction. He acts it, because he cannot as yet write it or even read it; but he
> never allows his moral sanity to be clouded by it. To him no two things
> could possibly be more totally contrary than playing at robbers and steal-
> ing sweets. No possible amount of playing at robbers would ever bring
> him an inch nearer to thinking it is really right to rob. . . . Though I might
> fill the world with dragons, I never had the slightest real doubt that heroes
> ought to fight with dragons.[25]

Chesterton really does want us to think sincerely about momentous things,
and his paradoxes are not obstructions to that end, they are the very means
to it.

Chesterton's magnanimity conditions his apodictic style, and these
must always be taken in conjunction. He operates with an anthropological
maximalism which makes the object of his hospitality coextensive with the
whole human family, as two early entries from his notebooks show.

> *An Invitation.*

> Mr. Gilbert Chesterton
> requests the pleasure
> Of humanity's company
> to tea on Dec. 25th 1896.
> Humanity Esq., The Earth, Cosmos E.

> Once I found a friend
> "Dear me," I said, "he was made for me."
> But now I find more and more friends

> Who seem to have been made for me
> And more and yet more made for me,
> Is it possible we were all made for each other
> all over the world? [26]

Because he liked people, when he duelled with someone his target was the ideology, not the person. This was perhaps nowhere truer than in his re-lationship with George Bernard Shaw, a relationship in which the two of them argued "on almost every subject in the world" and almost always "on opposite sides, without affectation or animosity." Chesterton defended "the institution of the family against [Shaw's] Platonist fancies about the State"; the institutions of "Beef & Beer against his hygienic severity of vegetarian-ism and total abstinence"; and the political ideal of the old Liberal notion of nationalism "against the new Socialist notion of internationalism." Yet at the end of his life, Chesterton includes a "salute to the duelist."

> It is not easy to dispute violently with a man for twenty years, about sex, about sin, about sacraments, about personal points of honor, about all the most sacred or delicate essentials of existence, without sometimes being irritated or feeling that he hits unfair blows or employs discreditable in-genuities. And I can testify that I have never read a reply by Bernard Shaw that did not leave me in a better and not a worse temper or frame of mind; which did not seem to come out of inexhaustible fountains of fairmindedness and intellectual geniality; which did not savour some-how of that native largeness which the philosopher attributed to the Mag-nanimous Man. [27]

It would be a worthy accomplishment if, in this age of acrid dispute, we could say of our own ideological opponents that discussion with them left us in a better and not a worse frame of mind.

Lest the reader think Chesterton refrains from sarcasm simply because he is incapable of it, we can contrast this appreciative appraisal of Shaw's disputation with the valuation Chesterton gives of a controversy over re-ligion once conducted in a newspaper. He compares the newspaper to a conservative colonel "who swears himself red in the face that he is not going to talk politics, but that damning to hell all those bloody blasted Socialists is not politics." In this case, the newspaper presented a defense of what it called "Progressive Faith" in the name of brotherly religion, but done in the form of a diatribe against Catholicism. Chesterton points out:

> So long as the writer employs vast and universal gestures of fellowship and hospitality to all those who are ready to abandon the irreligious beliefs, he is allowed to be as rude as he likes to all those who venture to retain them. The Dean of St. Paul's permits himself genially to call the Catholic Church a treacherous and bloody corporation; Mr. H. G. Wells is allowed to compare the Blessed Trinity to an undignified dance; the Bishop of Birmingham to compare the Blessed Sacrament to a barbarous blood-feast. It is felt that phrases such as these cannot ruffle that human peace and harmony which all such humanitarians desire; there is nothing in these expressions that could possibly interfere with brotherhood and the sympathy that is the bond of society; we may be sure of all this, for we have the word of the writers themselves that their whole aim is to generate an atmosphere of liberality and love.[28]

Chesterton does not skirt an issue, and he does utilize all of his considerable talents when disputing a point, including a sense of humor, expressed either as biting sarcasm or as a deep, generous chuckle at what he considers to be a ludicrous position deserving of a joke at its own expense. But he does not get personally nasty. He is so sure of his ground as to be irritating to those who disagree with him, but Chesterton pays them the dignity of disagreeing with them truly. When he frivols he is not being scornful.

> Now I for one greatly prefer the sort of frivolity that is thrown to the surface like froth to the sort of frivolity that festers under the surface like slime. To pelt an enemy with a foolish pun or so will never do him any grave injustice; the firework is obviously a firework and not a deadly fire. It may be playing to the gallery; but even the gallery knows it is only playing. But to associate an enemy always with certain ugly-sounding words, and never with their logical synonyms that sound a little better, is in a very real sense to poison our own minds. . . . The professed impartiality of certain academic historians stinks with their buried prejudice. Compared with this, I do think there is something sporting about conscious buffoonery.[29]

The issues tackled by Chesterton in print are multitudinous, but they are all ways of gaining access to a central core of convictions he objects to being violated. This explains why no matter what subject he writes about, the reader has the feeling of being on familiar territory. "Gilbert said once he was willing to start anywhere and develop from anything the whole of his philosophy."[30] His understanding of grace and nature was such that he combined the most startling concepts. In the following passage, he is describing what makes Dickens a great writer, but the skill for which he applauds Dickens is one which exactly describes the size which we find in Chesterton himself.

> A man who deals in harmonies, who only matches stars with angels, or lambs with spring flowers, he indeed may be frivolous; for he is taking one mood at a time, and perhaps forgetting each mood as it passes. But a man who ventures to combine an angel and an octopus must have some serious view of the universe. . . . The mark of the light and thoughtless writer is the harmony of his subject matter; the mark of the thoughtful writer is its apparent diversity. The most flippant lyric poet might write a pretty poem about lambs; but it requires something bolder and graver than a poet, it requires an ecstatic prophet, to talk about the lion lying down with the lamb.[31]

Chesterton's view of reality is serious, but it can appear fanciful because, knowing only one reality, he combines things more fantastic than angels and octopuses: he combines wonder and asceticism, liberty and authority, doctrinal complexity and simple ritual, Catholicism and paganism (or, grace and nature), hierarchy and freedom, tradition and democracy, a particular Church and the universal.

Some people think paradoxes obfuscate; for Chesterton, they illuminate reality. Using paradox was far more than a matter of mere style (although they were stylishly applied), or personal preference (though he did exhibit a constant partiality to them). Maisie Ward admits that "his love of a joke led him into indefensible puns and suchlike fooleries" but records him as having once said that, in the case of a paradox, "it is God, and not I, who should have the credit of it." She sees his paradox as a way of expressing in a startling way a neglected truth, or a neglected side of a truth. "What it amounted to was roughly this: paradox must be of the nature of things because of God's infinity and the limitations of the world and of man's mind.

To us limited beings God can express His idea only in fragments. We can bring together apparent contradictions in those fragments whereby a greater truth is suggested. If we do this in a sudden or incongruous manner we startle the unprepared and arouse the cry of paradox. But if we will not do it we shall miss a great deal of truth."[32] I suggest that this is the ultimate apology which Chesterton makes for Catholicism: that it is capacious enough to accommodate the paradoxical combinations which reveal reality. The Catholic Church is "the trysting-place of all the truths in the world."[33]

It might be said that Chesterton did not begin with Catholicism, to be convinced later of the universal truths it proclaims; instead, he began with truths about life, and concluded that only the Catholic faith could sanction them. He one day found Catholicism to be larger than the world he was exploring, and on that day entered its roomy confines. After he had covered the world, he ended up discovering the Catholic Church. "The difficulty of explaining 'why I am a Catholic,'" he writes, "is that there are ten thousand reasons all amounting to one reason: that Catholicism is true. . . . I would say chiefly of the Catholic Church that it is catholic. I would try to suggest that it is not only larger than me, but larger than anything in the world; that it is indeed larger than the world."[34] If it is a fundamental Catholic tenet that grace perfects nature, then Chesterton's journey was an essentially Catholic one at every point because he found in Catholicism the perfection of the truth, beauty, and goodness to which he had been led by his own exploration of the world. The Church to which he finally espouses himself does not void that world, or ask the Christian to avoid it. Chesterton says of his approach to this Church that it "is a house with a hundred gates; and no two men enter at exactly the same angle. Mine was at least as much Agnostic as Anglican."[35]

Heresy deals with truth and falsity, of course, but something can be false without being heretical, and something can be true and still be heretical. The image Chesterton most frequently uses to describe heresy is narrowness. It is a mood which narrows the mind of Catholicism. "True consistent heresies generally look very clear indeed; like Calvinism then or Communism now. They sometimes even look very true; they sometimes even are very true, in the limited sense of a truth that is less than the Truth. . . . For a heresy is not often a mere lie; as Thomas More himself said, 'Never was there a heretic that spoke all false.' A heresy is a truth that hides all the other truths."[36] At the conclusion of his biography of St. Francis, when he must explain how it was that the Franciscan order came eventually under papal administration, the most accurate definition of heresy in Chesterton's writing surfaces.

> It shows that the Saints were sometimes great men when the Popes were small men. But it also shows that great men are sometimes wrong when small men are right. And it will be found, after all, very difficult for any candid and clear-headed outsider to deny that the Pope was right, when he insisted that the world was not made only for Franciscans.
>
> For that was what was behind the quarrel. St. Francis was so great and original a man that he had something in him of what makes the founder of a religion. Many of his followers were more or less ready, in their hearts, to treat him as the founder of a religion. They were willing to let the Franciscan spirit escape from Christendom as the Christian spirit had escaped from Israel. That was the point the Pope had to settle; whether Christendom should absorb Francis or Francis Christendom. And he decided rightly. . . . For the Church could include all that was good in the Franciscans and the Franciscans could not include all that was good in the Church. . . .
>
> *Every heresy has been an effort to narrow the Church.* If the Franciscan movement had turned into a new religion, it would after all have been a narrow religion. In so far as it did turn here and there into a heresy, it was a narrow heresy. It did what heresy always does; it set the mood against the mind. The mood was indeed originally the good and glorious mood of the great St. Francis, but it was not the whole mind of God, or even of man.[37]

Every heresy has been an effort to narrow the Church. Heresy, although sometimes true and usually enticing, is uncatholic for being narrow-minded in the sense of single-minded. Catholic means "a mind surviving a hundred moods"[38] while heresy is the mood of the moment. Heresy is a truth that hides other truths insofar as it is blown out of proportion. "In all [heresies] you find that some Catholic dogma is, first, taken for granted; then exaggerated into an error; and then generally reacted against and rejected as an error, bringing the individual in question a few steps back again on the homeward road. And this is almost always the mark of such a heretic; that while he will wildly question any other Catholic dogma, he never dreams of questioning his own favourite Catholic dogma and does not even seem to know that it could be questioned."[39] The life cycle of a heresy reflects this at every point. A single truth's expansion beyond its right measure distorts the veracity it once contained; it is this error which Catholicism restrains. "The birth and death of every heresy has been essentially the same. A morbid or unbalanced Catholic takes one idea out of the thousandfold throng of Catholic ideas; and announces that he cares for that Catholic idea more than for Catholicism. He takes it away with him into a wilderness, where the idea becomes an image and the image an idol. After a century or two, he suddenly wakes up and discovers that the idol is an idol; and, shortly after that, that the wilderness is a wilderness. If he is a wise man, he calls himself a fool. If he is a fool, he calls himself an evolutionary progressive who has outgrown the worship of idols."[40]

What is represented under a spatial image as balance or proportion, Chesterton sometimes alternatively represents as a matter of consistency. The Catholic Church holds in its collective mind centuries-long conversations about certain important matters, and it holds them despite the alluring, fluctuating moods of the age. "We know what is really meant by saying that the Church is merely conservative and the modern world progressive. It means that the Church is always continuous and the heresies always contradictory. . . . But one effect of this contrast between continuity and bewildering variety is that the Church is generally seen in the light of the last heresy. The Church is supposed to consist chiefly of the things of which that heresy happens to disapprove. . . . [A] hundred years hence the Church may look to her enemies something utterly different from what she looked like a hundred years ago. She will look different because she will be the same."[41] The mood of the age, or ideal, or nation, or individual can swing the pendulum to an extreme.[42] But an extreme, being that which is farthest removed from the ordinary, forgets the ordinary person and the orders of life. "The moral is that the half-truth must be linked up with the whole truth; and who is to link it up? . . . He should take his half-truth into the culture of the Catholic Church, which really is a culture and where it really will be cultivated. . . . That is, he can take his idea where it will be valued for what is true in it, where it will be balanced by other truths and often supported by better arguments."[43]

Chesterton depicts Catholic stability not as rigidity or narrowness, but as *flexibility* (i.e., the faculty of coordinating additional truths to truth already held) and *size* (i.e., holding a truth in proper proportion to other truths). "She [the Catholic Church] is slow and belated, in the sense that she studies a heresy more seriously than the heresiarch does."[44] When a person has a truth wrong it is called error; but if the truth itself goes wrong, by exaggeration or misplacement, then what was true in itself becomes heretical. "Every great heretic had always exhibited three remarkable characteristics in combination. First, he picked out some mystical idea from the Church's bundle or balance of mystical ideas. Second, he used that one mystical idea against all the other mystical ideas. Third (and most singular), he seems generally to have had no notion that his own favourite mystical idea was a mystical idea, at least in the sense of a mysterious or dubious or dogmatic idea. With a queer uncanny innocence, he seems always to have taken this one thing for granted. He assumed it to be unassailable."[45]

Chesterton is an apologist for a catholic Catholicism. The heresy standing behind all the heretics with whom he tilts is an attenuated perspective which dwindles the faith down to singular and insulated themes, agendas, or viewpoints. I have gathered together in one place passages scattered throughout Chesterton's writings which divulge his regular reaction to this heresy. The heretic cannot understand the great Catholic combinations, combinations such as gratitude and duty, and so chapter 2 examines the connection Chesterton makes between wonder and asceticism. The heretic thinks that Christianity vitiates the world (either the common life of humanity, or the pagan religious aspiration, or present ritual religion), so chapter 3 sketches Chesterton's defense of ordinary life, chapter 4 his affinity with paganism, and chapter 5 his defense of religious ritual. The heretic errs in finding obedience stifling, so chapter 6 considers Chesterton's defense of doctrinal complexity and chapter 7 his descriptions of authority in the Church. And this attenuating attitude found expression in a set of kindred objections coming from the liberal Protestantism of Chesterton's day, so chapter 8 considers his response to such characteristic objections.

One comment about the selection of material. The reason why Chesterton's writing is so compelling is because he put himself through what the

reader goes through by reading him. He was the first victim of his apologetic. Making a selection from such a large body of work is difficult, even
having made the decision to restrict myself to Chesterton's theological works
and leave aside his literary ones. I am also leaving aside most secondary
works about Chesterton so that the reader can encounter him as directly as
possible.[46] Even so, it is obvious that a redactor's fingerprints are all over the
selection of quotations and their organization, and it is only fair to tell the
reader of this present work that Chesterton put this author through a dupli-
cate maneuver: I also have been a victim of his apologetic for Catholicism.
The ultimate criterion for the selection of material in this study will come
clear in the epilogue when a final word on this is mentioned.

Chesterton enjoyed himself when he was arguing because he was un-
pretentious: the claims were extravagant, he was not. The claims he made
were hardly modest, but the man who made them did so in all modesty.
Therefore he could combine personal amiability with a confidence about
the argument which fairly swaggered. What good would a Church be that
could not accommodate all the truths in the world? Not only truths we are
capable of seeing, but also truths which our ancestors saw and our descen-
dants will see, but to which we are blinded by the mood of the moment?
"There is no other case of one continuous intelligent institution that has
been thinking about thinking for two thousand years."[47] Nothing disturbed
him more than the modern hubris of trying to be ten minutes ahead, always
dismissing the ordinary (in the original sense of "regulated") because it was
ordinary (in the popular sense of "unexceptional"). Chesterton was allergic to these symptoms because he had once suffered the disease himself,
before taking the cure. He was as surprised about where he finally found the
cure as an Englishman would be who discovered England.

> I have often had a fancy for writing a romance about an English yachts-
> man who slightly miscalculated his course and discovered England under
> the impression that it was a new island in the South Seas. . . . I am that
> man in a yacht. I discovered England. . . . I am the man who with the
> utmost daring discovered what had been discovered before. . . . I did, like
> all the other solemn little boys, try to be in advance of the age. Like them I
> tried to be some ten minutes in advance of the truth. And I found that
> I was eighteen hundred years behind it. . . . When I fancied that I stood

alone I was really in the ridiculous position of being backed up by all Christendom. It may be, Heaven forgive me, that I did try to be original; but I only succeeded in inventing all by myself an inferior copy of the existing traditions of civilized religion. The man from the yacht thought he was the first to find England; I thought I was the first to find Europe. I did try to found a heresy of my own; and when I had put the last touches to it, I discovered that it was orthodoxy.[48]

A sense of wonder was the north star by which he navigated his yacht to the coast of Christendom, and a "mystical minimum of gratitude" was the compass which led him into the cove of orthodoxy, so it is to this sense of wonder that we turn first.

TWO

The Fairy
Godmother Philosophy

Chesterton sees the world with different eyes because of his fairy godmother. In that most revealing chapter of how his mind works, "The Ethics of Elfland," he explains the fairy godmother philosophy: resist a rule if it is evil, but not merely because it is mysterious.[1] During his dark nihilistic days, days which he never fully details but refers to in his autobiography as "how to be a lunatic," his fairy godmother held him fast by one thin thread. "I invented a rudimentary and makeshift mystical theory of my own. It was substantially this; that even mere existence, reduced to its most primary limits, was extraordinary enough to be exciting. . . . I hung on to the remains of religion by one thin thread of thanks. I thanked whatever gods might be, not like Swinburne, because no life lived for ever, but because any life lived at all. . . ."[2] This way of looking at things is a sort of "mystical minimum of gratitude" and is for Chesterton the fundamental philosophical riddle. It is how he describes the contents of *Orthodoxy*. He wants to know "How can we contrive to be at once astonished at the world and yet at home in it? How can this queer cosmic town, with its manylegged citizens, with its monstrous and ancient lamps, how can this world give us at once the fascination of a strange town and the comfort and honour of being our own town?"[3] His fairy godmother aids him in this.

It is perfectly compatible with Chesterton's theology to acknowledge this natural, almost pantheistic, pleasure in created things, considering how he describes his conversion. "I think I am the sort of man who came to Christ from Pan and Dionysius and not from Luther or Laud; that the conversion I understand is that of the pagan and not the Puritan."[4] Humanism and a near Dionysian enthusiasm for the world initially found satisfaction in the poetry of Walt Whitman, who remained a factor throughout

Chesterton's life, though possibly in a different setting than at first. After Chesterton's conversion he could still say the mood "is not dead in me. It remains real for me, not by any merit of mine, but by the fact that this mystical idea, while it has evaporated as a mood, still exists as a creed. . . . The truth is that Whitman's wild picture, or what he thought was a wild picture, is in fact a very old and orthodox picture. . . . [F]or Catholics it is a fundamental dogma of the Faith that all human beings, without any exception whatever, were specially made, were shaped and pointed like shining arrows, for the end of hitting the mark of Beatitude."[5] Chesterton needed more than the mood, but the creed he needed would have to profess a God who could justify the fundamental appetite for happiness. Thus his (theo)logical sequence that "there can only be fairy godmothers because there are godmothers; and there can only be godmothers because there is God."[6]

This mystical minimum of gratitude accounts for many features that make Chesterton who he is: the sense of magic in the ordinary, the thrill of domesticity and the resulting defense of the common life of ordinary people, "the wild romance of prudence" which he explains with the aid of Robinson Crusoe, a character who treasured each of the comforts he snatched from the sea as if it were magic. For Chesterton, only stories of magic could express his sense "that life is not only a pleasure but a kind of eccentric privilege." Could not citizens in the real world treasure things as dearly? "The greatest of poems is an inventory."[7] When life is viewed as an eccentric privilege, the most ordinary things in it are a marvel. "That there are two sexes and one sun, was like the fact that there were two guns and one axe. It was poignantly urgent that none should be lost; but somehow, it was rather fun that none could be added. The trees and the planets seemed like things saved from the wreck: and when I saw the Matterhorn I was glad that it had not been overlooked in the confusion."[8] The quality of preciousness which surrounds every thing, also surrounds every moment.

> *Evening*
>
> Here dies another day
> During which I have had eyes, ears, hands
> And the great world round me;
> And tomorrow begins another.
> Why am I allowed two?[9]

The thrill of gratitude derives from wonder at the world; the greater the wonder, the greater the gratitude. Surely we have all had, at some moment, flashes of this sort of precious wonder, and occasionally, irregularly, it might even cause us to pause and notice life's gracefulness, but it was Chesterton's charism to do this consistently, almost constantly.[10] In a letter to his fiancée, Frances, he confesses to being stained with a certain ink from that day's work, and then thinks to write, "I like the Cyclostyle ink; it is so inky. I do not think there is anyone who takes quite such fierce pleasure in things being themselves as I do. The startling wetness of water excites and intoxicates me: the fieriness of fire, the steeliness of steel, the unutterable muddiness of mud. It is just the same with people. . . . When we call a man 'manly' or a woman 'womanly' we touch the deepest philosophy."[11] Chesterton's brand of wondering has an immediate quality to it, as if nothing stood between himself and raw existence. Because he does not look through a smudged glass, he seems more to look into the world than merely at it. He has an immediate interest in things. It is such an interesting world, he has decided to look into it.

There is a primitive quality to this outlook, which he describes in one place as belonging to a child, and in another remembers having experienced in his own childhood.[12] In the biography of St. Thomas Aquinas, Chesterton must try to explain what he thinks Thomas meant by the scholastic category *Ens* ("being"). To do so he resorts to a child's early experience of being. "When a child looks out of the nursery window and sees anything, say the green lawn of the garden, what does he actually know; or does he know anything? . . . [St. Thomas] says emphatically that the child is aware of *Ens*. Long before he knows that grass is grass, or self is self, he knows that something is something. Perhaps it would be best to say very emphatically (with a blow on the table), 'There *is* an is.'"[13] The being of things is wonderful to a child. Most grownups have grown accustomed to taking the miracle for granted, but Chesterton celebrated such experiences during his entire life. He did not lose the child in the adult; instead he found the adult version of childhood's astonishments. He does not consider the childhood sense of wonder childish.

The very first thing I can ever remember seeing with my own eyes was a young man walking across a bridge. He had a curly moustache and an attitude of confidence verging on swagger. He carried in his hand a disproportionately large key of a shining yellow metal and wore a large golden or gilded crown. . . . To those who may object that such a scene is rare in the home life of house-agents living immediately to the north of Kensington High Street, in the later seventies of the last century, I shall be compelled to admit, not that the scene was unreal, but that I saw it through a window more wonderful than the window in the tower; through the proscenium of a toy theatre constructed by my father; and that (if I am really to be pestered about such irrelevant details) the young man in the crown was about six inches high and proved on investigation to be made of cardboard. . . . The scene has to me a sort of aboriginal authenticity impossible to describe. . . .

If this were a ruthless realistic modern story, I should of course give a most heartrendering account of how my spirit was broken with dis-appointment, on discovering that the prince was only a painted figure. But this is not a ruthless realistic modern story. On the contrary, it is a true story. . . . I was pleased, and not displeased, when I discovered that the magic figures could be moved by three human fingers. And I was right; for those three human fingers are more magical than any magic figures; the three fingers which hold the pen and the sword and the bow of the violin; the three fingers that the priest lifts in benediction as the emblem of the Blessed Trinity. There was no conflict between the two magics in my mind.[14]

The aboriginal authenticity with which reality struck Chesterton never ceased; to the contrary, as his capacity to understand matured and made reality more complex, the causes for gratitude became more numerous.

Unfortunately, this does not happen automatically, just by growing up. In fact, growing up makes it harder to surmount our jadedness. It is adults, believes Chesterton, not children, who need fairy tales in order to enable them to recover the sense of "elementary wonder."[15] "Just as we all like love tales because there is an instinct of sex, we all like astonishing tales because they touch the nerve of the ancient instinct of astonishment. This is proved by the fact that when we are very young children we do not need fairy tales: we only need tales. Mere life is interesting enough. . . . These tales say that apples were golden only to refresh the forgotten moment when we found that they were green. They make rivers run with wine only to make us remember, for one wild moment, that they run with water."[16] Our tired adult eyes have been dulled by sin's cataracts, so we are tempted to overlook the repetitive and be wearied by it. "The curse that came before history has laid on us all a tendency to be weary of wonders. If we saw the sun for the first time it would be the most fearful and beautiful of meteors. Now that we see it for the hun-dredth time we call it . . . 'the light of common day.'"[17]

This, incidentally, is the purpose and value of art, in Chesterton's opin-ion, not only the literary art of telling astonishing stories, as mentioned above, but the plastic arts as well. It is tantamount to saying, theologically, that the arts exist to show forth the glory of God and, psychologically, that the arts exist to awaken and keep alive the sense of wonder in human beings. "The success of any work of art is achieved when we say of any subject, a tree or a cloud or a human character, 'I have seen that a thousand times and I never saw it before.'" To accomplish this, artists must change their attack; throw new light on things; vary the perspective and surprise the viewer in some fashion. Insofar as artists can do this, Chesterton admires them. But sometimes it happens (and he thought it was already happening too often in his day) that the artist extends the experiment from art to real life. And then it is as if the absentminded sculptor has turned "his chisel from chipping at the bust to chipping at the bald head of the distinguished sitter." Then it is no longer art that is being experimented with but morals and metaphysics.

> We feel inclined to welcome even wild variations in the decorative style; and to admire the new artist who will paint the rose black, lest we should forget that it is a deep red, or the moonshine green, that we may realize it is something more subtle than white. But the moon is the moon and the rose is the rose; and we do not expect the real things to alter. Nor is there any reason to expect the rules about them to alter. . . . Because a particular painter, for a particular purpose, might paint the red rose black, the pes-simist deduced that the red rose of love and life was really as black as it was painted. . . . It is insane that there should be a new pattern of hearts or heads whenever there is a new pattern of hats.[18]

There is ultimately a limit to what can be accomplished by restless ex-perimentation. The ultimate solution to the pessimistic boredom which afflicts the modern age requires a change in the perceiver, not the perceived.

If our hearts were changed, then our eyes could see the world correctly, amazedly, wondrously. What is necessary in order to see the sun as a miracle is not a new sun but a new humility. "Humility is perpetually putting us back in the primal darkness. There all light is lightning, startling and instantaneous. Until we understand that original dark, in which we have neither sight nor expectation, we can give no hearty and childlike praise to the splendid sensationalism of things."[19] It is the sons of Adam and daughters of Eve who grow weary of seeing the same sun, in the same sky, following the same path; the God who choreographed its sky-dance is not bored. God is strong enough to "exult in monotony."

> Now to put the matter in a popular phrase, it might be true that the sun rises regularly because he never gets tired of rising. His routine might be due, not to a lifelessness, but to a rush of life. The thing I mean can be seen, for instance, in children, when they find some game or joke that they specially enjoy. A child kicks his legs rhythmically through excess, not absence, of life. Because children have abounding vitality, because they are in spirit fierce and free, therefore they want things repeated and unchanged. They always say, "Do it again"; and the grown-up person does it again until he is nearly dead. For grown-up people are not strong enough to exult in monotony. But perhaps God is strong enough to exult in monotony. It is possible that God says every morning, "Do it again" to the sun; and every evening, "Do it again" to the moon. It may not be automatic necessity that makes all daisies alike; it may be that God makes every daisy separately, but has never got tired of making them. It may be that He has the eternal appetite of infancy; for we have sinned and grown old, and our Father is younger than we.[20]

To be old in the way our age has grown old teeters on the verge of succumbing to a philosophy which tires of life, a philosophy which nihilistically and pessimistically despairs, not about any one thing, but that any things are. The way to be a lunatic is to indulge extremes of sterile isolation, skepticism, and thinking there is nothing but thought;[21] the way not to be a lunatic is to be humble. "Humility is a grand, a stirring thing, the exalting paradox of Christianity, and the sad want of it in our own time is, we believe, what really makes us think life dull, like a cynic, instead of marvelous, like a child."[22] Humility such as this is positively saintly and angelic. "Modern investigators of miraculous history have solemnly admitted that a characteristic of the great saints is their power of 'levitation.' They might go further; a characteristic of the great saints is their power of levity. Angels can fly because they can take themselves lightly. . . . The kings in their heavy gold and proud in their robes of purple will all of their nature sink downwards, for pride cannot rise to levity or levitation. Pride is the downward drag of all things into an easy solemnity. . . . For solemnity flows out of men naturally; but laughter is a leap. It is easy to be heavy; hard to be light. Satan fell by the force of gravity."[23]

Chesterton admits it was a struggle to deny pessimism when he as yet had no basis for optimism, and when he could not as yet turn for balm to the reasons being offered for optimism. "I had often called myself an optimist, to avoid the too evident blasphemy of pessimism. But all the optimism of the age had been false and disheartening for this reason, that it had always been trying to prove that we fit in to the world."[24] Yet the struggle was a worthwhile one, he was sure, because if grounds for optimism could not be found, then life would collapse in on itself, like a star imploding. "Pessimism is not in being tired of evil but in being tired of good. Despair does not lie in being weary of suffering, but in being weary of joy. It is when for some reason or other the good things in a society no longer work that the society begins to decline; when its food does not feed, when its cures do not cure, when its blessings refuse to bless."[25] It is wrong both to want out of the world, and to be content with only the world. The former is the sin of the suicide, the latter the sin of the hedonist; the former sins against our temporal creatureliness, the latter sins against our eternal soul. It was precisely the realization of this tension which inaugurated Chesterton's perception of a congruence between what he deduced experientially as necessarily true and what the Christian faith professed. He remembered "that it was actually the charge against Christianity that it combined these two things which I was wildly trying to combine. Christianity was accused, at one and the same time, of being too optimistic about the universe and of being too pessimistic about the world. The coincidence made me suddenly stand still."[26]

The thin thread by which his fairy godmother held him was happiness, and "the test of all happiness is gratitude; and I felt grateful, though I hardly knew to whom. Children are grateful when Santa Claus puts in their stockings gifts of toys or sweets. Could I not be grateful to Santa Claus when he put in my stockings the gift of two miraculous legs?"[27] He could wish for such a meeting between a fairy godmother and his friend George Bernard Shaw. Mr. Shaw would convince Chesterton that he saw things right if Chesterton could find him "staring with religious astonishment at his own feet. 'What are those two beautiful and industrious beings,' I can imagine him murmuring to himself, 'whom I see everywhere, serving me I know not why? What fairy godmother bade them come trotting out of elfland when I was born? What god of the borderland, what barbaric god of legs, must I propitiate with fire and wine, lest they run away with me?'"[28]

Chesterton might hear complaints from two directions at this point, from the pagan and the pietist. The one might feel that none of this has anything to do with religion; the other that it hasn't enough to do with religion, that at most it is a morality, or at least a human instinct—admirable, but hardly salutary. Had Chesterton agreed, he could have remained a happy agnostic, but a journey never begun into religion would never have concluded as a journey into Catholicism. So to the casual critic's question, "What nonsense all this is; do you mean that a poet cannot be thankful for grass and wild flowers without connecting it with theology; let alone your theology?" comes Chesterton's earnestly avowed answer, "Yes; I mean he cannot do it without connecting it with theology, unless he can do it without connecting it with thought. If he can manage to be thankful when there is nobody to be thankful to, and no good intentions to be thankful for, then he is simply taking refuge in being thoughtless in order to avoid being thankless."[29] The sense of wonder makes Chesterton wonder about the end of the world: as the end of a watch is to tell time, what is the end of man and woman? The sweet truths of beauty and goodness do not satisfy Chesterton's appetite, they stir it up. And when one discovers that no finite happiness can satisfy the infinite human appetite for beatitude, then one becomes convinced that the human race has lost its way and "been a tramp ever since Eden."[30] Chesterton felt the need for heaven because of the goodness of life, not because of its wickedness; his conversion was not from despair, it was from despair over despair, and from his desperate desire for a ground for optimism.

The important matter was this, that it entirely reversed the reason for optimism. And the instant the reversal was made it felt like the abrupt ease
when a bone is put back in the socket. I had often called myself an optimist, to avoid the too evident blasphemy of pessimism. But all the
optimism of the age had been false and disheartening for this reason, that it
had always been trying to prove that we fit in to the world. The Christian
optimism is based on the fact that we do not fit in to the world. . . .
I had been right in feeling all things as odd, for I myself was at once worse
and better than all things. . . . The modern philosopher had told me again
and again that I was in the right place, and I had still felt depressed even
in acquiescence. But I heard that I was in the wrong place, and my soul
sang for joy, like a bird in spring. I now knew why I could feel homesick
at home.[31]

Being homesick is a symptom of the Fall. That we suffer homesickness
is a sign that we are not now what we were meant to be, that our natures are
fallen, that our destiny is infinitely more than anything this finite world can
offer. For Chesterton, even the Christian doctrine of sin is not a cause for
berating humankind in a pessimistic funk over human nature; the doctrine
of original sin is the only cheerful view of human life there is, as a priest
once put it to him.[32] Or, as Chesterton himself puts it, the Fall "is not only
the only enlightening, but the only encouraging view of life. . . . It refers evil
back to the wrong use of the will, and thus declares that it can eventually be
righted by the right use of the will. . . . [It cries out that] happiness is not
only a hope, but also in some strange manner a memory; and that we are all
kings in exile."[33] Chesterton does not work from anthropological mini-
malism, even when defining sin. Instead, his anthropological maximalism
takes sin itself as a sign that our natures are made for beatitude.

> The main point is that the Fall, like every other large path of Chris-
> tianity, is embodied in the common language talked on the top of an
> omnibus. Anybody might say, "Very few men are really manly." Nobody
> would say, "Very few whales are really whaley."
> If you wanted to dissuade a man from drinking his tenth whisky you
> would slap him on the back and say, "Be a man." No one who wished to
> dissuade a crocodile from eating his tenth explorer would slap it on the

back and say, "Be a crocodile." For we have no notion of a perfect crocodile; no allegory of a whale expelled from his whaley Eden.[34]

Our sense of dis-ease is a stimulus. A dog cannot be any more canine than
he is (he is as doggy as he gets), but we could be more human than we are.
If certain behaviors of an animal are natural to its canine nature, then it is
ultimately a waste of effort to discipline them; but if certain behaviors of a
human being are unnatural to its human nature, then we are behooved to
discipline them. Disciplining a crocodile not to eat an explorer would make
the beast less a crocodile, but disciplining ourselves not to eat gluttonously
would make us more human. The doctrine of original sin precisely claims it
is not natural for people to sin, so while one might not be able to teach an
old dog new tricks, one can teach the old Adam new tricks, the original
tricks. Asceticism derives from *askesis,* which means "practice," or the sort of
disciplined practice by which an athlete trains. Chesterton believes that our
capacity for joy must be trained by such practice, and he calls the discipline
"the doctrine of conditional joy." In one of his more laconic descriptions of
it he says, "we should thank God for beer and Burgundy by not drinking
too much of them."[35]

Now Chesterton is walking a tightrope, an image which may seem
incredible if applied to him corporeally, but not if applied to his intellect,
considering his paradoxical powers. He instinctively understands that
God's grace and human works need not stand in inverse proportion. He
does not share the logic of inverse proportionality which states that the more
one agent causes, the less another agent can cause. For example, when two
people pull a weight, more work done by one means less work done by the
other. If the logic of inverse proportionality is applied to the salutary relationship between God and humanity, it results in the misjudgment that
the divine agent can be lauded only by devaluing the ascetical work of the
human agent. Chesterton does not commit this error. For him, wonder is a
cause of humility, and a source of gratitude, and therefore love is the key to
asceticism. Asceticism is the "discovery of an infinite debt."

> It may seem a paradox to say that a man may be transported with joy to
> discover that he is in debt. . . . It is the key of all the problems of Francis-
> can morality which puzzle the merely modern mind; but above all it is

the key of asceticism. It is the highest and holiest of the paradoxes that the man who really knows he cannot pay his debt will be forever paying it. He will be for ever giving back what he cannot give back, and cannot be expected to give back. He will always be throwing things away into a bottomless pit of unfathomable thanks. . . . We are not generous enough to be ascetics; one might almost say not genial enough to be ascetics.[36]

Asceticism cannot be understood outside of love, which is the cause of grace, and which causes the human response. Chesterton observes the same principle in romantic love. If ever romance fell out of fashion, we should have the same difficulty understanding behaviors caused by motivations then alien to us. "We should have the same sort of unintelligent sneers and unimaginative questions." The lengths to which lovers go might appear unconscionable. "Men will ask what selfish sort of woman it must have been who ruthlessly exacted tribute in the form of flowers, or what an avaricious creature she can have been to demand solid gold in the form of a ring: just as they ask what cruel kind of God can have demanded sacrifice and selfdenial," but this would only be because persons who have not understood the delight cannot understand the asceticism. "They will have lost the clue to all that lovers have meant by love; and will not understand that it was because the thing was not demanded that it was done. . . . The whole point about St. Francis of Assisi is that he certainly was ascetical and he certainly was not gloomy."[37] How can there be a dusky gloom where wonder at being has lit up the mind? Humility was described earlier as returning to the primal darkness against which the brilliance of being could be perceived. "Until we picture nonentity we underrate the victory of God."[38] But when a person has started from zero, in true humility, then he or she enjoys all things in a more intense fashion, "for there is no way in which a man can earn a star or deserve a sunset."[39]

To someone not head over heels in love with God, an ascetic like St. Francis certainly looks like a mass of contradictions, and Chesterton admits that the secular biographies of the saint which try to tell the story of the saint without God, do result in a figure who is a tangle of inconsistencies. The poet who praised his Lord the sun, hid himself in a dark cavern; the saint who was "so gentle with his Brother the Wolf was so harsh to his

Brother the Ass (as he nicknamed his own body)"; the troubador who said love set his heart on fire separated himself from women; the singer who praised God with the passion of a pagan for "our Sister, Mother Earth," ended the song with the words, "Praised be God for our Sister, the death of the body."[40] Such inconsistent contradictions would appear erratic and fickle to someone inexperienced with love, and likewise does asceticism appear to someone inexperienced with its true motive. For the modern reader of St. Francis's life, Chesterton suggests the clue to asceticism can best be found "in the stories of lovers when they seemed to be rather like lunatics." Tell the story like the tale of a troubador and the wild things a bard would do for his lady, and the puzzle disappears. "In such a romance there would be no contradiction between the poet gathering flowers in the sun and enduring a freezing vigil in the snow, between his praising all earthly and bodily beauty and then refusing to eat, between his glorifying gold and purple and perversely going in rags, between his showing pathetically a hunger for a happy life and a thirst for a heroic death. All these riddles would easily be resolved in the simplicity of any noble love; only this was so noble a love that nine men out of ten have hardly heard of it."[41]

Chesterton is not describing a prerequisite, he is describing reality. The doctrine of conditional joy is not an arbitrary decree by God, it is the decree by which reality has been constituted. It is decreed by God, but the conditions attached to joy are not accidental. It is not as if human beings could enjoy the world in a rampant, reckless way save that God does not allow it, though God could. The doctrine of conditional joy does not describe accidental conditions which must be met before joy will be released by whatever fate is restraining it (as it is necessary to eat your vegetables before your parents will give you dessert); the doctrine rather describes the ontological conditions necessary to the experience of joy (as it is necessary to eat to live, or to open your eyes to see). That a disordered will cannot love properly is not arbitrarily decreed, it is a state impossible by definition. To love properly requires an ordered will. Asceticism is not the condition (as "price") God demands before God will permit us to enjoy the world, it is the condition (as "capacity") for enjoying the world. The person who asked Chesterton why he was becoming more orthodox "was met by the now familiar Chestertonian argument for religion and humility; illustrated by the symbol [of] the sparks from the fire that was burning in front of them: 'Seduce a woman, and that spark will be less bright. Shed blood, and that spark will be less red.'"[42]

The thread spun by the fairy godmother linking thanks with good works is a natural one, both in the sense of evident and sensible and in the sense of belonging to the structure of reality. Therefore, completely absent is any consideration of winkling grace out of God with bribes of good behavior.

[The cynic] always imagines that there is an element of corruption about the idea of reward, about the position of the child who can say, as in Steven, son's verses, "Everyday when I've been good, I get an orange after food." To the man made ignorant by experience this always appears as a vulgar *bribe* to the child. . . . But it does not seem like that to the child. It would not seem like that to the child, if the Fairy Queen said to the Prince, "You will receive the golden apple from the magic tree when you have fought the dragon." For the child is not a Manichee. He does not think that good things are in their nature separate from being good. . . . To him the goodness and the gift and the golden apple, that is called an orange, are all parts of one substantial paradise and naturally go together. In other words, he re, gards himself on amiable terms with the natural authorities; not normally quarreling or bargaining with them. He has the ordinary selfish obstacles and misunderstandings; but he does not, in his heart, regard it as odd that his parents should be good to him, to the extent of an orange, or that he should be good to them, to the extent of some elementary experiments in good behavior. He has no sense of being corrupted. It is only we, who have eaten the forbidden apple (or orange) who think of pleasure as a bribe.[43]

Love is its own reward, on the one hand. On the other hand, "there are no things for which men will make such herculean efforts as the things of which they know they are unworthy," and it is no different in any other love relationship.

The truth is that there is no more conscious inconsistency between the hu, mility of a Christian and the rapacity of a Christian than there is between the humility of a lover and the rapacity of a lover. . . . There never was a man in love who did not declare that, if he strained every nerve to breaking, he was going to have his desire. And there never was a man in love who did not declare also that he ought not to have it. The whole secret of the practical success of Christendom lies in the Christian humility, however imperfectly fulfilled. For with the removal of all question of merit or payment, the soul is suddenly released for incredible voyages. . . . Thus comes the thing called Romance, a purely Christian product. A man cannot deserve adventures; he cannot earn dragons and hippogriffs.[44]

With dragons and hippogriffs come even more incredible sights: grass and stars, the sun and moon—and even a woman. "Keeping to one woman is a small price for so much as seeing one woman,"[45] says the doctrine of conditional joy. It should not be a surprise that precious realities, because they are precious, command a price. At any rate, it is not a surprise to those familiar with the ethics of elfland, and who remember the fairy godmother philosophy of resisting something if it is evil, but not merely because it is mysterious. "In the fairy tale an incomprehensible happiness rests upon an incomprehensible condition. A box is opened, and all evils fly out. A word is forgotten, and cities perish. A lamp is lit, and love flies away. A flower is plucked, and human lives are forfeited. An apple is eaten, and the hope of God is gone."[46] If we do not yet see the connection, it may be because we are not yet tall enough, or grownup enough, or practiced enough in life; it need not be immediately concluded that because the connection is not seen, it is not there. Some rudimentary experiments in good behavior might clarify the matter handily.

> [If someone asks] "Explain why I must not stand on my head in the fairy palace," the other might fairly reply, "Well, if it comes to that, explain the fairy palace." If Cinderella says, "How is it that I must leave the ball at twelve?" her godmother might answer, "How is it that you are going there till twelve?" If I leave a man in my will ten talking elephants and a hundred winged horses, he cannot complain if the conditions partake of the slight eccentricity of the gift. He must not look a winged horse in the mouth. . . . Surely one might pay for extraordinary joy in ordinary morals. Oscar Wilde said that sunsets were not valued because we could not pay for sunsets. But Oscar Wilde was wrong; we can pay for sunsets. We can pay for them by not being Oscar Wilde.[47]

We do not find it surprising that a certain behavior might be expected of guests in a dwelling as miraculous as the fairy godmother's palace, unless we have reached the point of no longer looking upon this world, our dwelling place, as miraculous.

Chesterton suggests that different generations have different conditions attached to their joy, and that the Catholic infirmary is stocked with whatever medicament is specially required to cure a generation's particular sins and infirmities. "The saint is a medicine because he is an antidote. Indeed that is why the saint is often a martyr; he is mistaken for a poison because he is an antidote. He will generally be found restoring the world to sanity by exaggerating whatever the world neglects, which is by no means always the same element in every age. Yet each generation seeks its saint by instinct; and he is not what the people want, but rather what the people need." The twentieth century "is already clutching at the Thomist rational theology, because it has neglected reason," while "St. Francis had a curious and almost uncanny attraction for the Victorians." It is the paradox of history that "each generation is converted by the saint who contradicts it most."[48]

In English we can use the word "order" in at least three ways—as end, structure, or command—and it is as if Chesterton detects a common source to these uses. In order that we might be ordered to God, morality orders obedience. Moral orders (the commands and the structures) are not arbitrary fiats, they are the imposition of reality's structure upon ourselves; or, if you prefer, alignments between our selves and reality. It is only because our natural sight is dimmed, that the fairy godmother's orders appear eccentric. In actual fact, her orders reflect the proper order of love, and we will only realize the wonder of life in the fairy palace if we understand the moral order.

> Morality did not begin by one man saying to another, "I will not hit you if you do not hit me"; there is no trace of such a transaction. There is a trace of both men having said, "We must not hit each other in the holy place." They gained their morality by guarding their religion. They did not cultivate courage. They fought for the shrine, and found they had become courageous. They did not cultivate cleanliness. They purified themselves for the altar and found that they were clean. . . . Only when they made a holy day for God did they find they had made a holiday for men.[49]

Chesterton finds a seamless, albeit mysterious, connection from wonder to gratitude to humility to morality to theology. Our attitude toward the world is ultimately determined by theology, i.e., our relationship with God. Chesterton does not put his face into the wind, gritting his teeth, struggling to find reason to put up with the world in order to justify existence. If we see his teeth at all, it is because he is smiling. His first memory of reality is of the man with the golden key, unlocking the marvels of being and awakening the homesick hunger of an exile for the true happiness of home. Eden did not disappear because we outgrew myths and fairy tales, but because we violated the conditions of our residency.

Yet even now there are holy things which speak to us of our origin and destiny. Holy days appoint the calendar, and light from stained-glass windows bejewel the landscape. "Decoration is not given to hide horrible things: but to decorate things already adorable. A mother does not give her child a blue bow because he is so ugly without it. A lover does not give a girl a necklace to hide her neck."[50] One of the things people have difficulty understanding, it would seem, is that the wastefulness of decorations is precisely their whole reason for being. Churches and holidays do not exist for cosmetic purposes, to disguise the ugliness of the world; they exist for the decorative purpose of enhancing the loveliness. God has not given humankind the holy day in order to flee the world. Chesterton waves the flag of the world and challenges that if people loved even the slums of "Pimlico as mothers loved children, arbitrarily, because it is *theirs*, Pimlico in a year or two might be fairer than Florence. . . . This, as a fact, is how cities did grow great. Go back to the darkest roots of civilization and you will find them knotted round some sacred stone or encircling some sacred well. People first paid honor to a spot and afterwards gained glory for it. Men did not love Rome because she was great. She was great because they had loved her."[51]

It is therefore totally wrong to charge Christian asceticism with hatred, gloom, pessimism, dualism, antiworldliness, or escapism—even though this is how it is customarily misperceived.

> Nothing is more common . . . than to find such a modern critic writing something like this: "Christianity was a movement of ascetics, a rush into the desert, a refuge in the cloister, a renunciation of all life and happi-

ness; and this was a part of a gloomy and inhuman reaction against nature itself, a hatred of the body, a horror of the material universe, a sort of
universal suicide of the senses and even of the self. . . ." Now the most
extraordinary thing about this is that it is all quite true; it is true in every
detail except that it happens to be attributed entirely to the wrong person.
It is not true of the church; but it is true of the heretics condemned by the
Church. . . .

The early Church was ascetic, but she proved that she was not pessimistic, simply by condemning the pessimists. The creed declared that
man was sinful, but it did not declare that life was evil, and it proved it by
damning those who did. The condemnation of the early heretics is itself
condemned as something crabbed and narrow; but it was in truth the very
proof that the Church meant to be brotherly and broad. It proved that the
primitive Catholics were specially eager to explain that they did *not* think
man utterly vile; that they did *not* think life incurably miserable; that they
did *not* think marriage a sin or procreation a tragedy. They were ascetic
because asceticism was the only possible purge of the sins of the world; but
in the very thunder of their anathemas they affirmed for ever that their asceticism was not to be anti-human or anti-natural; that they did wish to
purge the world and not destroy it.[52]

The key to Christian asceticism is the paradox that the person who knows
the debt cannot be paid will be forever paying it, just as the lover who knows
that the gift of love cannot be deserved will be forever committed to faithfulness. Both involve disciplined loyalty—*askesis*. Both monasticism and
marriage are ascetical vocations insofar as they involve a vow to love, and
do not depend just on the mood of love. Catholicism is roomy enough to
concurrently esteem the celibate ascetic and honor marriage as a sacrament.
Chesterton refers to reading a critic's review of a book on Augustine and
finding the "astounding statement that the Catholic Church regards sex as
having the nature of sin." He replies, "How marriage can be a sacrament if
sex is a sin, or why it is the Catholics who are in favor of birth and their foes
who are in favor of birth-control, I will leave to the critic to worry out for
himself."[53] The admiration Catholics feel toward extraordinary ascetical
saints is not at the expense of any respect accorded the ordinary institution of

marriage, because marriage too must be practiced: it is an *askesis*. The day will come when the creed will have to carry the mood. "In everything worth having, even in every pleasure, there is a point of pain or tedium that must be survived, so that the pleasure may revive and endure. . . . In everything on this earth that is worth doing, there is a stage when no one would do it, except for necessity or honor. It is then that the Institution upholds a man and helps him on to the firmer ground ahead. . . . If a man is bored in the first five minutes he must go on and force himself to be happy."[54] Disciplining the monastic heart in the desert is no more a sign of doubt about the goodness of creation than disciplining the heart to one spouse is a sign of doubt about the goodness of love.

It is a good creation, and one in which the monk has a special call. "Any human tradition would make more of the heroes who suffered for something than of the human beings who simply benefited by it. But that does not alter the fact that there are more human beings than heroes; and that this great majority of human beings has benefited by it."[55] Ascetics and martyrs are celebrated as heroes precisely because they do what not everyone has to do, and do so for the sake of everyone. Chesterton finds certain popular movements in his day—socialism, vegetarianism, prohibitionism—to be worse than asceticism, because by turning the individual ascetical act into an imposed general morality, these movements cannot simultaneously affirm the goodness of individuality, meat, and burgundy for human society while praising the hero who repudiates these values.

> Mr. Middleton Murry is an ascetic who wishes to transfer asceticism from the individual life, where it may be noble and beautiful, to the whole social and historical life, where it becomes simply vandalism or barbaric destruction. In this he is undoubtedly at one with the Puritan or the Prohibitionist or the more mechanical sort of pacifist. . . . Broadly considered, the fact that bulks biggest in the modern industrial world is this: that its moral movements are much *more* utterly and ruthlessly repressive than the past forms of mysticism or fanaticism that commonly affected only the few. Medieval men endured frightful fasts; but none of them would have dreamed of seriously proposing that nobody anywhere should ever have wine any more [as Prohibition does]. . . . Some pagan sages and some Christian saints have

been vegetarians, but nobody in the ancient world would ever have prophesied that flocks and herds would utterly vanish from the earth. . . . I admit that a saint may cut off his hand and enter heaven, and have a higher place there than the rest of us. But a plea for the amputation of the hands of all human beings, the vision of a Handless Humanity as the next evolu-tionary stage after that of the tailless ape, leaves me cold, however much it is commended as a splendid corporate self-sacrifice. . . . Though man may sacrifice anything, Everyman must not sacrifice everything.[56]

Preservation of this truth cannot be trusted to individual insights or moods of the day: it must be ensconced in teaching, carefully deliberated and ju-ridically defended. This is how dogma and charisms relate in the Catholic tradition. No matter how appealing an ecstatic spiritual movement may be, it is still necessary to examine the doctrine behind the practice, and to determine the effect the movement may have on the teaching. That the early Church was full of enthusiasms for renunciation and virginity made "all the more important the place where the dogma drew the line. A man might crawl about on all fours like a beast because he was an ascetic. He might stand night and day on the top of a pillar and be adored for being an ascetic. But he could not say that the world was a mistake or the marriage state a sin without being a heretic."[57]

As a means of stretching our minds to include what the heretic cannot include, namely, the other half of the whole truth, Chesterton recommends the experiment of telling the Christian story as if it were a heathen story. Tell the story of the God who died for humankind "without a capital G, as if it were the cult of some new and nameless tribe." Then people would sit up suddenly and say what a beautiful and touching pagan religion that must be, and in this context it could finally be explained to the pagan hedo-nist why the Catholic approves a fast of bread and water, and to the puritan prohibitionist why the Catholic approves a feast of beef and burgundy.

> When somebody says that a fast is the opposite to a feast, and yet both seem to be sacred to us, some of us will always be moved merely to say, "Yes," and relapse into an unobjectionable grin. When the anxious ethi-cal inquirer says, "Christmas is devoted to merry-making, to eating meat and drinking wine, and yet you encourage this pagan and materialistic

enjoyment," you or I will be tempted to say, "Quite right, my boy," and leave it at that. When he then says, looking even more worried, "Yet you admire men for fasting in caves and deserts and denying themselves ordinary pleasures; you are clearly committed, like the Buddhists, to the opposite or ascetic principle," we shall be similarly inspired to say, "Quite correct, old bean," or "Got it the first time, old top," and merely propose an adjournment for convivial refreshment. . . .

[S]uppose there appears on this earth a prodigy, a portent, or what is alleged to be a portent. In some way heaven has rent the veil or the gods have given some new marvel to mankind. Suppose, for instance, it is a fountain of magic water, said to be flowing at the top of a mountain. It blesses like holy water; it heals diseases; it inspires more than wine, or those who drink of it never thirst again. Well, this story may be true or false; but among those who spread it as true, it is perfectly obvious that the story will produce a number of other stories. It is equally obvious that those stories will be of two kinds. The first sort will say: "When the water was brought down to the valley there was dancing in all the villages; the young men and the maidens rejoiced with music and laughter. A surly husband and wife were sprinkled with the holy water and reconciled, so that their house was full of happy children. A cripple was sprinkled and he went capering about gaily like an acrobat. The gardens were watered and became gay with flowers," and so on. It is quite equally obvious that there will be another sort of story from exactly the same source, told with exactly the same motive. "A man limped a hundred miles, till he was quite lame, to find the sacred fountain. Men lay broken and bleeding among the rocks on the mountainside in their efforts to climb after it. A man sold all his lands and the rivers running through them for one drop of the water. A man refused to turn back from it, when confronted with brigands, but was tortured and died calling for it," and so on. There is nothing in the least inconsistent between these two types of legend. They are exactly what would naturally be expected, given the original legend of the miraculous fountain.[58]

In this contrast, Chesterton's power of paradox becomes evident again. He is capable of thinking two thoughts at once—the goodness of creation for many and the value of renunciation by some—because he is capable of thinking about two simultaneous facts about the world: it is good and it is fallen. The cure for disordered life in the world is not life out of this world, but ordered life in the world. Catholics believe "that there are no bad things, but only bad uses of things. If you will, there are no bad things but only bad thoughts; and especially bad intentions. . . . But it is possible to have bad intentions about good things; and good things, like the world and the flesh, have been twisted by a bad intention called the devil. But he cannot make *things* bad; they remain as on the first day of creation. The work of heaven alone was material; the making of a material world. The work of hell is entirely spiritual."[59] Escape from the world could be entertained as a salutary course of action only if disorderliness was confused with depravity. But the Catholic mind is not confused; it "moves upon two planes; that of the Creation and that of the Fall. . . . Any extreme of Catholic asceticism is a wise, or unwise, precaution against the evil of the Fall; it is *never* a doubt about the good of the Creation."[60]

There are various reactions to the problem of evil, Chesterton writes. The pessimist thinks the background is black and admits a speck or two of goodness, more or less accidental and insignificant; the Christian Scientist thinks the background is white and explains away dots and smudges; the dualist thinks black and white are equally represented, like a checkerboard with black and white squares. But that Catholic philosopher Thomas Aquinas thinks, on the one hand, "'Every existence, as such, is good.' On the other hand, something else tells him that it is unmanly and debased and even diseased to minimize evil to a dot or even a blot. He realizes that optimism is morbid. It is if possible even more morbid than pessimism. These vague but healthy feelings, if he followed them out, would result in the idea that evil is in some way an exception but an enormous exception; and ultimately that evil is an invasion or yet more truly a rebellion."[61]

Saints are few; the many live ordinary lives; but it is an accomplishment to be ordinary because it is an ascetical feat for our will to order our lives. To receive God's freshets of grace without pessimism or boredom is an ascetical humility, and in no way denigrated by the presence of saints in our midst. Nor is it treated so by any of these holy men and women whose saintliness is genuine.

A saint may be any kind of man, with an additional quality that is at once unique and universal. We may even say that the one thing which separates a saint from ordinary men is his readiness to be one with ordinary men. In this sense the word ordinary must be understood in its native and noble meaning; which is connected with the word order. A saint is long past any desire for distinction; he is the only sort of superior man who has never been a superior person. All this rises from a great central fact, which he does not condescend to call a privilege, but which is in its very nature a sort of privacy; and in that sense almost a form of private property. As with all sound private property, it is enough for him that he has it, he does not desire to limit the number of people who have it. He is always trying to hide it, out of a sort of celestial good manners; and Thomas Aquinas tried to hide it more than most.[62]

Sainthood is not a privilege. The saint, knowing himself or herself to be gifted, is humble.

This sense of celestial good manners is symbolized by Becket's unusual habit (I mean the monastic garb). "Becket wore a hair shirt under his gold and crimson, and there is much to be said for the combination; for Becket got the benefit of the hair shirt while the people in the street got the benefit of the crimson and gold. It is at least better than the manner of the modern mil-lionaire, who has the black and the drab outwardly for others, and the gold next his heart."[63] The saint is a flamboyantly private sort of person who does not think himself or herself superior to the ordinary person, because in this context "ordinary" does not mean commonplace, unimportant, or failed. The saint is God's midwife. The saint lives his or her life abnormally in order to assist ordinary people to live their lives normally. The saintly life is lived upside down so that the world, through the saint, can be seen aright. St. Francis's radical liberty from possessions assists those who manage pos-sessions to struggle against the upside-down perversity of using what should be enjoyed while enjoying what should be used. The service rendered by the professional ascetic (one who has professed a vow) to the ascetics who have not professed a vow (lay persons; nonprofessionals) is to turn the world right side up before their eyes by turning himself or herself upside down.

> If a man saw the world upside down, with all the trees and towers hanging head downwards as in a pool, one effect would be to emphasise the idea of dependence. There is a Latin and literal connection; for the very word de-

pendence only means hanging. It would make vivid the Scriptural text which says that God has hanged the world upon nothing. If St. Francis had seen, in one of his strange dreams, the town of Assisi upside down, it need not have differed in a single detail from itself except in being entirely the other way round. But the point is this: that whereas to the normal eye the large masonry of its walls or the massive foundations of its watchtowers and its high citadel would make it seem safer and more permanent, the moment it was turned over the very same weight would make it seem more helpless and more in peril. . . . Instead of being merely proud of his strong city because it could not be moved, he would be thankful to God Almighty that it had not been dropped; he would be thankful to God for not dropping the whole cosmos like a vast crystal to be shattered into falling stars. Perhaps St. Peter saw the world so, when he was crucified head-downwards.[64]

We do not all of us have to suffer these lengths; we may, any of us, choose to do so; we must, each of us, repair the fall by living life right side up.

The saint has sometimes been depicted as one who hurries ahead to the end of the pilgrimage on which all Christians have embarked. A few are called ahead. They run further ahead because they run faster because, by the vow of poverty, they run unburdened. The many will arrive by and by, but along the way their task is to gather up creation. They arrive at the same place, but carrying sanctified marriages, redeemed cities, evange-lized philosophies, and the raw material out of which Christ will make the new heavens and new earth. Chesterton called the saintly life "a form of private property"; but the lay person in his or her ordinary duties is not a "private person." The duties of stewarding creation and serving the King-dom's advance is a public work, a political work, conducted in service of the *polis*. Would the saint hurrying on blame the others for doing their duty? Would those doing their duty blame the saint for hurrying on? These two expressions of charity, public and private, are not in competition because ultimately, finally, they are dual expressions of what is the single source of asceticism: love. Love is the ingredient which makes gratitude grateful, which is why Chesterton said it is impossible to be grateful without the-ology. Chesterton was not just dumbfounded by *Ens*; he was grateful. That is why he was not disappointed when he found the human fingers inside the mysterious puppet: if the puppet was moved by a personal agent, then he had a personal recipient for his gratitude. For the identical reason, he was not disappointed when he found the Trinity behind his fairy godmother. "What Christianity says is merely this. That this repetition in Nature has its origin not in a thing resembling a law but a thing resembling a will."[65] Love is a personal capacity, only possible for persons, as gratitude is a personal attitude, only extended to persons.

The attempt to understand asceticism, meritorious works, the treasury of merit, or the relationship between the saint and the ordinary Christian will always end in failure unless one admits the possibility of wild, refreshing, bracing divine love. Chesterton states this truth most forcefully when he relates the story of St. Francis helping Clare at the tender age of seventeen run away to become a nun. "If we like to put it so, he helped her to elope into the cloister," Chesterton laughs, since the scene had "many of the elements of a regular romantic elopement." Clare escaped through a hole in the wall, fled against her father's wishes, and was received at midnight by the light of torches. "Now about that incident I will here only say this. If it had really been a romantic elopement and the girl had become a bride instead of a nun, practically the whole modern world would have made her a heroine. . . . The point for the moment is that modern romanticism entirely encourages such defiance of parents when it is done in the name of romantic love. For it knows that romantic love is a reality, but it does not know that divine love is a reality."[66]

We like love stories and adventure tales because they awaken our homesickness. They remind us that we were made for a world in which rivers run with wine and where bread can become the body of God. We are royalty in exile, made for blessing, battle, and beatitude. The professed ascetics are walking adventure tales who awaken our eagerness for whatever wild ascetical adventure is the condition for going home.

THREE

The Ordinary Life

Chesterton said of himself, "I am ordinary in the correct sense of the term; which means the acceptance of an order; a Creator and the Creation, the common sense of gratitude for Creation, life and love as gifts permanently good, marriage and chivalry as laws rightly controlling them, and the rest of the normal traditions of our race and religion."[1] When he champions the common person in the communal life known as a family, it is not an avocation tangential to his theological interests. Rather, as we saw in the last chapter, wonder which provokes gratitude results in an ascetical life, and Chesterton believes this to be a commonsense response to permanently good gifts. Regrettably, these permanently good, spiritual gifts are regularly devalued to the level of utilitarian goods. There is a reductive anthropology which tends to limit the human person to a function or a market, to a worker on an assembly line or a subject for a specialist to improve upon. Such modern heretics

> have taken what all ancient philosophers called the Good, and translated it as the Goods. . . . They ought to have said, not "Trade is Good," but "Living Is Good," or "Life Is Good." I suppose it would be too much to expect such thoroughly respectable people to say, "God is Good"; but it is really true that their conception of what is good lacks the philosophical finality that belonged to the goodness of God. When God looked on created things and saw that they were good, it meant that they were good in themselves and as they stood; but by the modern mercantile idea, God would only have looked at them and seen that they were the Goods. . . . All the flowers and birds would be ticketed with their reduced prices; all

creation would be for sale or all the creatures seeking employment; with all the morning stars making sky-signs together and all the Sons of God shouting for jobs. . . . The idea of a man enjoying a thing in itself, for himself, is inconceivable to them.[2]

Chesterton defends the common life of ordinary men and women because he believes that they were created by God to enjoy good things. He revolts against the various progressive movements appearing in his day which offered to improve the common institutions of family and school and home, wondering why the idea of a man and woman enjoying each other, their family, their children, and their home was so inconceivable to these specialists. Of course he has an answer in mind to the rhetorical question: it is because these heresies operate from a narrow anthropology dislodged from the broad, theological horizon. We shall consider three expressions of Chesterton's apologetic for the ordinary human life: (i) a defense of the common man and woman against the specialist, (ii) which can be seen in his definition of democracy, (iii) where such self-government is exercised in a liberty afforded by home and marriage.

Chesterton's conviction that religion is necessary in order to preserve the freedom of persons was the point on which he found his public voice. In 1903 Robert Blatchford declared in an article in his newspaper, the *Clarion*, that the case for science was complete and the structure upon which the religions of the world stood had been demolished. Blatchford sought to build a better religion of philanthropy which would not waste time gazing at the celestial spheres but would commit itself to the alleviation of human suffering in the slums, and he did so under the conviction that social improvements would come about by manipulation of environment. Improvement could therefore be best achieved if the individual would surrender certain liberties to the state, the uneducated person surrender certain plebian desires to the pundit, and the slum dweller surrender certain rights to the social engineer. After reading some articles by Chesterton critical of this deterministic outlook, Blatchford offered to print in the *Clarion* the unedited responses by Chesterton and several others. When Chesterton made his reply, he again exhibits his combined qualities of personal amiability and polemical verve, for he begins his remarks by offering Mr. Blatchford gratitude, "and something which is better than gratitude, our congratulations, upon the very magnanimous action which he has taken in thus putting his paper into the hands of his religious opponents. In doing so he has scored, in a generous unconsciousness, a real point."[3] On the other hand, Chesterton concludes his remarks with some of his most biting sarcasm, depicting Mr. Blatchford's cure by means of environmental and hereditary manipulation as the most enslaving threat of all.

> There is a liberty that has made men happy in dungeons, as it may make them happy in slums. It is the liberty of the mind, that is to say, it is the one liberty on which Mr. Blatchford makes war. That which all the tyrants have left, he would extinguish. . . . More numerous than can be counted, in all the wars and persecutions of the world, men have looked out of their little grated windows and said "at least my thoughts are free." "No, No," says the face of Mr. Blatchford, suddenly appearing at the window, "your thoughts are the inevitable result of heredity and environment. Your thoughts are as material as your dungeons. Your thoughts are as mechanical as the guillotine." So pants this strange comforter from cell to cell. . . .
>
> I know that this will never be. . . . But if ever it does I will very easily predict what will happen. Man, the machine, will stand up in these flowery meadows and cry aloud, "Was there not once a thing, a church, that taught us we were free in our souls?"[4]

Chesterton's constant refrain in his book of essays, *What's Wrong with the World,* is that "we do not ask what is right" (41); we cannot create anything good until we have conceived it, and we cannot conceive it until we know for what end it should exist (163); what's wrong is that we alter the person to fit his or her conditions rather than altering conditions to fit people (104). If we would right what's wrong with the means, we must begin by considering the end. And such consideration cannot be made except by the free human spirit. "Those who tell us, with a monotonous metaphor, that we cannot put the clock back, seem to be curiously unconscious of the fact that their own clock has stopped. And there is nothing so hopeless as clockwork when it stops. A machine cannot mend itself; it requires a man to mend it; and the future lies with those who can make living laws for men and not merely dead laws for machinery."[5] What's wrong with the world is that the "tyranny of precedent" (148) hoodwinks us into believing we cannot stop what has begun, or undo what has been done.

> If I am to discuss what is wrong, one of the first things that are wrong is this: the deep and silent modern assumption that past things have become impossible. There is one metaphor of which the moderns are very fond; they are always saying, "You can't put the clock back." The simple and obvious answer is, "You can." A clock, being a piece of human construction, can be restored by the human finger to any figure or hour. In the same way society, being a piece of human construction, can be reconstructed upon any plan that has ever existed. . . .
>
> This is the first freedom that I claim: the freedom to restore. I claim a right to propose as a solution the old patriarchal system of a Highland clan, if that should seem to eliminate the largest number of evils. . . . I claim the right to propose the complete independence of the small Greek or Italian towns, a sovereign city of Brixton or Brompton, if that seems the best way out of our troubles. . . . I merely claim my choice of all the tools in the universe; and I shall not admit that any of them are blunted merely because they have been used.[6]

In saying this, Chesterton is not just a nostalgist pining for the past. His primary interest is not to defend the past, it is to defend the right to choose.[7] To make such choice requires, first, against Blatchford, acknowledgment of a spiritual dimension in the human person wherein alone liberty is grounded. Second, it requires exercising that spiritual dimension against the "huge modern heresy of altering the human soul to fit its conditions, instead of altering human conditions to fit the human soul. If soap-boiling is really inconsistent with brotherhood, so much the worst for soap-boiling, not for brotherhood." Chesterton is not against modern invention, he is against what is against the human person. He is not measuring the present against the past, he is measuring every choice—past and present—by the human person. "Certainly, it would be better to do without soap rather than without society. Certainly, we would sacrifice all our wires, wheels, systems, specialties, physical science and frenzied finance for one half-hour of happiness such as has often come to us with comrades in a common tavern. I do not say the sacrifice will be necessary; I only say it will be easy."[8] Choices contrary to modern progress might not be necessary, but they will be easy if it comes to choosing between measuring and cutting the person to fit an industrial need or shaping any institution to human happiness.

> Mr. Middleton Murry . . . is content to say that industrialism has turned the world into One Man, who is aching in all his limbs. No doubt; and so would you and I, if we were all unnaturally tied to each other neck and heels, that we might make up together the monstrous and tottering figure of a pantomime ogre. But I do not want the ogre; I only want to cut him up. I am more revolutionary than Mr. Middleton Murry. I do not believe the unnatural monster will ache any the less, because he calls himself a Communist. I am more sceptical than Mr. Middleton Murry. I deny the pantomime myth of the One Man; and I should like to break him up again into men.[9]

Chesterton is not easily placed in an ideological camp, because in championing the ordinary life he attacks both ends of the political spectrum: the energetic progressive, whom he names Hudge, and the obstinate conservative, whom he names Gudge. Hudge would get people out of the slums at all costs, so runs up a row of tenements like beehives; Gudge persuades himself that slums and stinks are really very nice things.[10] At the end, Chesterton wonders whether they aren't in secret partnership, because what the good Hudge preaches turns out to be exactly what Gudge needs. Gudge wants cheap labor, docile employees, and an everincreasing supply of workers; Hudge preaches the lyric praises of anarchy, teetotalism, and pacifism, and contributes to the supply of cheap labor by advocating that women must also work in the factory.[11] More to the point, Chesterton's concern is theological and he is therefore committed to a thoroughgoing humanism. He does not, with the secularist, draw the line between God and humanity, as if these are antagonists. What is opposed is anything which mars human nature and disables human happiness, and such a thing would be opposed by both God and the humanist. We do not offend God except by doing something contrary to our own good. Human beings are the glory of God and for that reason are to be hallowed. Recreating the human person to feed the state's appetite damages the property of the Creator and is a trespass as well as a blasphemy. "Unless we have some doctrine of a divine man, all abuses may be excused," Chesterton warns, "since evolution may turn them into uses. Evolution has produced the snail and the owl; evolution can pro-duce a workman who wants no more space than a snail, and no more light than an owl. The employer need not mind sending a kaffir to work under-ground; he will soon become an underground animal, like a mole. . . . Men need not trouble to alter conditions; conditions will so soon alter men. The head can be beaten small enough to fit the hat. Don't knock the fetters off the slave; knock the slave until he forgets the fetters."[12]

It is important to ask what standard of state and family would ful-fill human happiness, and to first evaluate this ideal apart from whether it can be completely obtained. Such a question is exactly a theological anthro-pology, which is the concern of the Christian doctrine of the Fall. Ask what the human being was meant to do, do not ask what can be done with the human being. "It is rather as if a nurse had tried a rather bitter food for some years on a baby, and on discovering that it was not suitable, should not throw away the food and ask for a new food, but throw the baby out of the window, and ask for a new baby. Mr. Shaw cannot understand that the thing which is valuable and lovable in our eyes is man—the old beer-drinking, creed-making, fighting, failing, sensual, respectable man. And the things that have been founded on this creature immortally remain."[13] Living the general life is a human accomplishment, not improved upon by new speciation.

> The subconscious popular instinct against Darwinianism was not a mere offense at the grotesque notion of visiting one's grandfather in a cage in the Regent's Park. Men go in for drink, practical jokes and many other grotesque things; they do not much mind making beasts of themselves, and would not much mind having beasts made of their forefathers. The real instinct was much deeper and much more valuable. It was this: that when once one begins to think of man as a shifting and alterable thing, it is always easy for the strong and crafty to twist him into new shapes for all kinds of unnatural purposes. The popular instinct sees in such develop-ments the possibility of backs bowed and hunch-backed for their burden, or limbs twisted for their task. . . . It has therefore a vision of inhuman hy-brids and half-human experiments.[14]

Chesterton defends the general life against the specialist. He knows that the human organism can be developed so as to become adapted to a specific function or environment but finds universal humanity far more interest- ing and worth fighting for. He is suspicious about the ideal of improving ancient, democratic human institutions by specialization. He makes his point by sketching a parallel case of how objects lower on the spectrum of specialization have greater value and usefulness.

Cast your eye round the room in which you sit, and select some three or four things that have been with man almost since his beginning. . . . About each of these you will notice one specialty; that not one of them is special. Each of these ancestral things is a universal thing; made to supply many different needs. . . . The knife is meant to cut wood, to cut cheese, to cut pencils, to cut throats; for a myriad ingenious or innocent human ob- jects. The stick is meant partly to hold a man up, partly to knock a man down; partly to point with like a finger-post, partly to balance with like a balancing pole, partly to trifle with like a cigarette, partly to kill with like a club of a giant; it is a crutch and a cudgel; an elongated finger and an extra leg. The case is the same, of course, with the fire; about which the strangest modern views have arisen. A queer fancy seems to be current that a fire exists to warm people. It exists to warm people, to light their darkness, to raise their spirits, to toast their muffins, to air their rooms, to cook their chestnuts, to tell stories to their children, to make checkered shadows on their walls, to boil their hurried kettles, and to be the red heart of a man's house and that hearth for which, as the great heathens said, a man should die.

Now it is the great mark of our modernity that people are always proposing substitutes for these old things; and these substitutes always answer one purpose where the old thing answered ten. . . . If a man found a coil of rope in a desert he could at least think of all the things that can be done with a coil of rope; and some of them might even be practical. He could tow a boat or lasso a horse. He could play cat's cradle, or pick oakum. He could construct a rope-ladder for an eloping heiress, or cord her boxes for a traveling maiden aunt. He could learn to tie a bow, or he could hang himself. Far otherwise with the unfortunate traveler who should find a telephone in the desert. You can telephone with a telephone; you cannot do anything else with it. . . .

Spiritually, at least, it will be admitted that some all-round balance is needed to equalize the extravagance of experts.[15]

What he admires about the old, ancestral things, like the domicile, is its multifacetedness. The fire has many more uses to admire than merely its pragmatic one. He finds the home emancipatory not only because one can act freely there, as we shall see below, but because the variegation demanded in the home broadens a person. Although what moved Chesterton to argue this point the way he does was the particular claim by Hudge that the service provided by women in the factory was more valuable than any work done at home, the resultant apology for parenting might be used to defend the vocation by both sexes against the modern inclination to devalue this com-mitment.

> If drudgery only means dreadfully hard work, I admit the woman drudges in the home, as a man might drudge at the Cathedral of Amiens or drudge behind a gun at Trafalgar. But if it means that the hard work is more heavy because it is trifling, colorless and of small import to the soul, then as I say, I give it up; I do not know what the words mean. To be Queen Eliza-beth within a definite area, deciding sales, banquets, labors and holidays; to be Whiteley [a general goods store] within a certain area, providing toys, boots, sheets, cakes, and books, to be Aristotle within a certain area, teach-ing morals, manners, theology, and hygiene; I can understand how this might exhaust the mind, but I cannot imagine how it could narrow it. How can it be a large career to tell other people's children about the Rule of Three, and a small career to tell one's own children about the universe? How can it be broad to be the same thing to everyone, and narrow to be everything to someone? No; a woman's function is laborious, but because it is gigantic, not because it is minute. I will pity Mrs. Jones for the hugeness of her task; I will never pity her for its smallness.[16]

Against his age of professional specializations, Chesterton holds up a picture of the Victorian age as a time when one was not exhaustively defined by one's employment. He describes his father as someone who "sold houses for his living but filled his own house with his life." Leisure did not exist for the sake of work; work existed for the sake of leisure. After-hour hobbies at home were not just diversions or sports to relax the worker and enable greater toil upon returning to the workplace, these hobbies were "parallel lives." The toy theater built by his father required him to be the stage carpenter, "the architect and the builder and the draughtsman and the land-scape painter and the story-teller all in one."[17]

The social engineers who spin their visions of utopian bliss do so, they say, for the good of the common person; there is only one small fee. It will cost ordinary people their ordinary lives. The ordinary person will have to be re-thrown, like a clay pot, to fit special purposes. Chesterton, on the con-trary, sees no reason to put power or wealth or control in the hands of someone merely because he is an expert. "The expert is more aristocratic than the aristocrat, because the aristocrat is only the man who lives well, while the expert is the man who knows better. But if we look at the progress of our scientific civilization we see a gradual increase everywhere of the spe-cialist over the popular function. Once men sang together round a table in chorus; now one man sings alone, for the absurd reason that he can sing better. If scientific civilization goes on (which is most improbable) only one man will laugh, because he can laugh better than the rest."[18] In an essay criticizing H. G. Wells's optimism in *The Food of the Gods* that the lot of humankind will be improved by putting the common person in the hands of sociologists, scientists, doctors, and city planners, Chesterton suggests reading the book as "the tale of 'Jack the Giant-Killer' told from the point of view of the giant." No doubt "the giant whom Jack killed did regard himself as the Superman."

> It is likely enough that he considered Jack as a narrow and parochial person who wished to frustrate a great forward movement of the life-force. If (as not unfrequently was the case) he happened to have two heads, he would point out the elementary maxim which declares them to be better than one. . . . But Jack was the champion of the enduring human stan-dards, of the principle of one man one head and one man one conscience, of the single head and the single heart and the single eye. Jack was quite unim-pressed by the question of whether the giant was a particularly gigantic

giant. All he wished to know was whether he was a good giant—that is, a giant who was any good to us. What were the giant's religious views: what his views on politics and the duties of the citizen? Was he fond of children—or fond of them only in a dark and sinister sense? To use a fine phrase for emotional sanity, was his heart in the right place? Jack had some/ times to cut him up with a sword in order to find out.[19]

Being gigantic in ambition is no guarantee that the ambition is good. Or good for us. From their lofty height giants may have a difficult time seeing the small things, but in such small things is the good life lived by most of the human race, and if that race is made up of men and women created for a divine destiny beyond the factory, then no matter how pleasant life in the factory is made to be, it will never contain the human destiny. The tail must not wag the dog. Will the giant be any good to us, Chesterton wants to know, or are we only good for the giant because we are purchasers of his goods or practitioners of his ideology? Will society be crafted to fit human desires, or will human desires be reshaped by propaganda and government programs to fit the way a few giants have shaped society to suit themselves? Do political decisions serve to preserve the home, or are homes broken up into pieces to more easily refit the latest project by social engineers?

Chesterton spins an essay off a newspaper account of a bill passed in Parliament to shave short the hair of all little girls in the London slums be/ cause of an epidemic of lice. It ends in a battle cry for making humanity the measure of all things.

> When a crapulous tyranny crushes men down into the dirt, so that their hair is dirty, the scientific course is clear. It would be long and laborious to cut off the heads of the tyrants; it is easier to cut off the hair of the slaves. In the same way, if it should ever happen that poor children, screaming with toothache, disturbed any schoolmaster or artistic gentleman, it would be easy to pull out all the teeth of the poor; if their nails were disgustingly dirty, their nails could be plucked out; if their noses were indecently blown, their noses could be cut off. . . . It never seems to strike these people that the lesson of lice in the slums is the wrongness of slums, not the wrongness of hair. . . . If a house is so built as to knock a man's head off when he enters it, it is built wrong. . . .

With the red hair of one she-urchin in the gutter I will set fire to all modern civilization. Because a girl should have long hair, she should have clean hair; because she should have clean hair, she should not have an unclean home; because she should not have an unclean home, she should have a free and leisured mother; because she should have a free mother, she should not have a usurious landlord; because there should not be a usurious landlord, there should be a redistribution of property, because there should be a redistribution of property, there shall be a revolution. That little urchin with the gold-red hair, whom I have just watched toddling past my house, she shall not be lopped and lamed and altered; her hair shall not be cut short like a convict's; no, all the kingdoms of the earth shall be hacked about and mutilated to suit her. She is the human and sacred image; all around her the social fabric shall sway and split and fall; the pillars of society shall be shaken, and the roofs of ages come rushing down; and not one hair of her head shall be harmed.[20]

Is there a place for specialists? Chesterton admits they are valuable for the "particular and practical purpose of predicting the approach of enormous and admitted human calamities"; and experts can be called upon to amend abnormalities which the common person cannot rectify due to lack of skill or capacity or opportunity; but Chesterton draws the line when the solitary expert is given the authority to decide what is normal. A specialized expertise qualifies the specialist to solve calamities, it does not give him or her the right "to define what is a calamity; or to call things calamities which common-sense does not call calamities. . . . And as he has no moral authority to enforce a new conception of happiness, so he has no moral authority to enforce a new conception of sanity."[21] In other words, professionals are useful for serving the ends of persons but not for deciding the end of persons. And this is what Chesterton means by democracy, the second expression of the ordinary human life we will consider.

There are some activities which not everyone does well. By way of example, Chesterton thinks to mention such varied accomplishments as playing the church organ, painting on vellum, or discovering the North Pole. These are things we do not wish a person to do unless he or she does them well. But government, on the contrary, is not a thing in this class. It is a thing more "analogous to writing one's own love-letters or blowing one's own nose. These things we want a man to do for himself, even if he does them badly. . . . In short, the democratic faith is this: that the most terribly important things must be left to ordinary men themselves—the mating of the sexes, the rearing of the young, the laws of the state. This is democracy; and in this I have always believed."[22] The democratic view sees child-rearing and parenting to be responsibilities of the home, and the craze in Chesterton's day to give these responsibilities over to the state he saw as regress, not progress. Quite apart from the question of resources—even if officials of the state "grew like grass or bred like rabbits" so there was an endless supply of salaried persons to hire for these tasks—it would be abnormal for the state "to undertake all that human beings naturally do for themselves, including the care of children. . . . The actual effect of this theory is that one harassed person has to look after a hundred children, instead of one normal person looking after a normal number of them."[23]

Chesterton nuances what he means by "democratic." He says he does not simply mean "arbitrament by the majority," or "arbitrament by everybody," therefore he must not be simply playing to antigovernment sentiment. What he means by "democratic," properly put, is "arbitrament by anybody" because democracy consists of those things that could be inevitably assumed as held in common by oneself and a stranger. "Only the things that anybody may be presumed to hold have the full authority of democracy. Look out the window and notice the first man who walks by. The Liberals may have swept England with an over-whelming majority; but you would not stake a button that the man is a Liberal. . . . But you would bet your week's wages, let us say, that he believes in wearing clothes. You would bet that he believes that physical courage is a fine thing, or that parents have authority over children. . . . Of these universal dogmas that have full democratic authority the only test is this test of anybody."[24] The "test of anybody" seems to be what Chesterton calls "common sense," meaning a sense that is common. It is a common sense because it is available to ordinary people. It belongs to the common person, as the public person, not the private person privy to secret knowledge and peering at things from specialized viewpoints. Chesterton judges most modern philosophy (since the sixteenth century) to have failed to correspond to "everybody's sense of reality; to what, if left to

themselves, common men would call common sense," because each philosophy began with a paradox which turned out to be a peculiar point of
view demanding the sacrifice of a sane point of view. To follow these philosophies, "[a] man had to believe something that no normal man would
believe, if it were suddenly propounded to his simplicity; [such] as that law
is above right, or right is outside reason, or things are only as we think them,
or everything is relative to a reality that is not there."[25]

And the most common state of common persons, Chesterton claims,
the most ordinary way to live, is in a home. This is the third expression of his
apologetic for the common life we will consider. Even though the Superman
has designs on outgrowing marriage, Chesterton will champion the "thrill
of domesticity." Even lacking special skills, the average person can follow
God's general order to the residents of Eden to subdue the earth and cultivate
it. "The average man cannot cut clay into the shape of a man; but he can cut
earth into the shape of a garden; and though he arranges it with red gerani-
ums and blue potatoes in alternate straight lines, he is still an artist; because
he has chosen. The average man cannot paint the sunset whose colors he admires; but he can paint his own house with what color he chooses, and
though he paints it pea green with pink spots, he is still an artist; because
that is his choice."[26] In making such choices, the average person is freed from
the giant's gigantic claims, those claims which really do reach, excessively,
into realms where they do not belong. Jack the Giant Killer has the weapon
of religion at his disposal, just as David had a stone for his sling when he
faced Goliath; indeed, it is the only defense which is lethal to the giant. The
family feeling is a sure instinct, but for its protection against fluctuating
moods it must become an ideal; and "the obvious thing to protect an ideal is
a religion. The obvious thing to protect the ideal of marriage is the Christian
religion. . . . I do not dream of denying, indeed I should take every opportunity of affirming, that monogamy and its domestic responsibilities can be
defended on rational apart from religious grounds. But a religion is the practical protection of any moral idea which has to be popular and which has to
be pugnacious."[27] David has the rock named Peter in his sling.

Again and again Chesterton espouses the belief that because the
family is a sacred place, it is a free place. The home preserves a freedom of
such intensity that he calls the liberty found therein true anarchy. "It may be

said that this institution of the home is the one anarchist institution. That is to say, it is older than law, and stands outside the State."[28] Other anarchists seek their liberty by stepping outside all social structures; Chesterton finds liberty within the most social of all structures, marriage and the family. It is ludicrous to suggest that escape from the home is an escape into greater freedom when one considers the absence of constraint in the home and the ubiquity of constraints everywhere else.

> [T]he world outside the home is now under a rigid discipline and routine and it is only inside the home that there is really a place for individuality and liberty. Anyone stepping out of the frontdoor is obliged to step into a procession, all going the same way and to a great extent even obliged to wear the same uniform. . . . If the Duchess does want to play leapfrog, she must not start suddenly leaping in the manner of a frog across the ballroom of the Babylon Hotel, when it is crowded with the fifty best couples professionally practising the very latest dance, for the instruction of society. The Duchess will find it easier to practice leapfrog to the admiration of her intimate friends in the old oakpanelled hall of Fitzdragon Castle.[29]

Chesterton confesses, by an endearing and amusing example, to practice in his own home the anarchistic limits which are permitted: he and Frances often take evening supper as a picnic on the floor. The home "is the only spot on earth where a man can alter arrangements suddenly, make an experiment or indulge in a whim. Everywhere else he goes he must accept the strict rules of the shop, inn, club, or museum that he happens to enter. He can eat his meals on the floor in his own house if he likes. I often do it myself; it gives a curious, childish, poetic, picnic feeling. . . . For a plain, hardworking man the home is not the only tame place in the world of adventure. It is the one wild place in the world of rules and set tasks."[30]

Then how did the heretic come to mistake liberty as freedom *from* order, and believe that freedom is attained by denying home and marriage? How did anarchy come to be defined as disorder? The way the heretic always reaches his error: by seeing only half the truth. In a more serious discussion of the threats which moral lawlessness poses to persons, Chesterton acknowledges that, instead of his definition of anarchy as maximum freedom (one more adequately achieved within the home than without it), popular custom employs a definition of anarchy as freedom exercised against an order. In that definition, Chesterton admits, "[a]narchy is that condition of mind or methods in which you cannot stop yourself. It is the loss of that self-control which can return to the normal." But this is precisely the half-truth. Anarchy has been semi-defined as permission to start loosing the bonds of control; it has not been fully defined as enabling a person to keep control, and Chesterton can again draw upon his example of picnicking at home to make his point. "It is not anarchy because men are permitted to begin uproar, extravagance, experiment, peril. It is anarchy when people cannot *end* these things. . . . It was not anarchy in the Roman villa when, during the Saturnalia, the slaves turned masters or the masters slaves. It was (from the slave-owners' point of view) anarchy if, after the Saturnalia, the slaves continued to behave in a Saturnalian manner. . . . It is not anarchy to have a picnic; but it is anarchy to lose all memory of mealtimes. . . . It is this inability to return within rational limits after a legitimate extravagance that is the really dangerous disorder."[31]

It is in this context that we can appreciate one of Chesterton's wittier indictments of the modern mood about love, an opinion which considers love free when it is uncontrolled. "They talk of free love when they mean something quite different, better defined as free lust. But being sentimentalists they feel bound to simper and coo over the word 'love.' They insist on talking about Birth Control when they mean less birth and no control."[32]

If a marriage commitment was based on mood, even the deep and holy mood of love, it could not survive because human beings are too moody. We are never in the same humor for ten minutes together. In light of these flitting interests, "no man can say he will even be the same man by the next month or the next minute." But that makes impossible all those parts of life which only exist due to their construction over time, whether personal or professional identities. "A man cannot choose a profession; because, long before he has qualified as an architect, he may have mystically changed into an aviator, or be convulsed in rapid succession by the emotions of a ticket-collector, a trombone-player and a professional harpooner of whales . . . [T]he reply, not merely of religion but of reason and the rooted sanity of mankind is obvious enough. 'If you feel like that, why certainly you will not found families; or found anything else.'"[33] Marriage and the family are

longer-lasting things than the current mood can understand, because they
are eternal things, meaning they partake of the eternal and must be held in
place by an act of will through temporal vicissitudes.

> In everything worth having, even in every pleasure, there is a point of
> pain or tedium that must be survived, so that the pleasure may revive
> and endure. . . . In everything on this earth that is worth doing, there is a
> stage when no one would do it, except for necessity or honor. It is then that
> the Institution upholds a man and helps him on to the firmer ground
> ahead. . . . The essential element is not so much duration as security. Two
> people must be tied together in order to do themselves justice; for twenty
> minutes at a dance, or for twenty years in a marriage. In both cases the
> point is, that if a man is bored in the first five minutes he must go on and
> force himself to be happy. Coercion is a kind of encouragement. . . . If we
> all floated in the air like bubbles, free to drift anywhere at any instant, the
> practical result would be that no one would have the courage to begin a
> conversation. It would be so embarrassing to start a sentence in a friendly
> whisper, and then have to shout the last half of it because the other party
> was floating away into the free and formless ether.[34]

Happiness seems to be an effect not only of the affections but also of the
will. We have seen this already in Chesterton's doctrine of conditional joy.
Happiness is conditional upon an act of good faith, which as an act of will
in turn depends upon an act of faith. Thus are we returned to the theological basis for Chesterton's anthropological maximalism. To preserve the
human, one needs the divine; so in order to preserve the holiest human institution, one needs sacramental power. The faith which believes God became
incarnate in order to deify men and women believes the divine is committed
to defending what makes persons essentially human.

> The primary laws of man are to be found in the permanent life of man; in
> those things that have been common to it in every time and land, though
> in the highest civilisation they have reached an enrichment like that of the
> divine romance of Cana in Galilee. . . . For in such a case as the story of
> Cana, it may be remarked that the pedants are prejudiced against the
> earthly elements as much as, or more than, the heavenly elements. It is not

the supernatural that disgusts them, so much as the natural. And those of us who have seen all the normal rules and relations of humanity uprooted by random speculators, as if they were abnormal abuses and almost ac- cidents, will understand why men have sought for something divine if they wished to preserve anything human. They will know why common sense . . . has age after age sought refuge in the high sanity of a sacrament.[35]

Commitment of this sort will be a theological commitment or it will not be a commitment at all. It will be a salutary and sanctifying commitment. And even if not explicitly Catholic, it will be a shadow of the full truth which a Catholic fully knows. "If we are not of those who begin by in- voking a divine Trinity, we must none the less invoke a human Trinity; and see that triangle repeated everywhere in the pattern of the world."[36] This triangle was visible in the pattern which Chesterton saw in paganism even before he finally saw it in Christianity, and it is to this preparation for Catholic conversion that we next turn.

FOUR

Pan and Peter

Chesterton's path led ultimately to Catholicism because it was a home roomy enough to house ideals dismissed by the heretic for the narrow minded reason of being pagan. Chesterton's education had brought him into close contact with the world of antiquity, and he seemed to know this world imaginatively, not just recollectively. Remember that he professed to having come to Christ from Pan and Dionysius, not from Luther or Laud, and that he understood the conversion of the pagan better than that of the puritan. Although he reproves the dead end to which the pagan's natural religion ultimately led, he is a citizen of a Church which understands grace to perfect nature, and is therefore capable of perfecting natural religion. In a letter to Frances while they were still engaged to be married, he recommends that the two of them should by all means "have bad things in our dwelling and make them good things. I shall offer no objection to your having an occasional dragon to dinner, or a penitent Griffin to sleep in the spare bed."[1] He opines that the early Christians themselves "never seem to have entertained a doubt that the message would itself convert the world with a rapidity and ease which left no room for severe condemnation of the heathen societies."[2]

In order to overlay Chesterton's Catholic pagan axis on the Church world axis and the grace nature axis, I will, on the one hand, consider seriously the critique he makes of paganism and the purge which he believes Christianity effected. However, this purge was not made to protect the Church from paganism. It was made to protect paganism from its inordinate expression, so I will compare, on the other hand, the defense of pagan ideals he makes against the puritan allergic reaction.

Chesterton's Catholicism does not obscure paganism, it intersects it. This intersection transforms paganism, true; but it does not nullify or vilify the pagan world. When the human triangle and the divine trinity intersect, then grace perfects nature.

> If we are not of those who begin by invoking a divine Trinity, we must none the less invoke a human Trinity; and see that triangle repeated everywhere in the pattern of the world. For the highest event in history, to which all history looks forward and leads up, is only something that is at once the reversal and the renewal of that triangle. Or rather it is the one triangle superimposed so as to intersect the other, making a sacred pentacle of which, in a mightier sense than that of the magicians, the fiends are afraid. The old Trinity was of father and mother and child and is called the human family. The new is of child and mother and father and has the name of the Holy Family. It is in no way altered except in being entirely reversed; just as the world which is transformed was not in the least different, except in being turned upside-down.[3]

One result of this transformation is a saint, like St. Francis, and as we noted above, saints see the world upside down. But ordinary people find their ordinary worlds upended, too. The matter upon which Christian redemption works is the world. Therefore, this connection between creation and redemption assumes that the institutions of creation have a natural appetite for their final form. Chesterton features Christianity standing to pagan religion as the fulfillment of the rumors with which the religious history of humankind has been filled. "Mr. Blatchford and his school point out that there are many myths parallel to the Christian story; that there were Pagan Christs, and Red Indian Incarnations, and Patagonian Crucifixions, for all I know or care. But does not Mr. Blatchford see the other side of this fact? If the Christian God really made the human race, would not the human race tend to rumors and perversions of the Christian God? . . . If we are so made that a Son of God must deliver us, is it odd that Patagonians should dream of a Son of God?"[4]

Contradicting the many voices which fear that recognition of redemption's omega in creation's alpha will dilute evangelical purity, Chesterton replies that such voices miss the point of religion altogether. Critics who are suspicious of St. Francis for drawing inspiration from Ovid, or St. Thomas

for drawing inspiration from Aristotle, are misguided in wondering if humanism vitiates evangelicalism.

> Those who miss this, miss the point of the religion, even if it be a supersti-
> tion; nay, they miss the very point they would call most superstitious. I
> mean the whole staggering story of the God-Man in the Gospels. . . .
> [T]hey vaguely imagine that anybody who is humanising divinity must
> be paganising divinity; without seeing that the humanising of divinity
> is actually the strongest and starkest and most incredible dogma in the
> Creed. St. Francis was becoming more like Christ, and not merely more
> like Buddha, when he considered the lilies of the field or the fowls of
> the air; and St. Thomas was becoming more of a Christian, not merely
> more of an Aristotelian, when he insisted that God and the image of God
> had come in contact through matter with a material world. These saints
> were, in the most exact sense of the term, Humanists; because they were
> insisting on the immense importance of the human being in the theologi-
> cal scheme of things.[5]

Humanism is the consequence of a theology in which divinity itself was
humanized, literally. Sacramentalism and iconography is the consequence
of a materialized God. Answering inquirers who, after his conversion,
wondered whether he might someday tire of the Catholic faith (implying
that he had arrived at the Catholic faith from having tired of high Anglicanism after tiring of liberal Christianity) Chesterton muses that if he ever
did leave the Catholic Church he would not "go to any of those little social
sects which only express one idea at a time, because that idea happens to be
fashionable at the moment." He would not start sampling the many and
varied allergic reactions to a sacramental religion. "The best I could hope
for would be to wander away into the woods and become . . . a pagan, in the
mood to cry out that some particular mountain peak or flowering fruit tree
was sacred and a thing to be worshipped. That at least would be beginning
all over again; but it would bring me back to the same problem in the end.
If it was reasonable to have a sacred tree it was not unreasonable to have a
sacred crucifix."[6]

Chesterton believes the dialogue which Christianity had with paganism is a completed dialogue, because it has been an eternal dialogue: i.e., a
dialogue between human religious philosophy and the eternal. Paganism's

completion in Catholic Christianity was the fruition of religious philoso-phy, too. There are no other stones to be turned over in search of one more, last wisdom. "The limits that paganism had reached in Europe were the limits of human existence; at its best it had only reached the same limits any-where else. The Roman stoics did not need any Chinamen to teach them stoicism. The Pythagoreans did not need any Hindus to teach them about recurrence or the simple life or the beauty of being a vegetarian. . . . The Syn-cretists were as convinced as Theosophists that all religions are really the same. And how else could they have extended philosophy merely by ex-tending geography? It can hardly be proposed that they should learn a purer religion from the Aztecs or sit at the feet of the Incas of Peru."[7] "Pagans were wiser than paganism; that is why the pagans became Christians."[8]

So from what, then, did the pagan stand in need of salvation? In mod-ern fiction and light literature, one receives the impression that the pagan needed protection from atheism and hedonism, but Chesterton thinks this impression is mistaken at two points. First, the term "pagan" is taken to mean "a man without any religion, whereas a pagan was generally a man with about half a dozen." The term erroneously conjures to the uninformed mind an image of people continually dancing irresponsibly with flowers braided in their hair, "whereas, if there were two things that the best pagan civilization did honestly believe in, they were a rather too rigid dignity and a much too rigid responsibility." Second, on the civic front, "pagans are depicted as above all things inebriate and lawless, whereas they were above all things reasonable and respectable. They are praised as disobedient when they had only one great virtue—civic obedience."[9] The sum of these two mistakes, Chesterton claims, is that modern persons envy and admire pagans as shamelessly happy, while he assesses them as having in fact had the opposite, secret sin: despair. "When the pagan looks at the very core of the cosmos he is struck cold. Behind the gods, who are merely despotic, sit the fates, who are deadly. Nay, the fates are worse than deadly; they are dead."[10] Christianity's task, therefore, is not to protect the Church from pagans, but paganism from itself, by exuding a power which overcomes mortal despair.

In Chesterton's diagnosis this same mortal despair threatens to afflict us again. He thinks his own generation has become increasingly pagan, but with a difference, and in this case it is a difference which actually marks the superiority of the ancient pagan over the modern one. While ancient paganism suffered only a "practical materialism," modern pagans are under the delusion of a "theoretical materialism." While both modern and ancient pagans focus upon the material world, the latter's focus on the material did not preclude a sense of the transcendent Other. "The Pagan looks for his pleasures to the natural forces of this world; but he does not insist so strictly upon dry negations about the other; he has commonly admitted a vague borderland of the unknown, providing him with possibilities of inspiration or of awe which are forbidden to the cheap modern atheist with his clockwork cosmos. The worshippers of the Unknown God could at least build an altar, though they could not inscribe it with a name."[11] The pagan's humanism at least produced fruitful results, as his nature worship produced natural fruits. In this way the

> ancient sin was infinitely superior, immeasurably superior, to the modern sin. . . . It was at least on the side of Nature. It was at least on the side of Life. It has been left to the last Christians, or rather to the first Christians fully committed to blaspheming and denying Christianity, to invent a new kind of worship of Sex, which is not even a worship of Life. It has been left to the very latest Modernists to proclaim an erotic religion which at once exalts lust and forbids fertility. . . . Now the notion of narrowing property merely to *enjoying* money is exactly like the notion of narrowing love merely to *enjoying* sex. In both cases an incidental, isolated, servile and even secretive pleasure is substituted for participation in a great creative process; even in the everlasting Creation of the world.[12]

Paganism may have naturally come to an end, but at least it was a human end, an affirmation of the human, and its naturalism participated in the natural institutions. Probably this is why Chesterton felt a greater kinship with the world of antiquity than with the various modern attempts to recreate man and woman in service of a goal contrived against a godless horizon. For example, against the recommendation that individuals will derive greater happiness from serving the state than from being permitted the liberties of home and individuality (a position our century has seen brutally enforced on more than one occasion), Chesterton sarcastically posits an image from the insect world wherein the drone is supposed to find its greater good in "the soul of the hive," serving in the "temple of enormous entomology." Chesterton declares, "In resisting this horrible theory of the Soul of the Hive, we of Christendom stand not for ourselves, but for all humanity; for the essential and distinctive human idea that one good and happy man is an end in himself, that a soul is worth saving."[13] To treat a human being's happiness as the measure of progress seems to Chesterton more congruent with paganism than with certain modern movements.

Paganism is anthropocentric in the sense of centering upon the human, especially the human family gathered as a trin ty round the fire in the hearth. And it is not implausible to superimpose the divine Trinity on this natural scene when God has divinized human nature in order to place a pentecostal fire in the heart. The service which the Christian Gospel performs on behalf of paganism is to protect humanity's natural religious dreams lest they turn to nightmares.

> In the godhead of youth it seems easy to say, "Why cannot a man see God in a bird flying and be content?" But then comes a time when we go on and say, "If God is in the birds, let us be not only as beautiful as the birds; let us be as cruel as the birds; let us live the mad, red life of nature." And something that is wholesome in us resists and says, "My friend, you are going mad."
>
> Then comes the other side and we say: "The birds are hateful, the flowers are shameful. I will give no praise to so base a universe." And the wholesome thing in us says: "My friend, you are going mad."
>
> Now when Christianity came, the ancient world had just reached this dilemma. It heard the voice of nature worship crying, "All natural things are good: war is healthy as the flowers. Lust is as clean as the stars." And it heard also the cry of the hopeless stoics & idealists: "The flowers are at war: the stars are unclean: nothing but man's conscience is right and that is utterly defeated."
>
> Both views were consistent and philosophical and exalted: their only disadvantage was that the first leads logically to murder and the second to suicide.[14]

Paganism is natural, but by the Christian analysis we don't do nature naturally. Human appetites require ordering, or they will become inordinate appetites. To accomplish such ordering involves asceticism, and Christian tradition has always admitted that asceticism does violence to nature. But the violence is not to a natural thing (the world), it is to a thing become un-natural (the inordinate appetites of the human heart). It is no sin to pay attention to the world or to ourselves, but it is sin to idolize either. The true mistake "might almost as truly be called the mistake of being natural; and it was a very natural mistake. The Greeks...started out with the idea of some-thing splendidly obvious and direct; the idea that if man walked straight ahead on the high road of reason and nature, he would come to no harm; es-pecially if he was, as the Greek was, eminently enlightened and intelligent. We might be so flippant as to say that man was simply to follow his nose, so long as it was a Greek nose. . . . Nobody has seen the scale or the strangeness of the story. The wisest men in the world set out to be natural; and the most unnatural thing in the world was the very first thing they did."[15]

How could this happen? How is it to be explained that the very natural good we would do, we do not; and the most unnatural thing in the world which we would not do, is the first thing done? It is possible to examine the riddle close up, for it remains characteristic of the human heart still today. In Chesterton's opinion, the profound defect that destroyed paganism in its final phase is afoot again today. "We can already see men becoming un-healthy by the worship of health; becoming hateful by the worship of love; becoming paradoxically solemn and overstrained even by the idolatry of sport; and in some cases strangely morbid and infected with horrors by the perversion of a just sympathy with animals. . . . There is nothing in Pagan-ism to check its own exaggerations."[16] Truly healthy people do not think about health, because health exists for their use, that they may live. Health is simply nature, and no naturalist ought to have the impudence to make health or love or sport into God. "For God must mean, among other things, that mystical and multitudinous balance of all things, by which they are at least able to stand up straight and endure. . . . In the matter of fun-damental human rights, nothing can be above Man, except God."[17]

For want of ordinance, paganism toppled over the edge of sanity into despair. Anthropocentrism became egocentrism. "The pagan set out, with admirable sense, to enjoy himself. By the end of his civilization he had dis-covered that a man cannot enjoy himself and continue to enjoy anything else."[18] And despair often breeds cruelty after inordinate enjoyment. "I do not believe that mythology must begin with eroticism. But I do believe that mythology must end in it. I am quite certain that mythology did end in it. . . . There comes an hour in the afternoon when the child is tired of 'pre' tending'; when he is weary of being a robber or a Red Indian. It is then that he torments the cat. There comes a time in the routine of an ordered civilisation when the man is tired of playing at mythology and pretend' ing that a tree is a maiden or that the moon made love to a man. . . . [Then] men seek stranger sins or more startling obscenities as stimulants to their jaded sense."[19] The temptation is always with us, as Chesterton's cata' logue of heresies is meant to indicate. Modernism's malady is no different from paganism's—nor is modernism's hope. "If we do revive and pursue the pagan ideal of a simple and rational self'completion we shall end— where Paganism ended. I do not mean that we shall end in destruction. I mean that we shall end in Christianity."[20]

The word that comes to Chesterton's mind to describe the effect of Christianity upon paganism is "purge," and it is how he describes the effect of Christendom upon the pagan world in what is commonly known as the Dark Ages.

> Its very lusts are clean; for they have no longer any smell of perversion. Its very cruelties are clean; they are not the luxurious cruelties of the am' phitheatre. . . . The flowers and stars have recovered their first innocence. Fire and water are felt to be worthy to be the brother and sister of a saint. The purge of paganism is complete at last.
>
> For water itself has been washed. Fire itself has been purified as by fire. Water is no longer that water into which slaves were flung to feed the fishes. Fire is no longer that fire through which children were passed to Moloch. Flowers smell no more of the forgotten garlands gathered in the garden of Priapus; stars stand no more as signs of the far frigidity of gods as cold as those cold fires. . . . Man has stripped from his soul the last rag of nature'worship, and can return to nature.[21]

This cure took a number of centuries because the scar was very deep. Pagan Europe needed nothing less than a new heaven and a new earth because "they had really defiled their own earth and even their own heaven. How could their case be met by looking at the sky, when erotic legends were scrawled in stars across it; how could they learn anything from the love of birds and flowers after the sort of love stories that were told of them?" The antidote for natural religion gone bad was a religion that "was literally un, earthly. It was no good telling such people to have a natural religion full of stars and flowers; there was not a flower or even a star that had not been stained. They had to go into the desert where they could find no flowers or even into the cavern where they could see no stars. Into that desert and that cavern the highest human intellect entered for some four centuries; and it was the very wisest thing it could do."[22]

However, an unearthly religion is not finally a religion for the residents of Eden. The purge did not do away with religion and piety and ritual and sacrament. When Europe was baptized, the religious baby was not thrown out with the bathwater; the expurgation of natural religion still left nature to be enjoyed and a religion to be practiced. Therefore, Catholic Christianity was not allergic to the rhythms of nature, it did not fear the sacred wells and forests which the ancient pagan cartographers mapped across Europe, and it did not shun the celebrations which our pagan ancestors crafted. Chris, tianity can befriend nature truly, at last, as the pagan instinctively knew nature should be befriended, because the main point in Christianity is "that Nature is not our mother: Nature is our sister. We can be proud of her beauty, since we have the same father; but she has no authority over us; we have to admire, but not to imitate. This gives to the typically Christian plea, sure in this earth a strange touch of lightness that is almost frivolity. Nature was a solemn mother to the worshippers of Isis and Cybele. Nature was a solemn mother to Wordsworth or to Emerson. But Nature is not solemn to Francis of Assisi or to George Herbert. To Francis, Nature is a sister, and even a younger sister: a little, dancing sister, to be laughed at as well as loved."[23] After that long exile to the cavern, the Christian understanding of nature was first enunciated and enacted by St. Francis. He was neither afraid of Nature, nor unwilling to exercise the dominion which the human had been precisely created to wield in the garden.[24] "A bishop is said to have complained of a Nonconformist saying Paul instead of Saint Paul; and to have added 'He might at least have called him Mr. Paul.' So St. Francis is free of all obligation to cry out in praise or terror on the Lord God Apollo, but in his new nursery heavens, he salutes him as Mr. Sun. Those are the things in which he has a sort of inspired infancy, only to be paralleled in nursery tales. Something of the same hazy but healthy awe makes the story of Brer Fox and Brer Rabbit refer respectfully to Mr. Man."[25]

St. Thomas, too, affirms the sensual world and human rationality. Why, he even believes that the world known to the senses can be the start' ing point of a chain of reasoning begun by Aristotle which could lead to the conviction that God exists. "[I]t was a purely Christian miracle which raised the great Pagan from the dead. . . . [Only Thomas's] huge and solid orthodoxy could have supported so many things which then seemed to be unorthodox. . . . Whether or no he baptised Aristotle, he was truly the god' father of Aristotle; he was his sponsor; he swore that the old Greek would do no harm; and the whole world trusted his word."[26] Such a renewed interest in the material world and the corporeal body issues from the con' viction that the Incarnation has made a real difference to our real (cor' poreal) existence.

> The Body was no longer what it was when Plato and Porphyry and the old mystics had left it for dead. It had hung upon a gibbet. It had risen from a tomb. It was no longer possible for the soul to despise the senses, which had been the organs for something that was more than man. Plato might despise the flesh; but God had not despised it. The senses had truly become sanctified; as they are blessed one by one at a Catholic baptism. . . . After the Incarnation had become the idea that is central in our civili' sation, it was inevitable that there should be a return to materialism, in the sense of the serious value of matter and the making of the body. When once Christ had risen, it was inevitable that Aristotle should rise again.[27]

In returning to materialism, neither Francis nor Thomas are smuggling something heathen or heretical into Christianity; this is not pagan recidi' vism. They are smuggling God into the world. It is perhaps an undignified thought to imagine the Creator having to stoop so low as to be smuggled into his own creation, but, then, the Christmas story always did have such a note of defiance about it.

> By the very nature of the story the rejoicings in the cavern were rejoicings in a fortress or an outlaw's den; properly understood it is not unduly flip'

pant to say they were rejoicings in a dug-out. . . . It is not only that the very horse-hoofs of Herod might in that sense have passed like thunder over the sunken head of Christ. It is also that there is in that image a true idea of an outpost, of a piercing through the rock and an entrance into an enemy ter- ritory. There is in this buried divinity an idea of undermining the world; of shaking the towers and palaces from below; even as Herod the great king felt the earthquake under him and swayed with his swaying palace."[28]

The rude shepherd peasantry on the Bethlehem hillside may have been unre- fined in their metaphysics, but they were right in their mythology, as have been countless other peasantries. "Mythology is a search," says Chesterton, and the ancient world was searching vigorously. It may have been true that "Pan was dead and the shepherds were scattered like sheep" but the pagan and peasant population had not given up. They may have been wrong in many things, but there was one thing about which they had not been wrong. "[T]hey had not been wrong in believing that holy things could have a habitation and that divinity need not disdain the limits of time and space."[29]

Therefore Chesterton thinks it a patent misinterpretation to believe St. Francis forsook sacred doctrine for heathen nature, or that St. Thomas forsook revelation for philosophy, when the former used Nature to experi- ence God and the latter found an ally in Aristotle. It was never a matter of using "a Pagan goddess and a Pagan sage" to purge Christianity; to the contrary, "the truth in its simplest form [is] that they both reaffirmed the Incarnation, by bringing God back to earth."[30] St. Francis, that *jongleur de Dieu,* discovered when he obeyed the command of his Lady to stand on his head that pleasing the deity makes the world more pleasant, not less. "Our Lady's Tumbler stood on his head to please Our Lady. . . . The whole point of him was that the secret of recovering the natural pleasures lay in regarding them in the light of a supernatural pleasure."[31] Our Father is younger than we are, we heard Chesterton say when extolling the virtue of monotony, and just when the pagan world had become stale and banal, too weary to believe its own myths, God our Father frisked into the world in his own body, making true the stories which promise eternal youth.

Chesterton seems to feel that his own day, exhibiting inordinate ap- petites due to a severed theological ground, "stands much at the same stage

as it did at the beginning of the Dark Ages." The same temptation to
pursue health distracts from using health; an even worse theoretical materialism enslaves us to theories of determinism. Some people avert their eyes
from a nature they do not trust because they erroneously think of nature as
despoiled rather than correctly knowing themselves as corrupted, while
others look to nature alone for salvation because it can be manipulated more
easily than the human heart. The world stands at the same stage again. This
creates the agenda for the Church, if the Church is to be roomy enough to
save something of the world, and ambitious enough to save the world.

> The Church has the same task as it had at the beginning of the Dark
> Ages; to save all the light and liberty that can be saved, to resist the down-
> ward drag of the world, and to wait for better days. So much a real Church
> would certainly do; but a real Church might be able to do more. It might
> make its Dark Ages something more than a seed-time; it might make them
> the very reverse of dark. It might present its more human ideal in such
> abrupt and attractive a contrast to the inhuman trend of the time, as to in-
> spire men suddenly for one of the moral revolutions of history; so that men
> now living shall not taste of death until they have seen justice return.
>
> We do not want, as the newspapers say, a Church that will move
> with the world. We want a Church that will move the world.[32]

If this challenge is failed, then Church and world will be speciously cast as
antagonists, which is Chesterton's complaint about the puritan attitude
which objects to Catholicism on the grounds that it retains remnants of a
pagan heritage.

The defining characteristic of the heretic, as we have been abstract-
ing the heretic, is narrowness. When the heretic narrows his mind against
natural religion and pagan antiquity, he chafes at the otherwise natural rub
between nature and grace; he lacks the capaciousness to envelop the wide,
public spaces which make up Catholic history. Chesterton believes this in-
capacity is why Catholicism's connection with things called pagan nettled
the puritanical Protestants of his day.

> To put it shortly; the man who fears to enter the Church commonly fancies
> that what he feels is a sort of claustrophobia. As a fact, what he really feels,
> is rather a sort of agoraphobia. . . . These honest Protestants, like the imag-

inary nuns in the impossible romances, walk about in perpetual fear of being "walled up." For them the typical Catholic act is not going into a great thing like a church, but into a small thing like a confessional box.... As I have said, it was not claustrophobia, the fear of the crypt or the cell; it was agoraphobia, or the fear of the forum, of the market-place, of the open spaces and the colossal public buildings. To the really insular and indi- vidualistic type of sectarian, even the fear of the Church was also partly a fear of the world.... Of nearly all the non-Catholic types of our time we can truly say, that any such type must broaden his mind to become a Catholic. He must grow more used than he is at present to the long avenues and the large spaces. This is really what is meant by the Puritans who say that the church is Pagan; that it does open a very long avenue, which is the only avenue left connecting us with Pagan antiquity. That is largely what is meant by insisting that the Church covers all sorts of dubious or dis- reputable people; all the motley mobs of tramps and pedlars and beggars, who do make up the life of an open market-place.[33]

These colossal public buildings are of no interest to the agoraphobic who finds the vastness of the pagan sky unsettling; neither are the colossal public philosophies of Plato and Aristotle of interest, if the Bible alone suffices; or the colossal public art of Hellenism, if the interior walls of the church are to be whitewashed and the statues of the saints evicted; or the colossal public ritual of Rome or Byzantium, if truly sincere worship is conducted in the heart and not in public, ceremonial rites. Such a person will always feel a bit fearful before the long avenues (reaching back as far as pagan antiquity) and large spaces (spanning wide enough to envelop those vulgar persons and practices which constitute the bulk of human history), but Chesterton revels in this vulgarity. He defends the beer-drinking and creed-making common person against Mr. Shaw; he defends simple family pleasures of country folk against urban and urbane diversions;[34] he defends the honest greengrocer against the "shiny pebbly-eyed Theosophist";[35] he defends the drinking of beer against teetotalers and the eating of beef against vegetar- ians. A gusty, vivacious quality is precisely what he admires about pagan- ism, and why his midwives into Catholicism were Pan and Dionysius. He takes exception to a Tolstoyan simplicity which undercuts the natural pleasures.

The chief error of these people is to be found in the very phrase to which they are most attached—"plain living and high thinking." These people do not stand in need of, will not be improved by, plain living and high thinking. They stand in need of the contrary. They would be improved by high living and plain thinking. A little high living . . . would teach them the force and meaning of the human festivities, of the banquet that has gone on from the beginning of the world. . . . It would teach them that ritualism is older than any religion. . . . A man approaches, wearing sandals and simple raiment, a raw tomato held firmly in his right hand, and says, "The affections of family and country alike are hindrances to the fuller develop/ ment of human love"; but the plain thinker will only answer him, with a wonder not untinged with admiration, "What a great deal of trouble you must have taken in order to feel like that."[36]

There is some danger involved, of course. Coming into the presence of the Almighty is always a risky proposition. Paganism needs protection from itself—a sort of supernatural ballast lest it destabilize into despair and de/ generate from there into cruelty. Humankind must not be permitted to take itself too seriously. But the way to accomplish this is not to disparage human nature; instead, it is to take God more seriously than we take ourselves, the eternal more seriously than we take the finite. Because Chesterton believes in this ordered and maximal humanism, he does not right the ritual ban/ quet by serving raw tomatoes and a platter of self/deprecation, he rights it by situating the banquet before its true host. The ordinate relationship can be achieved by exalting the deity instead of by demeaning the human: there is a gratitude which can humble without humiliating. Gratitude's ritual countenance need not be sallow. "Let no man deceive himself; if by vul/ garity we mean coarseness of speech, rowdiness of behavior, gossip, horse/ play, and some heavy drinking, vulgarity there always was wherever there was joy, wherever there was faith in the gods. Wherever you have belief you will have hilarity, wherever you have hilarity you will have some dangers."[37]

Instincts of warm, natural religiosity, such as invoking a common primeval sky/god[38] or the fire upon the pagan hearthstone—instincts which continued in medieval Christianity for centuries—have been chilled of late, but not extinguished from Catholicism. "So long as Christianity contin/

ued the tradition of patron saints and portable relics, this idea of a blessing on the household could continue. If men had not domestic divinities, at least they had divine domesticities. When Christianity was chilled with Puritanism and rationalism, this inner warmth or secret fire in the house faded on the hearth. But some of the embers still glow or at least glimmer; and there is still a memory among the poor that their material possessions are something sacred."[39] We see once again that Chesterton's support of the family and the common life has a theological basis. These are worldly institutions, of course! They exist for the sake of the world.

> Catholicism is not a narrow thing; [it] knows more than the world knows about the potentialities and creative possibilities of the world, and that it will outlast all the worldly and temporary expressions of the same culture. Christianity has gone northward and established richer ports in colder seas; it has been changed and chilled for a time by colder heresies; but the same principle still stands for its expansion and exaltation; that which is expressed in the expansion and exaltation of great buildings; in the breadth of great gates declaring the brotherhood of men or the lifting of great domes pointing the way of their destiny. . . . Faith itself enlarges the world; which would be a small thing without it.[40]

If this inner warmth is missing from cold, modern materialism it will not be retrieved from any religion spawned in the Enlightenment because there these secret fires were already doused.

The Catholic tradition is not only a sacramental connection to transcendent things, it is also a historic connection to the ancient wisdoms. Catholic Christianity rests on natural religion's footing, not on rationalism. "The great intellectual tradition that comes down to us from Pythagoras and Plato was never interrupted or lost through such trifles as the sack of Rome, the triumph of Attila or all the barbarian invasions of the Dark Ages. It was only lost after the introduction of printing, the discovery of America, the founding of the Royal Society and all the enlightenment of the Renaissance and the modern world. It was there, if anywhere, that there was lost or impatiently snapped the long thin delicate thread that had descended from distant antiquity; the thread of that unusual human hobby; the habit of thinking."[41] Chesterton acknowledges that all religions contain certain

common features, deriving as they do from human nature, and cannot understand why the heretic believes the distinctiveness of Christianity is only
preservable by a sort of counter-religious attitude. "I fancy that all modern
religions are counter-religions; attacks on, or alternative to the Catholic
Church. They bear no likeness to the natural pagan speculations that existed before the Catholic Church, or would exist if it had never existed. The
attitude of Dean Inge is certainly much more like that of Plotinus than that
of Plato. But it is even more like that of Porphyry than that of Plotinus. He
is exactly like some pagan of the decline; it is not necessary for him to know
very much about the Christian superstition; as soon as he heard of it, he
hated it."[42]

The uniqueness of Christianity does not for Chesterton lie in its being
an exception to all other religious teachings, it lies in Christianity's con-
firmation, from beyond the bounds of natural religion (nature's boundary
being death), that religion's ultimate desire for eternal and beatific life is true.
The Church fulfills religion's longing. Therefore, when Christianity shares
common religious practices with the whole of humanity, Chesterton considers it to be a sign of the Church's solidarity with human nature, not an
insult to Christianity. "There is a phrase of facile liberality uttered again and
again at ethical societies and parliaments of religion: 'the religions of the
earth differ in rites and forms, but they are the same in what they teach.' It is
false; it is the opposite of the fact. The religions of the earth do not greatly
differ in rites and forms; they do greatly differ in what they teach. . . . They
agree in machinery; almost every great religion on earth works with the
same external methods, with priests, scriptures, altars, sworn brotherhoods,
special feasts. They agree in the mode of teaching; what they differ about
is the thing to be taught."[43] Chesterton is clear that Christ came not to found
a religion but to establish the Church.[44] Catholicism therefore believes the
Church is charged with permeating all life and culture for the purpose of ordering what has become inordinate, or balancing what has become
lopsided. "Catholic doctrine and discipline may be walls; but they are the
walls of a playground. Christianity is the only frame which has preserved
the pleasure of Paganism. . . . The unpopular parts of Christianity turn out
when examined to be the very props of the people. The outer ring of Christianity is a rigid guard of ethical negations and professional priests; but

inside that inhuman guard you will find the old human life dancing like children, and drinking wine like men; for Christianity is the only frame for pagan freedom."[45] For that reason it hails the broad avenue back to pagan antiquity, just as it continues to salute every contribution from the public forum. The Church gives (re)birth to its ancestors, and adopts its parents into the household of grace. When pagan feasts and rituals are invited to participate at the Table of the Mass (as Gilbert & Frances thought of inviting dragons and griffins to supper) it is for the purpose of inviting their perfection. What is true, good, and beautiful is real and eternal, and it is a chief function of the eternal liturgy to preserve eternal things. There is only one reality, and, as St. Thomas avers, being is good. "All good things are one thing. Sunsets, schools of philosophy, babies, constellations, cathedrals, operas, mountains, horses, poems—all these are merely disguises. One thing is always walking among us in fancy-dress. . . . And that is what the savage old Hebrews, alone among the nations, guessed, and why their rude tribal god has been erected on the ruins of all polytheistic civilisations. For the Greeks and Norsemen and Romans saw the superficial wars of nature and made the sun one god, the sea another, the wind a third. They were not thrilled, as some rude Israelite was, one night in the wastes, alone, by the sudden blazing idea of all being the same God: an idea worthy of a detective story."[46]

Hence Chesterton feels no chagrin when critics of Catholicism complain that certain "ritual feasts, processions or dances are really of pagan origin."

> They might as well say that our legs are of pagan origin. Nobody ever disputed that humanity was human before it was Christian; and no Church manufactured the legs with which men walked or danced, either in a pilgrimage or a ballet. What can really be maintained, so as to carry not a little conviction, is this: that where such a Church has existed it has *preserved* not only the processions but the dances; not only the cathedral but the carnival. One of the chief claims of Christian civilisation is to have preserved things of pagan origin. In short, in the old religious countries men *continue* to dance; while in the new scientific cities they are often content to drudge.

But when this saner view of history is realised, there does remain something more mystical and difficult to define. Even heathen things are Christian when they have been preserved by Christianity. Chivalry is something recognisably different even from the *virtus* of Virgil. Charity is something exceedingly different from the plain city of Homer. Even our patriotism is something more subtle than the undivided lover of the city; and the change is felt in the most permanent things, such as the love of landscape or the love of woman.[47]

When Christian Europe came out of the Dark Ages, its time of purga-torial exile, it had a freshness which could restore naturalness to religion. So it is not surprising if St. Francis in some degree discouraged books and book-learning in favor of a message to be put so simply "that the village idiot could understand it. The whole point of his point of view was that it looked out freshly upon a fresh world, that might have been made that morning. Save for the great primal things, the Creation and the Story of Eden, the first Christmas and the first Easter, the world had no history. But is it desired or desirable that the whole Catholic Church should have no history? . . . In short, it is really quite right and quite desirable that St. Francis should never have heard of Virgil. But do we really desire that Dante should never have heard of Virgil?"[48] The Catholic Church, including as it does so many par-ticipants in the parade along that broad avenue, refuses to choose between being a novitiate for Francis's fresh Christianity and being the depository for old Christianity, not to mention being a depository for some truths even older than that. Because the Catholic Church refuses to choose between simple practice and complex theology, therefore at the same time that it ap-plauds St. Francis for his choice, it lauds St. Thomas for the opposite choice. The Church further refuses to choose between theology and philosophy. In the Greek and Roman world, Chesterton muses, religion was one thing and philosophy quite another, and usually those who became good philosophers became bad believers. This is because "the rivers of mythology and philoso-phy run parallel and do not mingle till they meet in the sea of Christen-dom. . . . The truth is that the Church was actually the first thing that ever tried to combine reason and religion. There had never before been any such union of the priests and the philosophers."[49] It was not altogether unnatural, then, "that many bishops and doctors feared that the Thomists might become good philosophers and bad Christians," but on the whole "Aquinas convinced most of his critics that he was quite as good a Catholic as they were. . . . His main business was to defend the Faith against the abuse of Aristotle; and he boldly did it by supporting the use of Aristotle."[50]

As a result, the Church found that philosophy and culture and the sensual world could all be used for constructing the temple of God, and in that temple could be found justification for being. St. Thomas hatched an optimism about being which had not been seen since paganism sighed its deep despair. "If the morbid Renaissance intellectual is supposed to say, 'To be or not to be—that is the question,' then the massive medieval doctor does most certainly reply in a voice of thunder, 'To be—that is the answer.' . . . Something milder and more amiable may be made out of the deliquescence of theology, and the mixture of the creed with everything that contradicts it; but among consistent cosmic creeds, this is the only one that is entirely on the side of life."[51] A plenitude of philosophies have aided theology, and a legion of cultures have contributed forms by which Christians express themselves. Francis did not need to know Virgil, but many Christians were happier for Dante having read both Thomas and Virgil. They were so happy that they said "Virgil was almost a Christian. It is almost as if two great tools or toys of the same timber, the divine and the human, had been in the hands of Providence; and the only thing comparable to the Wooden Cross of Calvary was the Wooden Horse of Troy. So, in some wild allegory, pious in purpose if almost profane in form, the Holy Child might have fought the Dragon with a wooden sword and a wooden horse."[52]

Putting it symbolically, Chesterton could say he understood "what Coventry Patmore meant when he said calmly that it would have been quite as Catholic to decorate his mantelpiece with the Venus of Milo as with the Virgin."[53]

The truths known to pagan antiquity were "crystallized in Christendom."[54] What in the pagan myths were faint foreshadowings of the Christian mysteries have been given more substantial reality than the original mythmakers could have thought. They had mythical images of a god appearing human, but how could they have imagined God appearing as a human? "When all imaginative kinship has been explored or allowed for, it is not true that mythology ever rose to the heights of theology. It is not true that a thought so bold or so subtle as this one ever crossed the mind that created the centaurs and the fauns. In the wildest and most gigantic of the primitive epic fancies, there is no conception so colossal as the being who is both Zeus and Prometheus."[55]

However, even if paganism dares not imagine such incredibilities, it does provide forms to celebrate that incarnate fact. It is as if the puppets used by his fairy godmother to instruct him in Pan's toy theater have come to life for Chesterton. He seems especially certain and pleased to find that Christmas fulfills pagan humanism and festivity and warmth and hope. "All that genuinely remains of the ancient hymns or the ancient dances of Europe, all that has honestly come to us from the festivals of Phoebus or Pan, is to be found in the festivals of the Christian Church. If any one wants to hold the end of a chain which really goes back to the heathen mysteries, he had better take hold of a festoon of flowers at Easter or a string of sausages at Christmas."[56] Only the miracle of eternal youth belongs not just to the world of myth but also to the world of history. "Peter Pan does not belong to the world of Pan but the world of Peter."[57] Chesterton does acknowledge that paganism ended in a kind of despair from which Christianity rescued it, but he does seem to positively prefer a Dionysian's optimistic desperation about how to fully realize the possibilities of religion to a Lutheran's despondent conclusion that religious cult is impossible for the totally depraved soul. Chesterton is very happy to discover that the hearth fire in a stable on the outskirts of Bethlehem has a kinship to the fires round which pagan antiquity built human civilization.

> It is as if a man found his own parlour and fireside in the heart of the Great Pyramid. It is as if a child's favourite doll turned out to be the oldest sacred image in the world, worshipped in Chaldea or Nineveh. . . . Everything that men called sentimental in Roman Catholic religion, its keepsakes, its small flowers and almost tawdry trinkets, its figures with merciful gestures and gentle eyes, its avowedly popular pathos and all that Matthew Arnold meant by Christianity with its "relieving tears"—all this is a sign of sensitive and vivid vitality in anything so vast and settled and systematic. There is nothing quite like this warmth, as in the warmth of Christmas, amid ancient hills hoary with such snows of antiquity. It can address even God Almighty with diminutives. In all its varied vestments it wears its Sacred Heart upon its sleeve.[58]

That God had a mother makes God even more at home in the world than were the pagan domestic divinities. The name given by a peasant mother to her God-child makes it easier for people to make God's acquain- tance than if they had to rely on visits to the altar of the Unknown God. Christmas is an insatiable longing met, a homesickness satisfied. "No other birth of a god or childhood of a sage seems to us to be Christmas or any- thing like Christmas. It is either too cold or too frivolous, or too formal and classical, or too simple and savage, or too occult and complicated. Not one of us, whatever his opinions, would ever go to such a scene with the sense that he was going home."[59] And this satisfaction remains long in the heart, longer even than if, one day, for whatever incomprehensible reason, it would be discarded by the mind. That is why there is really a difference as a result of being brought up in a home that keeps the Christmas ritual.

The difference is that every Catholic child has learned from pictures, and even every Protestant child from stories, this incredible combination of contrasted ideas as one of the very first impressions on his mind. It is not merely a theological difference. It is a psychological difference which can outlast any theologies. . . . Any agnostic or atheist whose childhood has known a real Christmas has ever afterwards, whether he likes it or not, an association in his mind between two ideas that most of mankind must regard as remote from each other; the idea of a baby and the idea of un- known strength that sustains the stars. His instincts and imagination can still connect them, when his reason can no longer see the need of the con- nection; for him there will always be some savour of religion about the mere picture of a mother and a baby; some hint of mercy and softening about the mere mention of the dreadful name of God. But the two ideas are not naturally or necessarily combined. . . . It is no more inevitable to connect God with an infant than to connect gravitation with a kitten. It has been created in our minds by Christmas because we are Christians; because we are psychological Christians even when we are not theological ones.[60]

And with that remark, we have already crossed the threshold into Chester- ton's understanding of ritual.

FIVE

Practically Practicing Religion

The nuance of a certain English word has changed, making it difficult to communicate exactly Chesterton's understanding about the topic of this chapter. What I really want to say is that he finds religion "practical" in the older sense of "pertaining to practice or action," but not in the newer sense of businesslike, sensible, and efficient. Perhaps I could add "practicable" in its sense of "capable of being done, capable of being used," since Chesterton remembers how startling it was the first time he met a person who actually practiced religion: Frances Blogg, the future Mrs. Chesterton. She had, he writes in *The Autobiography,*

> a sort of hungry appetite for all the fruitful things like fields and gardens and anything connected with production; about which she was quite practical. She practised gardening; in that curious cockney culture she would have been quite ready to practise farming; and on the same perverse principle, she actually practised a religion. This was something utterly unaccountable both to me and to the whole fussy culture in which she lived. Any number of people proclaimed religions, chiefly oriental religions, analysed or argued about them; but that anybody could regard religion as a practical thing like gardening was something quite new to me and, to her neighbors, new and incomprehensible.[1]

This chapter will compile Chesterton's understanding of religion as ritual, considering its practicality on three fronts: religion's origin, its vulgar expression, and some irksome Catholic habits. First, Chesterton disputes the narrow definition of religion proposed by theories which trace the origin of religion to superstition, a definition which implies that a more advanced class of society should have outgrown it by now. Second, he articulates a favorable view of religious practice by ordinary people, people such as those described in chapter 3 and practices such as his ideological opponents only see as vulgar. Chesterton prefers the greengrocer's gaudy Christmas to the sophisticate's aseptic theories. Third, although criticisms of religious ritual can come from various sources, churched and unchurched, Chesterton associates certain remonstrations with Protestant sources. I will deal with Chesterton's apology to certain other Protestant concerns in our final chapter, but contention about ritual will be considered here.

We saw earlier that Chesterton preferred the general to the specific because of the former's greater practicality, the way that he would prefer a rope to a telephone in the desert because of the number of useful acts that could be performed with it. He places religion in this same class of the generally useful. When the heretic thinks about religion, it is narrowed to a single, useful, and usually preconceived purpose; when Chesterton thinks about religion, it is flooded into as many compartments of human life as there are components to human life. "Religion, the immortal maiden, has been a maid-of-all-work as well as a servant of mankind. She provided men at once with the theoretic laws of an unalterable cosmos; and also with the practical rules of the rapid and thrilling game of morality. She taught logic to the student and told fairy tales to the children; it was her business to confront the nameless gods whose fears are on all flesh, and also to see the streets were spotted with silver and scarlet, that there was a day for wearing ribbons or an hour for ringing bells."[2] It is the modern person who has a simple religion because it is confined to narrowly isolated moments; it is the common person, called simple by the modernist, who has a complex religion because it is implemented in all the ordinary parts of common life.

In so construing the problem, Chesterton is objecting to the prevailing opinion in his day that the uneducated vulgar class thoughtlessly engages in formal, artificial, and empty ritual practices, while the educated sophisticated class is free from ritualistic oppression. To the contrary, says Chesterton, it is really the modern sophisticate whose life is tyrannized by a choreographed ritual dance which is actually "complex, and many coloured, and elaborate, and needlessly formal."

It consists not of plain things like wine and fire, but of really peculiar, and local, and exceptional, and ingenious things—things like door-mats, and door-knockers, and electric bells, and silk hats, and white ties, and shiny cards, and confetti. The truth is that the modern man scarcely ever gets back to very old and simple things except when he is performing some religious mummery. The modern man can hardly get away from ritual except by entering a ritualistic church. . . . The symbols employed are in most cases symbols which belong to a primary human poetry. The most ferocious opponent of the Christian ceremonials must admit that if Catholicism had not instituted the bread and wine, somebody else would most probably have done so.[3]

The sophisticate's prejudice against religious ritual cuts in two directions— down and backward. This elitism looks down upon the lower class as being vulgar, and back at the primitive origins of religion as being supersti- tious. Thus it should be clear to us that when Chesterton contests the then prevailing view that religion was generated by prescientific primitives, he is simultaneously defending the lower class against the charge that they only practice religion because they are credulous. (This is also the source of any kinship the reader may have felt between Chesterton's justification of the ordinary life and his apology for the ancient pagan.)

The irreligious critic who does not practice religion considers anyone who does—the pagan, the vulgar citizen, or Catholic Christians—guilty of superstition, because the critic supposes ceremony to be mere nonsense. Nonsense, says Chesterton. The ceremony looks superstitious because it looks irrational, but it only looks irrational to an outside observer who cannot see the reason for the behavior. If we could look at our own behavior from the outside, it would appear irrational to us, too; and a practice would stop looking strange if we stopped looking at the practitioner as a stranger but recognized a common human emotion. "This total misunderstanding of the real nature of ceremonial gives rise to the most awkward and dehu- manized versions of the conduct of men in rude lands or ages. The man of science, not realizing that ceremonial is essentially a thing which is done without a reason, has to find a reason for every sort of ceremonial, and, as might be supposed, the reason is generally a very absurd one— absurd because it originates not in the simple mind of the barbarian, but in the sophisticated mind of the professor." Chesterton goes on to offer an example. The scientific mind chuckles at the primitive belief that the dead can eat, which it assumes from the ceremony of putting food in the grave. This misses the point, which can be shown by holding up a mirror to our own practices.

> It is like saying, "The English in the twentieth century believed that a dead man could smell. This is attested by the fact that they always covered his grave with lilies, violets, or other flowers. Some priestly and tribal terrors were evidently attached to the neglect of this action, as we have records of several old ladies who were very much disturbed in mind because their wreaths had not arrived in time for the funeral." . . . I believe they put food or weapons on the dead for the same reason that we put flowers, because it is an exceedingly natural and obvious thing to do. We do not understand, it is true, the emotion which makes us think it obvious and natural; but that is because, like all the important emotions of human existence, it is essentially irrational.[4]

A second example is offered to aid our reflexive vision. "I imagine that Mr. Kensit takes off his hat to a lady; and what can be more solemn and absurd, considered in the abstract, than symbolizing the existence of the other sex by taking off a portion of your clothing and waving it in the air?"[5] Chesterton sees flowers on graves and food in tombs and ritualized social acknowledgments as common human experiences because he believes in a common human nature. In fact, the more common, the better. The more extraordinary we fancy ourselves, the more singular we are, having little in common with either our ancestors or our neighbors.

Two theories about the origin of religion come particularly under Chesterton's criticism. They may appear unrelated at first glance, but they can be thought of as two versions of the same mistaken anthropology which Chesterton lances with the same blade. The first theory treats religion under human psychology because it treats God as a human projection. It surmises that religious beliefs exist to ballast our fears: we fear nature so postulate a personal god, we fear death so postulate a personal judge with whose good graces we can barter, we fear ill fortune so believe personal providence stands behind all things, accessible to prayer. This theory is called anthropomor- phism, of course, but it does not inveigle Chesterton. "Possibly the most pathetic of all the delusions of the modern students of primitive belief is the notion they have about the thing they call anthropomorphism. They believe that primitive men attributed phenomena to a god in human form in order to explain them, because his mind in its sullen limitation could not reach any further than his own clownish existence."[6] The efficient assumption here is that religion anthropomorphizes nature in order to make nature more reasonable and comforting to us, like calling thunder a human voice makes it not so awful. Chesterton thinks this puts the original religious motivation exactly backward, since it is not religion's purpose to lessen awe, but to increase it. The final cure for this misunderstanding is to walk down a lane at night.

> Anyone who does so will discover very quickly that men pictured some-thing semihuman at the back of all things, not because such a thought was natural, but because it was supernatural; not because it made things more comprehensible, but because it made them a hundred times more incom-prehensible and mysterious. For a man walking down a lane at night can see the conspicuous fact that as long as nature keeps to her own course, she has no power with us at all. So long as a tree is a tree . . . it does not frighten us at all. It begins to be something alien, to be something strange, only when it looks like ourselves. When a tree really looks like a man our knees knock under us. And when the universe looks like a man we fall on our faces.[7]

The intent of the scientifically minded gentleman in the top hat may be to make nature more intelligible and less awesome, but it is not the intent of religion, nor will this motive explain religion. Religion is the flower of a reverent fear. Awe explains religion, and less awe is not more of an expla-nation; and Chesterton found being itself awesome.

The second theory "puts a highly elaborate cart before a really primitive horse." Chesterton's criticism appears in the context of *The Everlasting Man,* wherein he disputes pure materialists who believe that the human being has no transcendent element, or soul. Now, Chesterton is sophisticated enough to understand that the soul is not a ghost in the machine; his objection is not with evolution per se. He does not think it erroneous to say the human is an animal; he only thinks it wrong not to say the human is a qualitatively different kind of animal. Spelunking anthropologists exploring the environs of the creature they call the Cave Man have depicted him as a beastly being who automatically grew into a human being, like a small child automatically grows into a bigger pair of pants. But why would an animal, big or small, want a pair of pants? Clothing is human vesture; Christians believe it has to do with a sense of shame connected with a doctrine of sin; but all this is the life of the spirit, not simply the life of the animal. Chesterton makes his point by the phenomenon of art. The drawings discovered by a young boy exploring a grotto, while primitive in style, already prove that human beings and animals differ in kind and not just in degree. We know what "professors who simplify the relation of men and beasts to a mere evolutionary variation" would make of these paintings, but what should the boy think who is uncontaminated by pure materialism? "What would be for him the simplest lesson of that strange stone picturebook? After all, it would come back to this; that he had dug very deep and found the place where a man had drawn the picture of a reindeer. But he would dig a good deal deeper before he found a place where a reindeer had drawn a picture of a man." The strict material evolutionist could find a trail of fossils likè the ruins of lost dynasties, a trail of monsters blindly developing and "groping and grasping and touching life with every extravagant elongation of horn and tongue and tentacle. . . . [b]ut nowhere would he find one finger that had traced one significant line upon the sand; nowhere one claw that had even begun to scratch the faint suggestion of a form," because it is "the simple truth that man does differ from the brutes in kind and not in degree; and the proof of it is here. . . . Art is the signature of man."[8]

It is in the context of this popular image of the Cave Man, half animal, frightened by nature's thunder and lightning, wishing to make appeal to some benevolent being for a good hunt or, later, a good crop, that the second theory places the origin of religion. It considers religion a merely human instinct, the natural instinct of a human being who has been duped into thinking there is something supernatural. Chesterton first objected to anthropomorphism making the god an overblown person; now he objects to the idol as an underinflated deity, to a god who is merely a product of our animal instinct. Chesterton suggests that religion is a uniquely human activity because religion is a uniquely human capacity.

A cow in a field seems to derive no lyrical impulse or instruction from her unrivalled opportunities for listening to the skylark. And similarly there is no reason to suppose that live sheep will ever begin to use dead sheep as the basis of a system of elaborate ancestor-worship. It is true that in the spring a young quadruped's fancy may lightly turn to thoughts of love, but no succession of springs has ever led it to turn however lightly to thoughts of literature. And in the same way, while it is true that a dog has dreams, while most other quadrupeds do not seem even to have that, we have waited a long time for the dog to develop his dreams into an elaborate system or religious ceremonial. . . .

It is not impossible, in the sense of self-contradictory, that we should see cows fasting from grass every Friday or going on their knees as in the old legend about Christmas Eve. It is not in that sense impossible that cows should contemplate death until they can lift up a sublime psalm of lamentation to the tune the old cow died of. It is not in that sense impossible that they should express their hopes of a heavenly career in a symbolic dance, in honour of the cow that jumped over the moon. . . . The materials for religion had lain there for countless ages like the materials for everything else; but the power of religion was in the mind.[9]

The first theory thinks religion to be a projection upon the screen of nature by the human mind; the second theory thinks religion to be a natural product of bucolic life. The first considers religion to be the mistake of looking at the celestial sphere when our true home is earth; the second considers it a religious mistake to treat a mundane experience as hallowed and heavenly. Both heresies narrow the human scope to nature, instinct, or animal behavior, while Chesterton finds religion to be the prerogative of a soul, a soul created to enjoy God. "That an ape has hands is far less interesting to the philosopher than the fact that having hands he does next to nothing with them; does not play knuckle-bones or the violin; does not carve marble or carve mutton. . . . Who ever found an ant-hill decorated with the statues of celebrated ants? Who has seen a bee-hive carved with the images of gorgeous queens of old? No; the chasm between man and other creatures may have a natural explanation, but it is a chasm."[10]

That is why religious ritual is more difficult to analyze than the heretic can understand. Religion is practicable, but it is not functional, in the sense

that it can be reduced to serving a utilitarian end, no matter the end conceived: forming morality or educating believers or enthusing disciples.
These alone do not adequately account for religion. The things people do for
enjoyment are not always justifiable to reason, though they are eminently reasonable. This immortal tutor and companion of the human race exists for
many more reasons than the heretic narrowly considers, but this went unob-
served by the century into which Chesterton was born, an age which tried
to justify religion for its sagacious beliefs, minus the practices. Auguste
Comte's positivism had tried to obviate the embarrassment of ritual by re-
placing practicable religion with a general creed, yet when even he eventually invested this universal creed with prayers and rituals, Chesterton could
no longer stifle himself. He mocks that Comte "alone saw that men must
always have the sacredness of mummery," and that "while the brutes have all
the useful things, the things that are truly human are the useless ones."

> Ritual is really much older than thought; it is much simpler and much
> wilder than thought. A feeling touching the nature of things does not only
> make men feel that there are certain proper things to *say*; it makes them
> feel that there are certain proper things to *do*. The more agreeable of these
> consist of dancing, building temples, and shouting very loud; the less
> agreeable, of wearing green carnations and burning other philosophers
> alive. But everywhere the religious dance came before the religious hymn,
> and man was a ritualist before he could speak. . . . A man who has faith
> must be prepared not only to be a martyr, but to be a fool. It is absurd to
> say that a man is ready to toil and die for his convictions when he is not
> even ready to wear a wreath round his head for them. I myself, to take
> a *corpus vile,* am very certain that I would not read the works of Comte
> through for any consideration whatever. But I can easily imagine myself
> with the greatest enthusiasm lighting a bonfire on Darwin Day.[11]

It is lamentable, Chesterton taunts, that while proponents of this artificial, positivist religion seem to approve the idea of celebration in theory,
they seem hesitant to practice any such rituals themselves. They lionize the
great human festivals in history, like the Olympian games or the maypole,
but they absent themselves from the common and rowdy festivals in today's
streets with the excuse that these are too mean and coarse for their sensitive
spirits.

[T]here is about these people a haunting and alarming something which suggests that it is just possible that they don't keep Christmas. It is painful to regard human nature in such a light, but it seems somehow possible that Mr. George Moore does not wave his spoon and shout when the pudding is set alight. It is even possible that Mr. W. B. Yeats never pulls crackers. If so, where is the sense of all their dreams of festive traditions? Here is a solid and ancient festive tradition still plying a roaring trade in the streets, and they think it vulgar. If this be so, let them be very certain of this, that they are the kind of people who in the time of the maypole would have thought the maypole vulgar; who in the time of the Canterbury pilgrimage would have thought the Canterbury pilgrimage vulgar; who in the time of the Olympian games would have thought the Olympian games vulgar. Nor can there be any reasonable doubt that they were vulgar. . . . Vulgarity there always was wherever there was joy, wherever there was faith in the gods. . . . If we ever get the English back on to the English land they will become again a religious people, if all goes well, a superstitious people.[12]

Chesterton encountered such people throughout his life, and he speaks of their hypocrisy and haughtiness a final time in his autobiography where he recalls having disliked their attitudes even before coming to disagree with their beliefs. Since he describes himself as "almost entirely Pagan and Pantheist" before his own conversion, it was not for theological reasons that he disliked theosophy. "I did not dislike [Theosophists] because they had erroneous doctrines, when I myself had no doctrines. . . . I disliked them because they had shiny pebbly eyes and patient smiles. Their patience mostly consisted of waiting for others to rise to the spiritual plane where they themselves already stood. It is a curious fact, that they never seemed to hope that *they* might evolve and reach the plane where their honest greengrocer already stood. They never wanted to hitch their own lumbering waggon to a soaring cabman; or see the soul of their charwoman like a star beckon to the spheres where the immortals are."[13]

If one is logical, like the theosophist, there appears to be no reason why one could not arbitrarily found holidays on any pretense and create celebration *ex nihilo,* but if one is anthropological, as Chesterton was when analyzing the greengrocer, then one can realize the true connection between the temporal and the divine. "Man cannot love mortal things. He can only love immortal things for an instant. . . . Ultimately a man cannot rejoice in anything except the nature of things. Ultimately a man can enjoy nothing except religion."[14] The greengrocer and the sausage-seller do not practice ritual religion in order to express some positivist creed logically deduced on the gnostic heights. Theirs is an even more mystical approach: they want to touch other worlds. The holiday does not exist in order to enable the working class to work harder for the leisured class; it exists because in the leisure of the holy-day, in temporal moments and material monuments, men and women can love the immortal for an instant. Practicing religion naturalizes the world; without supernature nature is unnatural.

> It is hard to see at first sight why so human a thing as leisure and larkiness should always have a religious origin. Rationally there appears no reason why we should not sing and give each other presents in honor of anything—the birth of Michael Angelo or the opening of Euston Station. But it does not work. As a fact, men only become greedily and gloriously material about something spiritualistic. Take away the Nicene Creed and similar things, and you do some strange wrong to the sellers of sausages. Take away the supernatural, and what remains is the unnatural.[15]

Religious myth may speak of rivers running with wine, or trees growing golden apples, but only in order to overcome our walking amnesia and revive our first ontological memory. "At the back of our brains, so to speak, there was a forgotten blaze or burst of astonishment at our own existence. The object of the artistic and spiritual life was to dig for this submerged sunrise of wonder; so that a man sitting in a chair might suddenly understand that he was actually alive, and be happy."[16] The natural world is sufficient raw material for the mystical life. The moment rivers running with water and trees growing green apples no longer appear to us as supernatural largesse, we will be left with an unnatural world. Our lassitude will become unbearable and our ruptured spirits will acquiesce to death, as Chesterton briefly experienced during his (lunatic) days of nihilism. Mystery and poetry and myth are not schizophrenic escapes from reality by the sick mind, they are constituents of the sound mind. "Poetry is sane because it floats easily in an infinite sea; reason seeks to cross the infinite sea, and so make it finite. The result is mental exhaustion. . . . The poet only asks to get his head into the heavens. It is the logician who seeks to get the heavens into his head. And it is his head that splits."[17] Take religion away, and the world becomes a collection of dead atoms. It would be the most ironical of all tragedies were the supernatural to be elided in the name of improving on religion. The sophisticates' attempted sanitization of religion by removing its natural and mystic rituals would not accomplish their intended goal of a saner, healthier human because

> Mysticism keeps men sane. As long as you have mystery you have health; when you destroy mystery you create morbidity. The ordinary man has always been sane because the ordinary man has always been a mystic. He has permitted the twilight. He has always had one foot in earth and the other in fairyland. He has always left himself free to doubt his gods; but (unlike the agnostic of today) free also to believe in them. He has always cared more for truth than for consistency. If he saw two truths that seemed to contradict each other, he would take the two truths and the contradiction along with them. His spiritual sight is stereoscopic, like his physical sight: he sees two different pictures at once and yet sees all the better for that.[18]

Religious rituals do not look inconsistent to those who see them from the inside, close up, with both eyes wide open, stereoscopically; they only look inconsistent to those who look at them from afar, as through a telescope, with one eye squeezed shut and the other squinted. Religious ritual always seems a trifle vulgar to the expert, but, then, we have seen Chesterton's opinion of the expert. The expert is more aristocratic than the aristocrat, because the latter is only the person who lives well, while the former is the person who thinks he knows better than the rest of us.

> Once men sang together round a table in chorus; now one man sings alone, for the absurd reason that he can sing better. If scientific civilization goes on (which is most improbable) only one man will laugh, because he can laugh better than the rest.
>
> Now, in all commonwealths dominated by a religion—in the Christian commonwealths of the Middle Ages and in many rude societies—this habit of dancing was a common habit with everybody, and was not necessarily confined to a professional class. A person could dance without

being a dancer; a person could dance without being a specialist; a person could dance without being pink. And, in proportion as Mr. McCabe's scientific civilization advances—that is, in proportion as religious civilization (or real civilization) decays—the more and more "well trained," the more and more pink, become the people who do dance, and the more and more numerous become the people who don't. . . . Mr. McCabe is trying to create a world in which there will be no life for dancing to have a place in. The very fact that Mr. McCabe thinks of dancing as a thing belonging to some hired women at the Alhambra [a ballet hall] is an illustration of the same principle by which he is able to think of religion as a thing belonging to some hired men in white neckties. Both these things are things which should not be done for us, but by us. If Mr. McCabe were really religious he would be happy. If he were really happy he would dance.[19]

When we come to Protestant charges against Catholic ritual religion, they might be summed up by the objection contained inchoately in Mr. McCabe's concern. There is some anxiety about letting people practice religion who don't know the theory. Five objections to ritual Catholicism will be isolated, ones which are typically Protestant: attitudes toward the Bible, the accusation of mindless repetition, the question of natural religion, the case of sacrament and sacrifice, and sentimentality.

First, in the Protestant mood, religion is a religion of the book. Faith is a matter of belief. Unlike that ancient ascetical work *The Ladder of Divine Ascent*, Protestantism believes in the ladder of divine assent, and how can one give assent unless one has heard, and how can one hear if the content of the book is not proclaimed? This is why Bible reading is urged at all times and in all places. In Chesterton's day, some even urged it in the schools. There was in the Education Bill of 1902 a proposal brought by the Conservative Party to give financial support to church schools, and Chesterton found himself in general agreement with the Liberal attacks on the bill, thinking it not fair that the country should support specifically Catholic schools. However, he took exception to the Liberal "compromise" of simple Bible teaching for all children in the state schools, and in a letter to the *Daily News* he explains why this could not be expected to satisfy Catholics.

Protestant Christianity believes that there is a Divine record in a book; that everyone ought to have free access to that book; that everyone who gets hold of it can save his soul by it, whether he finds it in a library or picks it off a dustcart. Catholic Christianity believes that there is a Divine army or league upon earth called the Church; that all men should be induced to join it; that any man who joins it can save his soul by it without ever opening any of the old books of the Church at all. The Bible is only one of the institutions of Catholicism, like its rites or its priesthood; it thinks the Bible only efficient when taken as part of the Church.[20]

Chesterton remembers thinking it odd, even before his conversion, to remove this one institution of Catholicism Scripture, and isolate it from the rest, as if a part can be played off against the whole. He found unintelligible the everlasting cry that Catholic traditions are condemned by the Bible. Coming without a tradition (remember, he describes his approach having been as much agnostic as Anglican), he could imagine how a sensible skeptic or pagan would react to the Protestant protest that "the Church of Rome is afraid of the Bible." Suppose a man was standing in the street watching a procession go by, a procession of

the priests of some strange cult, carrying their object of worship under a canopy, some of them wearing high head-dresses and carrying symbolical staffs, others carrying scrolls and sacred records, others carrying sacred images and lighted candles before them, others sacred relics in caskets or cases, and so on. I can understand the spectator saying, "This is all hocus-pocus"; I can even understand him, in moments of irritation, breaking up the procession, throwing down the images, tearing up the scrolls, dancing on the priests and anything else that might express that general view. I can understand his saying, "Your croziers are bosh, your candles are bosh, your statues and scrolls and relics and all the rest of it are bosh." But in what conceivable frame of mind does he rush in to select one particular scroll of the scriptures of this one particular group (a scroll which had always belonged to them and been a part of their hocus-pocus, if it was hocus-pocus); why in the world should the man in the street say that one particular scroll was *not* bosh, but was the one and only truth by which all the other things were to be condemned? Why should it not be as superstitious to worship the scrolls as the statues, of that one particular procession?[21]

In such a case, the scriptural scroll would be excised from the body of the religion by the scalpel of some secret exception, making that one, single part of the historical Western Catholic faith true while all the rest of it was rubbish. Yet already the clan of surgeons "who had just proved that Rome did not believe the Bible, were excitedly discovering that they did not believe the Bible themselves."[22] The inconsistency boggled Chesterton's mind. Perhaps, he thought, the Bible is best served and most serviceable when taken as part of the Church. Perhaps Scripture is of chief importance to the Christian religion, as the head is of chief importance to the body, but even the head is part of the body and works more efficiently when left attached.

Second, as assent to intelligible propositions explains the Protestant emphasis upon the Bible, it equally explains the objection to ritual religion on the grounds that rites are not always done consciously, determinedly, meaningfully. Chesterton's apology for repetitive ritual includes an apology in the conventional sense of expressing regret. Sometimes, he concedes, perfunctoriness does happen, despite the Church's real teaching about such things or "her numberless recommendations of attention and vigilance." When it does, both the caviler and the Catholic will see a defect in the procedure, like a spot on the carpet, but the latter "will know better than the first man that there ought not to be a spot on the carpet. [And] he will know, unlike the first man, why there is a carpet."[23]

To say that the ritual is not done attentively is a picayune objection from someone who does not believe the ritual ought to be done at all, or from someone else who does not believe the ritual can do what it promises. It is a contradictory pair of horns on which Catholic ceremony is impaled when one side denounces the words as magical, and the other side faults the priest who fails to pronounce the words with conviction. At least in this ritual the words are kept alive by a tradition which extends through countless communities which have made them their life. Contrast that with other speech which has died but remains on our lips.

[The truth is] that *all* human forms of speech tend to fossilize into formalism; and that the Church stands unique in history, not as talking a dead

language among everlasting languages; but, on the contrary, as having pre⁄
served a living language in a world of dying languages. When the great
Greek cry breaks into the Latin of the Mass, as old as Christianity itself,
it may surprise some to learn that there are a good many people in
church who really do say *Kyrie eleison* and mean exactly what they say. But
anyhow, they mean what they say rather more than a man who begins a
letter with "Dear Sir" means what he says. "Dear" is emphatically a dead
word; in that place it has ceased to have any meaning. It is exactly what the
Protestants would allege of Popish rites and forms; it is done rapidly, ritu⁄
ally, and without any memory even of the meaning of the rite. . . . Now,
life, ordinary, jolly, heathen, human life, is simply chockfull of these dead
words and meaningless ceremonies. You will not escape from them by
escaping from the Church into the world.[24]

It is a shame if the Mass is prayed indifferently, yes, and it is a shame because
the Catholic is supposed to believe the words. When the critic says that
Catholics "are only required to make a material or mechanical attendance
at mass, he says something which is *not* true about the ordinary Catholic in
his feelings about the Catholic Sacraments. But he says something which *is*
true about the ordinary official attending official functions."[25] The unfortu⁄
nate fact that repetition desensitizes us may be harmless, Chesterton muses,
or melancholy, or a mark of the Fall of man, but as a characteristic human
frailty it will not only be found in the person attending Mass.

Third, there are concerns about natural religion. The difference be⁄
tween the Catholic and Protestant positions on natural religion is rooted in
the disagreement over whether grace perfects nature or not. Is Christianity
the perfection of humankind's natural religious proclivity, or is it the sal⁄
vation of humankind from its corrupted tendency to appease God by re⁄
ligious behavior? If the latter, then it is only proper to dispose of all the
bits of the religious machinery littering the history of humankind: relics in
the altars and refrigeriums at the graveside, icons and statues in candlelit
temples, sacred days and holy oils and hallowed fasts. The broad avenue
reaching back to the Roman public forum should be swept clean of the
rubble of religious practice so that on this cleansed surface an edifice of wor⁄
ship may be built untainted by any vestiges of natural religion. If revealed

religion is the demise of natural religion, then this would be the strategy. But Chesterton suggests that the true forces of life are in fact with the other side. The Protestant religions, he writes, were fossilized, almost immediately.

> [T]hey really died almost as soon as they were born. And this was due to a fact not always emphasised, but which always strikes me as the most out-standing fact of the mysterious business; the incredible clumsiness of the Reformers. The real Protestant theologians were such very bad theo-logians. They had an amazing opportunity; the old Church had been swept out of their way, along with many things that were really unpopular, and some things that were deservedly unpopular. One would suppose it was easy enough to set up something that would at least look a little more popular. When they tried to do it, they made every mistake that they could make. They waged an insane war against everything in the old faith that is most normal and sympathetic to human nature; such as prayers for the dead or the gracious image of a Mother of Men. They hardened and fixed themselves upon fads which anybody could see would pass like fashions. Luther lashed himself into a sort of general fury, which obviously could not last; Calvin was logical, but used his logic for a scheme which hu-manity manifestly would not long find endurable.[26]

The religious craving is natural, but it is not selfish; sacrifice is tribute, it is not barter. If a child is on amiable terms with his parents, and does not normally bargain with them over an orange or quarrel with them over some rudimentary experiments in good behavior, then the natural instinct of the religious child to sacrifice would not be regarded as a bribe. Only if religion were turned into nothing more than a means to private redemption would religious sacrifice be misinterpreted as an act of bribery instead of an act of love. But even Greek sacrifice was more than bribery.

> [Greek sacrifice] did satisfy a thing very deep in humanity indeed; the idea of surrendering something as the portion of the unknown powers; of pour-ing out wine on the ground, of throwing a ring into the sea; in a word, of sacrifice. It is the wise and worthy idea of not taking our advantage to the full; of putting something in the other balance to ballast our dubious pride, of paying tithes to nature for our land. This deep truth of the danger of

insolence, or being too big for our boots, runs through all the great Greek tragedies and makes them great. But it runs side by side with an almost cryptic agnosticism about the real nature of the gods to be propitiated. Where that gesture of surrender is most magnificent, as among the great Greeks, there is really much more idea that the man will be the better for losing the ox than that the god will be the better for getting it.[27]

Losing the ox is an act of humility, which is a very necessary moral act; giving the ox to God is a very necessary religious act; but there is a greater perfection of sacrifice than even the ancient Greeks in their natural hellenic hubris could conceive. It is the Christian audacity to believe that because of Jesus' paschal mystery there is now a sacrifice wherein we truly participate in the divine self-love which was manifested as the Son's crucified self-giving to the Father in the Holy Spirit. The sacrifice of the Mass is perfect ecstatic love.

This dovetails with the fourth complaint, regarding sacraments. I have attempted to link in the reader's mind the chapters on the ordinary life, paganism, and ritual religion because it seems that in Chesterton's mind they are three links in the chain binding Christianity to reality. Christianity does not do a new world, it does this world anew. Although Catholic rituals do not acquiesce to sin's derangement of nature, neither are they fractured from creation. The Gospel delivers paganism from despair, it does not deliver people from their corporeality. Catholic Christianity will always look too coarse for a puritanism that wants an unearthly religion, and too magical for Manichaeism. "As compared with a Jew, a Moslem, a Buddhist, a Deist, or most obvious alternatives, a Christian *means* a man who believes that deity or sanctity has attached to matter or entered the world of the senses."[28] Dean Inge fired charges at Catholic sacramental practices in the name of a more rational and material world, but the funny thing is that "the strange bigotry, which leads the Bishop to scream and rail at all sacramentalism as Magic, is in its inmost essence the very reverse of materialism."

> The root of this prejudice is not so much a trust in matter as a sort of horror of matter. The man of this philosophy is always asking that worship shall be wholly spiritual, or even wholly intellectual; because he really does feel a disgust at the idea of spiritual things having a body and a solid form. . . .

Indeed the Dean uttered an unconscious truth when he said the sacramen-talists must be "natural idolators." He shrinks from it not only because it is idolatrous, but also because it is natural. He cannot bear to think how natural is the craving for the supernatural. He cannot tolerate the idea of it actually working through the elements of nature.[29]

The stones of the Christian temple are spiritualized matter. Excise the supernatural from nature and you do some strange wrong to the seller of sausages; excise matter from the Church and you do some strange wrong to the body of Christ. Freeing the spirit from matter does not produce a health-ier religion, like freeing the spirit from the human body does not produce a healthier human being; it leaves a corpse.

Finally, Chesterton offers a rebuttal to the Protestant charge that Catholics always succumb to the temptation of sentimentalism when they practice their religion. His comments are provoked by a Protestant bish-op's remark that Catholics see St. Francis "in a halo of false sentiment, or through a haze of false sentiment." It is to be admitted that an exercise of sentiment really is a hazard when religion is treated as practicable instead of merely theoretical, but Chesterton finds it an acceptable hazard and an honest one. (It is, at any rate, more honest behavior than that shown by those who "take off their hats in [Christ's] churches while denying that he was present on his altars.") So, the clear-eyed Catholic might criticize certain te-dious expressions of religion, and even admit that not every "pink and blue doll from an Art Repository is a satisfactory symbol of the Mother of God," but this is

> less of a contradiction than exists in a person who says there is no Original Sin in anybody, and then calls it Mariolatry to say there was no Original Sin in Mary. There may be devotional expressions that are emotional, even extravagantly emotional; but they do not actually distort any definition that is purely intellectual. . . . We are under no illusions about the literary quality of a large number of hymns in our hymn-books. But we modestly submit that though they are doggerel they are not nonsense. . . . Devo-tional art and literature are often out of balance or broken in expression; sometimes because the emotion is too real and too strong for the reason, the same thing which makes the love-letters of the wisest men like the letters of lunatics.[30]

Those of the bibliocentric persuasion may believe that theology must expunge florid sentiment; the capacious Catholic does not see the contra, diction so long as Catholicism will not admit sentiment as a substitute for statement.

Having spoken in part about the relationship between doctrine and practical religious expression, we are obliged to treat the question more fully in the next two chapters. What is Chesterton's understanding of the role of doctrine and the place of the hierarchy? If he has defended Catholicism from the charge of sentimentality, he has yet to protect it from two charges from the opposite side: that Catholicism is militantly doctrinal and suffo, catingly hierarchical.

SIX

The Key in the Lock

The images one uses to think about a thing will condition the way one thinks about that thing, because thought is facilitated by imagination. Chesterton's mind is very imaginative, and his paradoxes enjoy upending normal expectations, but his thoughts always express his experience, and he experiences doctrine as liberating rather than confining, vivifying instead of asphyxiating, brightening and not darkening the world. Therefore, he goes against the grain and defends doctrine on the grounds that it makes us more free to think and act, not less. Doctrine is a way of thinking, and for Chesterton thought is a way of accomplishing something. "When things will not work, you must have the thinker, the man who has some doctrine about why they work at all. It is wrong to fiddle while Rome is burning; but it is quite right to study the theory of hydraulics while Rome is burning."[1] Chesterton is first in line to volunteer to consider the very practical, useful, functional discipline of theorizing. "I perceive that it is far more practical to begin at the beginning and discuss theories. . . . I for one have come to believe in going back to fundamentals." He claims to revert to the doctrinal methods of the thirteenth century, inspired by "the general hope of getting something done" and provides a parable to defend his choice.

> Suppose a great a commotion arises in the street about something, let us say a lamp-post, which many influential persons desire to pull down. A grey-clad monk, who is the spirit of the Middle Ages, is approached upon the matter, and begins to say, in the arid manner of the Schoolmen, "Let us first of all consider, my brethren, the value of Light. If Light be in itself good—." At this point he is somewhat excusably knocked down. All the people make a rush for the lamp-post, the lamp-post is down in ten minutes, and they go about congratulating each other on their unmediaeval

practicality. But as things go on they do not work out so easily. Some people have pulled the lamp-post down because they wanted the electric light; some because they wanted old iron; some because they wanted darkness, because their deeds were evil. Some thought it not enough of a lamp-post, some too much; some acted because they wanted to smash municipal machinery; some because they wanted to smash something. And there is war in the night, no man knowing whom he strikes. So, gradually and inevitably, to-day, tomorrow, or the next day, there comes back the conviction that the monk was right after all, and that all depends on what is the philosophy of Light. Only what we might have discussed under the gas-lamp, we now must discuss in the dark.[2]

I have gone to some length, about three chapters' worth, to indicate Chesterton's attempt to give new valuation to the vulgar elements in ordinary life, pagan naturalism, and ritual religion in the face of that high-handedness which sneers at the common person. However, it would be a mistake as grave as that committed by these progressive heretics to think Chesterton's attack on haughty thought means an attack on thought itself. Remember, the size of the faith which Chesterton is circumscribing is sufficient to accommodate both practical religion, whose primary mode is not analysis, and doctrinal complexity, whose primary mode is. Though the sausage-seller may practice the creed simply, the creed which he practices is not simple; it is a complex thing, composed of many parts, and to grasp it in its fullness has required a considerable amount of intellectual effort over a considerable number of centuries. Thus the history of doctrine. Not everyone must perform this task (one of the advantages of belonging to a cooperative like the Church), but someone must perform this task, because "[c]ommon things are never commonplace. And in the last analysis most common things will be found to be highly complicated." Chesterton ridicules the strategem of reduction as a means of avoiding complicated analysis. "Some men of science do indeed get over the difficulty by dealing only with the easy part of it: thus, they will call first love the instinct of sex, and the awe of death the instinct of self-preservation. But this is only getting over the difficulty of describing peacock green by calling it blue. There is blue in it."[3] The reductionist strategy of naming only one component of the com-

plex is but a variant of the heretical procedure of doing injustice by decre-
mentalism. Chesterton would have us widen our vision.

A thing can be said to be communal not only by virtue of being shared,
but also by virtue of possessing multiple facets: like white light is a communion of colors. Although naming a rainbow "blue" is not false, because
there is blue in it, this does not yet name the whole composite. Catholicism
is a community of beliefs, simple in the sense that it is accessible to the
average person, but complex in the sense that it is not monochromatic.
Therefore, Chesterton takes the charge that Catholicism is complex as a
compliment. Against the feeling in his day that the heartfelt and intuitive religion of the Galilean is superior to complicated Roman creeds, Chesterton
crows: "When once one believes in a creed, one is proud of its complexity,
as scientists are proud of the complexity of science. It shows how rich it is in
discoveries. If it is right at all, it is a compliment to say that it's elaborately
right."[4]

Four images will be noted by which Chesterton argues against doctrinal pointillism in favor of Catholic complexity: a key, vitality, a map, and
single-mindedness. In other words, he says that doctrines are complex in
the way a key is complex; that they are vital in the sense of life-producing
and life-protecting; that they show a map to the mind which maintains by
conviction what is otherwise maintained only by custom; and he says that
doctrinal complexity, while single-minded, does not suffer the narrow-
mindedness which cleaves revelation from reason and science.

First, we have already seen that Chesterton described his journey
to orthodoxy as a sailor whose attempted excursion to an uncharted island
ultimately landed him upon a completely mapped shore. His point of em-
barkation was not a church catechism but a Dionysian love of the world
which nonetheless felt a pang of despair. He describes the final moment of
anchorage thus:

And then followed an experience impossible to describe. It was as if I
had been blundering about since my birth with two huge and unmanage-
able machines, of different shapes and without apparent connection—
the world and the Christian tradition. I had found this hole in the world:
the fact that one must somehow find a way of loving the world without

trusting it; somehow one must love the world without being worldly. I found this projecting feature of Christian theology, like a sort of hard spike, the dogmatic insistence that God was personal, and had made a world separate from Himself. The spike of dogma fitted exactly into the hole in the world—it had evidently been meant to go there—and then the strange things began to happen. When once these two parts of the two machines had come together, one after another, all the other parts fitted and fell in with an eerie exactitude. I could hear bolt after bolt over all the machinery falling into its place with a kind of click of relief. . . . Instinct after instinct was answered by doctrine after doctrine.[5]

Chesterton returns often to the image of the dogmatic key fitting exactly into the world's cavity, not only to affirm that Church doctrines fit the circumstances encountered in life, but also to suggest that only a complex key could fit a circumstance as complex as existence. "A stick might fit a hole or a stone or a hollow by accident. But a key and a lock are both complex. And if a key fits a lock, you know it is the right key."[6]

Of course, Catholics do not "worship a key";[7] the key's value is in unlocking a door. And the early Christian "was very precisely a person carrying about a key, or what he said was a key. The whole Christian movement consisted in claiming to possess that key."[8] Chesterton explicitly enumerates the three characteristics possessed by a key which drew him to image a creed in this way. First, "a key is above all things a thing with a shape," and its value to us, as well as its own integrity, "depends entirely upon keeping its shape." Second, "the shape of a key is in itself a rather fantastic shape."

A savage who did not know it was a key would have the greatest difficulty in guessing what it could possibly be. And it is fantastic because it is in a sense arbitrary. A key is not a matter of abstractions; in that sense a key is not a matter of argument. It either fits the lock or it does not. It is useless for men to stand disputing over it, considered by itself; or reconstructing it on pure principles of geometry or decorative art. It is senseless for a man to say he would like a simpler key; it would be far more sensible to do his best with a crowbar. And thirdly, as the key is necessarily a thing with a pattern, so this was one having in some ways a rather elaborate pattern. When people complain of the religion being so early complicated with theology and things of the kind, they forget that the world had not only got into a hole, but had got into a whole maze of holes and corners. . . . If the faith had faced the world only with the platitudes and peace and simplicity some moralists would confine it to, it would not have had the faintest effect on that luxurious and labyrinthine lunatic asylum. . . . [T]here was un-doubtedly much about the key that seemed complex; indeed there was only one thing about it that was simple. It opened the door.[9]

The image influences how one thinks about a thing, and Chesterton thinks of Christianity as something which came at the ancient world (or ours, too) not with the deconstructive force of a battering ram, but with the effectiveness of a key. The tool for opening the door is small, smaller than a crowbar, but it is sufficient because the shape of the key was made by the locksmith who fashioned the lock. We may open the world—if we have the key. Christianity is not, then, locked in an eternal, antagonistic struggle with the world. Christianity is the one thing which will permit the won-ders of the world to open to us if only we would be directed to where the struggle really belongs, namely, the heart. The pagan has the right instinct in being drawn to the world, which is why the pagan could find the incar-nate Christ; but when the pagan set out to enjoy himself, he soon found he could enjoy nothing else. The key to enjoying the world was lacking.

The complexity of the key permits Chesterton to accent the givenness of the creed, affirming that it is God's revelation and not our construction, and at the same time permits him to account for the complexity of doctrine, which does bear the mark of the human mind.

Man can be defined as an animal that makes dogmas. As he piles doctrine on doctrine and conclusion on conclusion in the formation of some tremendous scheme of philosophy and religion, he is, in the only legiti-mate sense of which the expression is capable, becoming more and more human. When he drops one doctrine after another in a refined scepticism, when he declines to tie himself to a system, when he says that he has out-grown definitions, when he says that he disbelieves in finality, when, in his own imagination, he sits as God, holding no form of creed by contem-plating all, then he is by that very process sinking slowly backwards into the vagueness of the vagrant animals and the unconscious of the grass. Trees have no dogmas. Turnips are singularly broad-minded.[10]

Doctrines are not puzzles we must figure out before God will let us occupy heaven. They are the product of a mind gifted by grace and commanded to figure out how on earth to be happy. Both faith and morality require thoughtfulness; a simplistic creed is inapt for mature faith. "To say with the optimists that God is good, and therefore everything is good; or with the universalists that God is Love, and therefore everything is love; or with the Christian Scientists that God is Spirit, and therefore everything is spirit; or, for that matter, with the pessimists that God is cruel, and therefore everything is a beastly shame; to say any of these things is to make a remark to which it is difficult to make any reply, except 'Oh'; or possibly, in a rather feeble fashion, 'Well, well.' The statement is certainly, in one sense, very complete; possibly a little too complete; and we find ourselves wishing it were a little more complex."[11] Catholic complexity attempts to hold "the complete philosophy which keeps a man sane; and not some single fragment of it. . . . [T]hose who tried to make the Faith more simple invariably made it less sane."[12] In the past century we have had our share of simple religions, Chesterton contends, each trying "to be more simple than the last. And the manifest mark of all these simplifications was, not only that they were finally sterile, but that they were very rapidly stale. A man had said the last word about them when he had said the first."[13]

Chesterton points out the inconsistency of desiring to keep the divine science in a retarded state even though we acknowledge the advantage of being deliberative in other departments of life. There appeared in the newspapers of his day a cry for religion to be simplified, discarding both ritual and theology in favor of simple morality, in order to propound only loving one another, and the golden rule, and so forth, "as if the moral problem of man were perfectly simple" and one could address that problem without "long technical words, and talking about senseless ceremonies." Chesterton counters:

> [I]t is exactly as if somebody were to say about the science of medicine: "All I ask is Health; what could be simpler than the beautiful gift of Health? Why not be content to enjoy for ever the glow of youth and the

fresh enjoyment of being fit? Why study dry and dismal sciences of anatomy and physiology; why inquire about the whereabouts of obscure organs in the human body? Why pedantically distinguish between what is labelled a poison and what is labelled an antidote, when it is so simple to enjoy Health? Why worry with a minute exactitude about the number of drops of laudanum or the strength of a dose of chloral, when it is so nice to be healthy? Away with your priestly apparatus of stethoscopes and clinical thermometers; with your ritualistic mummery of feeling pulses, putting out tongues, examining teeth, and the rest! The god Aesculapius came on earth solely to inform us that Life is on the whole preferable to Death; and this thought will console many dying persons unattended by doctors."[14]

The elementary love of the fishermen who left their boats to follow their Lord round the shores of Galilee was adequate to found the divine society, but would rudimentary doctrine and discipline be adequate for a Church rigged to sail to every corner of the world with the key to transfigure every philosophy and every civlization? "Quite apart from the theory of a Church, if Christ had remained on earth for an indefinite time, trying to induce men to love one another, He would have found it necessary to have some tests, some methods, some way of dividing true love from false love, some way of distinguishing between tendencies that would ruin love and tendencies that would restore it. You cannot make a success of anything, even loving, entirely without thinking."[15]

A second image Chesterton uses to think about doctrine is vitality, meant both in the sense that doctrines are vitally important and in the sense that doctrines are animated, living, vital things themselves. We earlier saw Chesterton's opinion that one cannot make a success of asceticism without the controlling pressure of a creed because it is dogma that keeps asceticism from vilifying the body when it vivifies the spirit. It is no less true that a success cannot be made of mysticism without ecclesiastical and theological pressure. "Nothing on earth needs to be organised so much as Mysticism. You say that man tends naturally to religion; he does indeed; often in the form of human sacrifice of the temples of Sodom. Almost all extreme evil of that kind is mystical. The only way of keeping it healthy is to have some rules, some responsibilities, some definitions of dogma and moral function."[16] Neither can one make a success of human culture without debating the boundary lines. Creeds and doctrines identify the pressure points on the fault line, and though the points are minor, intellectual shifts can be seismic.

> It is exactly this which explains . . . the monstrous wars about small points of theology, the earthquakes of emotion about a gesture or a word. It is only a matter of an inch; but an inch is everything when you are balanc-ing. The Church could not afford to swerve a hair's breadth on some things if she was to continue her great and daring experiment of the ir-regular equilibrium. Once let one idea become less powerful and some other idea would become too powerful. It was no flock of sheep the Chris-tian shepherd was leading, but a herd of bulls and tigers, of terrible ideals and devouring doctrines, each one of them strong enough to turn to a false religion and lay waste the world. Remember that the Church went in specifically for dangerous ideas; she was a lion tamer. The idea of birth through a Holy Spirit, of the death of a divine being, of the forgiveness of sins, or the fulfillment of prophecies, are ideas which, any one can see, need but a touch to turn them into something blasphemous or fero-cious. . . . If some small mistake were made in doctrine, huge blunders might be made in human happiness. A sentence phrased wrong about the nature of symbolism would have broken all the best statues in Europe. A slip in the definitions might stop all the dances; might wither all the Christmas trees or break all the Easter eggs.[17]

If doctrines consisted of nothing more vital than the esoteric prattle between opinionated pundits we would not be so concerned, but because doctrines will affect Christmas trees and holiday dances, statues and sacraments, Easter eggs and Easter hope, correctly formulating them is vitally important business. They concern the things that keep us alive, and the things that threaten to kill us. The Church has rarely had the luxury of deliberating in fields of serene quietude; the decibel level is usually quite high inside the world of conflicting ideals wherein the Church is called to keep its concen-tration on the run. Nothing is so simple as dying; it is staying alive and stay-ing human that is complex. That's why the Church is in possession of many ideas. "To us, Christian Scientists are simply people with one idea, which they have never learnt to balance and combine with all the other ideas. That is why the wealthy business man so often becomes a Christian Scientist. He is not used to ideas and one idea goes to his head, like one glass of wine to a starving man. But the Catholic Church is used to living with ideas and walks among all those very dangerous wild beasts with the poise and the lifted head of a lion-tamer."[18] Besides having the head for it, and keeping one's feet on the ground when considering such heady matters, we must be able to evaluate ideas that come into our heads. As we have already established, ideas are dangerous, "but the man to whom they are least dangerous is the man of ideas. He is acquainted with ideas, and moves among them like a lion-tamer. . . . The man of no ideas will find the first idea fly to his head like wine to the head of a teetotaller. . . . Many, for example, avowedly followed Cecil Rhodes because he had a vision. They might as well have followed him because he had a nose; a man without some kind of dream of perfection is quite as much of a monstrosity as a noseless man. People say of such a figure, in almost feverish whispers, 'He knows his own mind,' which is exactly like saying in equally feverish whispers, 'He blows his own nose.'"[19]

It is evident from these images why Chesterton does not think dogmas are dull: the matter out of which faith is formed is too rambunctious to ever be called drear, and the stakes are too high for the work to ever be called tedious. It would be surprising, indeed, to hear described as dull or trifling the struggle against forces which impede life, even if they are noetic forces; or, if Chesterton is right about the seismic consequences of ideas, precisely *because* they are noetic. "Dogmas are not dull. Even what are called the fine doctrinal distinctions are not dull. They are like the finest operations of surgery; separating nerve from nerve, but giving life. It is easy enough to flatten out everything for miles round with dynamite, if our only objective is to give death. But just as the physiologist is dealing with living tissues, so the theologian is dealing with living ideas; and if he draws a line between them it is naturally a very fine line."[20]

Not shying away from the implications of his vivacious metaphor, Chesterton goes so far as to say, several times, that doctrines are analogous to sex: they breed. (And in both cases things seem to fare better with an element of monogamy.) As human procreation cannot come from a single individual, neither can a single and individual thought sire doctrine. Trini-

tarian monotheism seems to Chesterton more fertile than unitarian monotheism. "The Moslem had one thought, and that a most vital one; the great-
ness of God which levels all men. But the Moslem had not one thought
to rub against another, because he really had not another. It is the friction
of two spiritual things, of tradition and invention, or of substance and symbol, from which the mind takes fire. The Creeds condemned as complex
have something like the secret of sex; they can breed thoughts."[21] There are
thoughts, Chesterton says, which feel too complete, and which therefore
leave us with nothing to say in return. That is the problem with a simple
thought, a complete thought.

> We find ourselves wishing it were a little more complex. That is exactly the
> point. It is not complex enough to be a living organism. It has no vitality
> because it has no variety of function. . . . And, meanwhile, any one
> Catholic peasant, while holding one small bead of the rosary in his fingers,
> can be conscious, not of one eternity, but of a complex and almost a con-
> flict of eternities; as, for example, in the relations of Our Lord and Our
> Lady, of the fatherhood and the childhood of God, of the motherhood and
> childhood of Mary. Thoughts of that kind have, in a supernatural sense,
> something analogous to sex; they breed. They are fruitful and multiply;
> and there is no end to them.[22]

The person is wrong, therefore, who complains for the thousandth time that
a living religion does not need dull and dusty dogmas. "[W]e must stop
him with a sort of shout and say, 'There—you go wrong at the very start.' If
he would condescend to ask what the dogmas are, he would find out that it
is precisely the dogmas that are living, that are inspiring, that are intellec-
tually interesting. Zeal and charity and unction are admirable as flowers
and fruit; but if you are really interested in the living principle you must be
interested in the root or the seed."[23]

Living ideas share another characteristic with living things: they develop. Not only do doctrines increase in the sense of multiplying in number, but a doctrine itself can be said to increase, in the sense of developing.
Of course, Chesterton does not mean develop in the sense of change, in the
sense of going out of date, as if doctrine thought true by our ancestors can no
longer possibly be thought so by us. Doctrinal development does not equal
doctrinal dilution. However, he does definitely mean that it is not unnatural

for doctrines to develop, if we understand the natural meaning of the word "development."

> [T]here seems to be a queer ignorance, not only about the technical, but the natural meaning of the word Development. The critics of Catholic theology seem to suppose that it is not so much an evolution as an evasion; that it is at best an adaptation. They fancy that its very success is the success of surrender. But that is not the natural meaning of the word Development. When we talk of a child being well-developed, we mean that he has grown bigger and stronger with his own strength; not that he is padded with borrowed pillows or walks on stilts to make him look taller. When we say that a puppy develops into a dog, we do not mean that his growth is a gradual compromise with a cat; we mean that he becomes more doggy and not less. Development is the expansion of all the possibilities and implications of a doctrine, as there is time to distinguish them and draw them out.[24]

And neither does the Church compromise its identity when it welcomes an occasional dragon to dinner or a penitent griffin to sleep in the spare bed. In fact, the way in which the faith becomes catholic is for St. Francis to invite Pan to Peter's liturgy, and St. Thomas to invite Aristotle to submit categories to describe the indescribable repast. These two saintly persons are a moment of what Chesterton would call development in doctrine. "St. Thomas, every bit as much as St. Francis, felt subconsciously that the hold of his people was slipping on the solid Catholic doctrine and discipline, worn smooth by more than a thousand years of routine; and that the Faith needed to be shown under a new light and dealt with from another angle. . . . It needed something like the shrewd and homely touch of Aristotle to turn it again into a religion of common sense."[25] God works on both sides of the Church-world equation. Baptizing into service of the Kingdom of God whatever truths of nature have been uncovered is a perfectly natural course of development for a Church entrusted with the key to transfiguring the world.

Chesterton's third image of doctrine is that of a map through the world imagined as a walled maze. However, this map is not an escape map.

> Nine out of ten of what we call new ideas are simply old mistakes. The Catholic Church has for one of her chief duties that of preventing people

from making those old mistakes; from making them over and over again forever, as people always do if they are left to themselves. The truth about the Catholic attitude towards heresy, or as some would say, towards liberty, can best be expressed perhaps by the metaphor of a map. The Catholic Church carries a sort of map of the mind which looks like a map of a maze, but which is in fact a guide to the maze. It has been compiled from knowledge which, even considered as human knowledge, is quite without any human parallel. There is no other case of one continuous intelligent institution that has been thinking about thinking for two thousand years. Its experience naturally covers nearly all experiences; and especially nearly all errors. The result is a map in which all the blind alleys and bad roads are clearly marked, all the ways that have been shown to be worthless by the best of all evidence: the evidence of those who have gone down them.

On this map of the mind the errors are marked as exceptions. The greater part of it consists of playgrounds and happy hunting-fields, where the mind may have as much liberty as it likes; not to mention any number of intellectual battle-fields in which the battle is indefinitely open and un-decided. But it does definitely take the responsibility of marking certain roads as leading nowhere or leading to destruction, to a blank wall, or a sheer precipice. By this means, it does prevent men from wasting their time or losing their lives upon paths that have been found futile or disastrous again and again in the past. . . . She does dogmatically defend humanity from its worst foes, those hoary and horrible and devouring monsters of the old mistakes.[26]

This map shows the way through the maze; it shows where the fences should be put up for the protection of human life; it leads to artesian springs and away from infectious swamps; it distinguishes grass from poison, showing us meadows capable of supporting life; but it does not, as an insular and sectarian piety would have it, show us an escape tunnel leading out of this public and pagan *polis*. Doctrines are not for walling out the world, but for safeguarding our paradisiacal playing field. "Catholic doctrine and discipline may be walls; but they are the walls of a playground. Christianity is the only frame which has preserved the pleasure of Paganism. We might fancy some children playing on the flat grassy top of some tall island in the sea. So long as there was a wall round the cliff's edge they could fling themselves into every frantic game and make the place the noisiest of nurseries. But the walls were knocked down, leaving the naked peril of the precipice. They did not fall over; but when their friends re-turned to them they were all huddled in terror in the centre of the island; and their song had ceased."[27]

Human beings, being "doctrinal animals," search for truth; and under the assumption that reality is complex, truthful expressions about reality will be complex. "I began to examine more exactly the general Christian the-ology which many execrated and few examined. I soon found that it did in fact correspond to many of these experiences of life; that even its paradoxes corresponded to the paradoxes of life."[28] The elaborateness of a doctrine sig-nifies that the whole truth is being seen and not just that part of it visible to a very local vision. By reductionism, one philosopher can see one truth, like one person can see one color in the peacock tail, but to speak the real color or the real truth requires more than one word, maybe more than one speaker. Catholic theology is a two-thousand-year-old mind which has kept intact its memory of what other speakers have said.

> [I]t is the only theology that has not only thought, but thought of every-thing. That almost any other theology or philosophy contains a truth, I do not at all deny; on the contrary, that is what I assert; and that is what I complain of. Of all the other systems or sects I know, every single one is content to follow a truth, theological or theosophical or ethical or meta-physical; and the more they claim to be universal, the more it means that they merely take something and apply it to everything. . . . I have only found one creed that could not be satisfied with a truth, but only with the Truth, which is made of a million such truths and yet is one. . . . Flowers grow best in a garden, and even grow biggest in a garden. . . .[29]

The kind of truth with which Chesterton is concerned—the kind opposed to heresy, I maintain—is not only the truth of verity but the truth of the garden. Heresy is not false because it has never thought a truth; heresy is diminutive because outside the Catholic garden it cannot grow big. A Catholic's sense of being free derives from possessing "the range of two thou-sand years full of twelve-hundred thousand controversies, thrashed out by thinker against thinker, school against school, guild against guild, nation against nation, with no limit except the fundamental logical fact that the things were worth arguing, because they could be ultimately solved and settled."[30]

In our modern wilderness we have withered worse than paganism, for at least in their wilderness they struggled to grow truth, believing that the questions were worth arguing. "All previous ages have sweated and been crucified in an attempt to realize what is really the right life, what was really the good man. A definite part of the modern world has come beyond question to the conclusion that there is no answer to these questions, that the most we can do is to set up a few notice-boards at places of obvious danger."[31] Catholic doctrine is more ambitious than setting up signs warning of thin ice or absolving itself of liability with warning labels on packages. It has the ambitious plan to build a firm foundation for living. The Church wills not only to preserve past truth by protecting it within the gardener's wall, it wills also to persevere in its search for further truth. If an age no longer believes that truth can be found, then it will have lost its resoluteness and will no more inaugurate a quest for truth than embark on a search for unicorns. The argument in ages past between the heretic and the orthodox was about who was which. "In former days the heretic was proud of not being a heretic. . . . But a few modern phrases have made him boast of it."[32] What this means is that people have lost concern for whether they are philosophically right, and at that point one can hardly get a good discussion off the ground, much less a productive argument.

Before Chesterton can arrive at the point of disagreement with heretics, these flighty minds would have to be able to arrive at a point of commitment themselves. One can't argue about what is true when the heretic is more interested in being interesting than in being correct. That is the difficulty which Chesterton had felt with such people. "The truth of the matter is, I imagine, that these particular people never did believe or disbelieve in anything. They liked to go and hear stimulating lecturers; and they had a vague preference, almost impossible to reduce to any definable thesis, for those lecturers who were supposed to be in some way heterodox and unconventional. . . . I had begun to discover that, in all that welter of inconsistent and incompatible heresies, the one and only real unpardonable heresy was orthodoxy."[33] Perhaps this also accounts for the change in attitude toward creed. Perhaps doctrinal creeds looked less restrictive to a medieval person who wanted to reason things out than to a modern person who does not want to be held by the oppressive constraints of reasonability. To someone who doesn't believe truth can be stated, the person who believes a stated truth looks gullible. "Creed and credence and credulity are words of the same origin and can be juggled backwards and forwards to any extent. But when a man assumes the absurdity of anything that anybody else believes, we wish first to know what he believes; on what principle he believes; and, above all, upon what principle he disbelieves."[34] Christian doctrine looks adamantine not because our age suffers want of freedom, but because it suffers want of reason. In an earlier world, one which "was too stolid, Christianity returned in the form of a vagabond [i.e., Francis]; in a world that has grown a great deal too wild, Christianity has returned in the form of a teacher of logic [i.e., Thomas]. In the world of Herbert Spencer men wanted a cure for indigestion; in the world of Einstein they want a cure for vertigo."[35]

Just as the complexity of a key is a sign that it was made to fit a lock, so the labyrinthian quality of the map is a sign that it is a blueprint. The map might seem a canard if we never get anywhere by following it, but when we discover that this particular path does lead to happiness and that this particular wall does protect us from danger, just as the map predicts, then we determine that the maker of the map was also the maker of our minds and of our world. Chesterton's argument for revelation is not in the least an argument against reason, and in this he follows St. Thomas. Every turn revealed by the map is a reasonable turn; each truth to which it leads, a reasonable truth. St. Thomas is inclined to admit "that truth could be reached by a rational process, if only it were rational enough; and also long enough. . . . That is, he does emphatically believe that men can be convinced by argument; when they reach the end of the argument. Only his common sense also told him that the argument never ends. . . . [Therefore] men must receive the highest moral truths in a miraculous manner; or most men would not receive them at all."[36] Revelation does not short-circuit human rationality by disclosing things reason could never believe. Revelation is a source of truths which not every person has the luxury of time to arrive at by reasonable argument. Revelation delivers us from having to discover the dead ends by personal harm and detriment, but even the pagan, without benefit of revelation, would agree which ends are fatal for human beings. Revelation does not reveal anything contrary to reason.

Chesterton illustrates this understanding of natural law and revelation through the subject of human dignity and equality. Some say that belief "in the brotherhood of men was only founded on certain texts in the Bible, about all men being the children of Adam and Eve." If this is true, if doctrine is grounded solely on revealed text without any ground of reason, then those who don't believe those texts don't have to believe the teaching. But Chesterton thinks the texts aren't required to make us start believing the teaching; in fact, the texts are most required when we stop believing the teaching. Millions of plain people all over the world have assumed obligations toward their neighbor without ever having clapped eyes on any sacred text, so it is not true that without revelation the belief would be unreasonable.

What is true is this: that if the nonsense of Nietzsche or some such sophist submerged current culture, so that it was the fashion to deny the duties of fraternity; then indeed it might be found that the group which still affirmed fraternity was the original group in whose sacred books was the text about Adam and Eve. Suppose some Prussian professor has opportunely discovered that Germans and lesser men are respectively descended from two such very different monkeys that they are in no sense brothers, but barely cousins (German) any number of times removed. And suppose he proceeds to remove them even further with a hatchet; suppose he bases on this a repetition of the conduct of Cain, saying not so much "Am I my brother's keeper?" as "Is he really my brother?" And suppose this higher philosophy of the hatchet becomes prevalent in colleges and cultivated circles, as even more foolish philosophies have done. Then I agree it probably will be the Christian, the man who preserves the text about Cain, who will continue to assert that he is still the professor's brother; that he is still the professor's keeper. He may possibly add that, in his opinion, the professor seems to require a keeper. . . .

It is the Christian church which continues to hold strongly, when the world for some reason has weakened on it, what many others hold at other times. . . . But anybody who holds it at all will hold it as a philosophy, not hung on one text but on a hundred truths.[37]

The doctrinal map is not nearly so private as the heretic would have us believe. The ancient Greeks called a private person an "idiotes," meaning "not public"—self-contained in one's own world. The Catholic believes the Bible is true because what it contains is public and can be recognized by reason; but the heretic, wishing to demonstrate revelation's truth on the grounds that it is too unique for reason to recognize, would have us believe the Bible is true because it is idiotic. If this disjunction between revelation and reason comes about, then there is nothing to talk about, since dialogue requires that we have both a reason to talk and reason to talk with. Then civilized dialogue breaks off and civilization's acerbic tongue makes its appearance. "As a matter of fact, it is generally the man who is not ready to argue, who is ready to sneer. That is why, in recent literature, there has been so little argument and so much sneering."[38]

It was not in St. Thomas's character to sneer. "There is not a single occasion on which he indulged in a sneer. His curiously simple character, his lucid but laborious intellect, could not be better summed up than by saying that he did not know how to sneer."[39] And this remained true although he thought combatively, apologetically, and indulged in arguments of inordinate length. A sneer was not only not in his character, it was not in his theology. In his Catholic theology, revelation did not end an argument, it began it, made sense of it, and revealed its end. Therefore the engagement between revelation and reason enlarged both the faith and the mind. St. Thomas thought one must understand the opponent's position better than the opponent understood it himself.

It is no good to tell an atheist that he is an atheist; or to charge a denier of immortality with the infamy of denying it; or to imagine that one can force an opponent to admit he is wrong, by proving he is wrong on somebody else's principles, but not on his own. After the great example of St. Thomas, the principle stands, or ought always to have stood as established; that we must either not argue with a man at all, or we must argue on his grounds and not ours. We may do other things instead of arguing, according to our views of what actions are morally permissible; but if we argue we must argue [as Thomas put it] "on the reasons and statements of the philosophers themselves."[40]

In a related way, one must understand the principle behind a practice better than the person who holds the position without reason. It is not enough to be right only by prejudice, even if it is a valid prejudice, because without a principle the prejudice can't be corrected when it starts to go awry. In evidence, Chesterton submits that although "most of our friends and acquaintances continue to entertain a healthy prejudice against cannibalism," there are nevertheless attitudes appearing today toward the human body (our corporal mode of being human), which do not think the bodies of humans very much different from the bodies of animals. "Among people who have reached this position, the *reason* for disapproving of cannibalism has already become very vague. It remains as a tradition and an instinct. Fortunately, thank God, though it is now very vague, it is still very strong." But social sanities which we take for granted shan't remain strong without a theological creed for a grounding principle. "[A]ll such social sanities are now the traditions of old Catholic dogmas. Like many other Catholic dogmas, they are felt in some vague way even by heathens, so long as they are healthy heathens. . . . They have the prejudice; and long may they retain it! We have the principle, and they are welcome to it when they want it."[41] If the heretic finds revelation unreasonable, it is because he has surrendered his principle of reason; at least the healthy heathen is in the position of being able to ascertain in revelation what he has reasonably expected. "Some people do not like the word 'dogma.' Fortunately they are free, and there is an alternative for them. There are two things, and two things only, for the human mind, a dogma and a prejudice. The Middle Ages were a rational epoch, an age of doctrine. Our age is, at its best, a poetical epoch, an age of prejudice. A doctrine is a definite point; a prejudice is a direction. That an ox may be eaten, while a man should not be eaten, is a doctrine."[42]

This brings us to Chesterton's fourth image. It is true that Catholic doctrine is rather single-minded: it persistently harps about love of God and justice on earth, eternal happiness and how one becomes capacitated for it, beatitude and other such topics which do tend to grab the mind's attention. But single-mindedness should not be mistaken for narrow-mindedness.

While it is true that Catholic doctrine has a quality which may be called undeviating, assiduous, and constant (so constant that those who were already too tired to hear it the first time will find it monotonously tiring the millionth time they hear it), it is not true that Catholic doctrine may be called narrow in ambition or modest in scope. This theology really does want to reconcile such diverse things as angels and octopuses, heaven and earth, revelation and reason, faith and science, Church and world, and all this because it believes grace perfects nature. Failure to perceive this is the cause of the puritan's agoraphobia as New Rome invited Old Rome to help decorate St. Peter's Basilica.

St. Thomas must make corrections to Aristotle where this philosopher has not accounted for a fact of revelation to come after him, but all that this wise pagan had right, Thomas keeps. Of whatever other faults scholasticism may be culpable, it cannot be charged with narrow-mindedness when it tries to accommodate, simultaneously, all the reality which heaven reveals and reason discovers. In its broad-mindedness, scholasticism is unwilling to live in twin worlds, which is at the root of Thomas's objection to his schizophrenic opponent, Siger of Brabant.

Siger of Brabant said this: the church must be right theologically, but she can be wrong scientifically. There are two truths; the truth of the supernatural world, and the truth of the natural world, which contradicts the supernatural world. While we are being naturalists, we can suppose that Christianity is all nonsense; but then, when we remember that we are Christians, we must admit that Christianity is true even if it is nonsense. In other words, Siger of Brabant split the human head in two, like the blow in an old legend of battle; and he declared that a man has two minds, with one of which he must entirely believe and with the other may utterly disbelieve. To many this would at least seem like a parody of Thomism. As a fact, it was the assassination of Thomism. It was not two ways of finding the same truth; it was an untruthful way of pretending that there are two truths. And it is extraordinarily interesting to note that this is the one occasion when the Dumb Ox really came out like a wild bull. . . .

Those who complain that theologians draw fine distinctions could hardly find a better example of their own folly. In fact, a fine distinction can be a flat contradiction. It was notably so in this case. St. Thomas was willing to allow the one truth to be approached by two paths, precisely *be- cause* he was sure there was only one truth. Because the Faith was the one truth, nothing discovered in nature could ultimately contradict the Faith. Because the Faith was the one truth, nothing really deduced from the Faith could ultimately contradict the facts. It was in truth a curiously daring confidence in the reality of his religion; and though some may linger to dis- pute it, it has been justified.[43]

"A man is not really convinced of a philosophic theory when he finds that something proves it. He is only really convinced when he finds that everything proves it."[44] That is why it was necessary for Chesterton, and for St. Thomas, that the Catholic faith be stretched large enough to cover everything. In the scholastic's case, it resulted in "books enough to sink a ship or stock a library";[45] a review of Chesterton's own bookshelves, and the range of interests they reveal, proves that it is not much different for him. If he had only needed a single truth, he could have been satisfied with any phi- losophy, because every half-truth contains some truth; but to be really convinced that Catholicism had the one whole truth, he tilted with a range of heresies. "Now anybody driven to the defence of what he does really mean must cover all the strategic field of the fight, and must fight at many points which he would not have chosen in fancy, but only in relation to fact. He cannot hope to deal only with heresies that amuse him; he must, in common fairness, deal seriously with heresies that bore him."[46]

Catholic doctrine is still being stretched; the flowers in the garden are still growing. The matter which doctrine uses to develop, like the food which a child uses to grow, increases as actual, novel, historical events come to pass and the sum total of facts to chew on increases. As the world in- creases for us, doctrine will be animated, and thoughts will breed. So unless Siger of Brabant is right, and surely he isn't, Catholicism does not have a conflicted mind about scriptural truth and scientific truth.

[I]n the matter of the inspiration of Scripture, [Thomas] fixed first on the obvious fact . . . that the meaning of Scripture is very far from self-evident; and that we must often interpret it in the light of other truths. If a literal interpretation is really and flatly contradicted by an obvious fact, why then we can only say that the literal interpretation must be a false interpretation.

But the fact must really be an obvious fact. And unfortunately, nineteenth-century scientists were just as ready to jump to the conclusion that any guess about nature was an obvious fact, as were seventeenth-century sectarians to jump to the conclusion that any guess about Scripture was the obvious explanation. Thus, private theories about what the Bible ought to mean, and premature theories about what the world ought to mean, have met in loud and widely advertised controversy . . . and this clumsy collision of two very impatient forms of ignorance was known as the quarrel of Science and Religion. . . . If the matter had been left to [Thomas], and men like him, there never would have been any quarrel between Science and Religion.[47]

Interpreting the meaning of Scripture in the light of other truths is an ongoing proposition, not a fundamentalist proposition which pulls the shade on the world's bright lights: Plato, Aristotle, Copernicus, Newton, and so forth. In fact, a new pile of empirical fact was dumped in the university square at Paris for St. Thomas's consideration by a new attitude toward empiricism cultivated by his teacher, Albert the Great.

It is not really so much a question of access to the facts, as of attitude to the facts. Most of the Schoolmen, if informed by the only informants they had that a unicorn has one horn or a salamander lives in the fire, still used it more as an illustration of logic than an incident of life. What they really said was, "If a unicorn has one horn, two unicorns have as many horns as one cow." And that is not one inch the less a fact because the unicorn is a fable. But with Albertus in medieval times, as with Aristotle in ancient times, there did begin something like the idea of emphasising the question: "But *does* the unicorn only have one horn or the salamander a fire instead of a fire-side?" Doubtless when the social and geographical limits of medieval life began to allow them to search the fire for salamanders or the desert for unicorns, they had to modify many of their scientific ideas. A fact which will expose them to the very proper scorn of a generation of scientists which has just discovered that Newton is nonsense, that space is limited, and that there is no such thing as an atom.[48]

From this world of facts sprang cosmological arguments as the natural world became grist for the reasoning of faith.

It does seem to be agreed upon that the unruly child, Science, is really Christianity's child. The willingness to poke Mother Nature with empiri‐ cal syringes could not have come out of a pagan worldview which treated nature as quasi‐divine. It required a worldview in which Nature is not our mother, but our sister. "We can be proud of her beauty, since we have the same father; but she has no authority over us."[49] "Are you surprised that the same civilisation which believed in the Trinity discovered steam?"[50] With the discovery also comes obligations. As Chesterton has repeatedly told us, what's wrong with the world is that we act without knowing to what end we are obliged. Our sister, Nature, is not mute about this knowledge, so St. Thomas listens to her, making him Huxley's ideal agnostic: one com‐ mitted to the method of following reason as far as it will go.

> Now the modern Anthropologists, who called themselves Agnostics, completely failed to be Anthropologists at all. Under their limitations, they could not get a complete theory of Man, let alone a complete theory of nature. They began by ruling out something which they called the Un‐ knowable. . . . But it rapidly became apparent that all sorts of things were unknowable, which were exactly the things that a man has got to know. It is necessary to know whether he is responsible or irresponsible, perfect or imperfect, perfectible or unperfectible, mortal or immortal, doomed or free, not in order to understand God, but in order to understand Man. . . . Has a man free will; or is his sense of choice an illusion? Has he a con‐ science, or has his conscience any authority; or is it only the prejudice of the tribal past? Is there any real hope of settling these things by human reason; and has *that* any authority? Is he to regard death as final; and is he to regard miraculous help as possible?[51]

Where St. Thomas and the agnostic part company is not in their answer— Thomas is supremely confident that God lies at the end of reason—but in the fact that only St. Thomas, and not the agnostic, really asks "Where does it go?" Because theology is not disjunctive to reason or empiricism, investi‐ gations of nature will contribute to the discussion about the end and essence of human beings, but only if that is being discussed. Unfortunately, the in‐ vestigation will not treat what it declares at the outset as unknowable.

Thus it happens, says Chesterton, that the Catholic tradition can affirm both mystical knowledge and intellectual knowledge, for the very simple reason that they are both right. Again, the heretic's ungainly position is to stand on a single footing, waving his arms frantically in apprehension of falling to either one side or the other—reason or mysticism. The Catholic stands upon both feet, on a base broad enough to house both Franciscans and Dominicans.

> The Franciscan [Bonaventure] may be represented as the Father of all the Mystics; and the Mystics can be represented as men who maintain that the final fruition or joy of the soul is rather a sensation than a thought. The motto of the Mystics has always been, "Taste and see." Now St. Thomas also began by saying, "Taste and see"; but he said it of the first rudimentary impressions of the human animal. It might well be maintained that the Franciscan puts Taste last and the Dominican puts it first. It might be said that the Thomist begins with something solid like the taste of an apple, and afterwards deduces a divine life for the intellect; while the Mystic exhausts the intellect first, and says finally that the sense of God is something like the taste of an apple. . . . They are both right; if I may say so, it is a privilege of people who contradict each other in their cosmos to be both right. The Mystic is right in saying that the relation of God and Man is essentially a love-story; the pattern and type of all love-stories. The Dominican rationalist is equally right in saying that the intellect is at home in the topmost heavens; and that the appetite for truth may outlast and even devour all the duller appetites of man.[52]

Our hankering for love stories reminds us that we were made for love, and our craving for understanding reminds us that we were made for intellectual fulfillment. "Whether the supreme ecstasy is more affectional than intellectual is no very deadly matter of quarrel among men who believe it is both, but do not profess even to imagine the actual experience of either."[53]

SEVEN

Room to Run Wild

If the last chapter presented Chesterton clearly on doctrine, we should be able to ascertain his attitude toward authority clearly in this chapter. He connects them because he believes doctrine requires a living authority. Some people eschew authority because they believe that freedom's increase comes only in proportion to authority's decrease; from such a starting point, both doctrine and authority are unwelcome impositions. Chesterton finds Catholic doctrine and authority imposing, to be sure, but he experiences them as an imposition in the way gravity imposes upon a body so it can walk the surface of the planet, or logic imposes itself on thought so that conversation can take place, or social rules impose on a society so we can cross a street without harm or enjoy a festive dinner party without anxiety. In this chapter such an attitude toward authority will be presented. The first objective will be to consider the paradox of freedom and limits, the second to organize the roomy images Chesterton uses to describe the Church, and the third to consider why he believes doctrine and authority require a real Church and do not function in the abstract.

We saw that Chesterton images doctrine as a map to a maze. But anyone who has been in a maze knows that the experience involves coming up against walls, fences, or gates which obstruct one's original intentions. When one encounters such forced modifications of direction, what should be one's general principle?

> In the matter of reforming things, as distinct from deforming them, there is one plain and simple principle; a principle which will probably be called a paradox. There exists in such a case a certain institution of law; let us say, for the sake of simplicity, a fence or gate erected across a road. The more modern type of reformer goes gaily up to it and says, "I don't see the use of

this; let us clear it away." To which the more intelligent type of reformer
will do well to answer: "If you don't see the use of it, I certainly won't let
you clear it way. Go away and think. Then, when you can come back and
tell me that you *do* see the use of it, I may allow you to destroy it.". . . .

The truth is that nobody has any business to destroy a social institution until he has really seen it as an historical institution. If he knows how
it arose, and what purposes it was supposed to serve, he may really be able
to say that they were bad purposes, or that they have since become bad
purposes, or that they are purposes which are no longer served. But if he
simply stares at the thing as a senseless monstrosity that has somehow
sprung up in his path, it is he and not the traditionalist who is suffering
from an illusion.[1]

What appear at first to be impositions placed upon us by an authority, turn
out to be markers on an uncharted shore (which turns out to be England):
someone has pioneered this path and has left warning markers if a certain
way has been found dangerous or dehumanizing, or if it ill-serves the cause
of happiness. The purpose of the markers is the purpose of boundary lines
on a playing field. "There was room for wrath and love to run wild. And
the more I considered Christianity, the more I found that while it had established a rule and order, the chief aim of that order was to give room for
good things to run wild."[2]

As usual, Chesterton's paradox operates by upsetting or inverting our
normal assumptions. He suggests that the world conceives liberty "as something that merely works outwards," whereas he has always "conceived it
as something that works inwards." This house is a strange and marvelous
edifice: its inside is bigger than its outside. As the convert peers into the
Catholic Church from the outside, "he often feels as if he were looking
through a leper's window. He is looking through a little crack or crooked
hole that seems to grow smaller as he stares at it; but it is an opening that
looks towards the Altar. Only, when he has entered the Church, he finds
that the Church is much larger inside than it is outside."[3] The house, as any
house, must be designed and ordered in deference to certain laws, just as any
house must take account of the law of gravity if it plans to keep the roof from
crashing in. But within the limits laid down by authority there is more room

for good things to run wild than if they dwelled in a wild, albeit limitless, wasteland. Domestic does not mean servile; it means that by limitations, like that of four walls, a roof, and a cozy hearth, a place becomes holy and habitable. The sense of limits stimulates a memory Chesterton carries from childhood, the source of so many of his paradoxes.

It is plain on the face of the facts that the child is positively in love with limits. He uses his imagination to invent imaginary limits. The nurse and the governess have never told him that it is his moral duty to step on alternate paving-stones. He deliberately deprives this world of half its paving-stones, in order to exult in a challenge that he has offered to himself. I played that kind of game with myself all over the mats and boards and carpets of the house; and, at the risk of being detained during His Majesty's pleasure, I will admit that I often play it still. In that sense I have constantly tried to cut down the actual space at my disposal; to divide and subdivide, into these happy prisons, the house in which I was quite free to run wild. . . . The charm of Robinson Crusoe is not in the fact that he could find his way to a remote island; but in the fact that he could not find any way of getting away from it. It is the fact which gives an intensive interest and excitement to all the things that he had with him on the island; the axe and the parrot and the guns and the little hoard of grain. . . . This game of self-limitation is one of the secret pleasures of life.[4]

Limits permit creativity not only in the child's game but in an artist's drawing as well. "It is impossible to be an artist and not care for laws and limits. Art is limitation; the essence of every picture is the frame. . . . The moment you step into the world of facts, you step into a world of limits. . . . Do not free a camel of the burden of his hump: you may be freeing him from being a camel."[5] And even on a metaphysical level it is evident that, "every act of will is an act of self-limitation."[6] At every real moment we are faced with a multitude of potentialities. To act is to make one choice, and to choose one act is to delimit the other possible acts. We are not faced with an infinity of potentialities. This belongs to the infinite Creator, not to finite creatures. "God is that which can make something out of nothing. Man (it may truly be said) is that which can make something out of anything. In other words, while the joy of God be unlimited creation, the special joy of man is limited creation, the combination of creation with limits. Man's pleasure, therefore, is to possess conditions, but also to be partly possessed by them. . . . The excitement is to get the utmost out of given conditions; the conditions will stretch, but not indefinitely."[7]

Chesterton really does want good things to run wild, but to do so good things must not themselves become wild things, because goodness lies in being proportioned to an end; disarrayed and erratic things cannot run to their good. That is why there is more room living within reason than without reason. Hence creeds and hierarchies were not organized, "as is ignorantly said, for the suppression of reason. They were organized for the difficult defence of reason. Man, by a blind instinct, knew that if once things were wildly questioned, reason could be questioned first."[8] We can be reasonably sure that a religion which liberates us from authority would leave us lighter, but we fear it would also, at the same time, liberate us from essential human goods the way a robber would leave us lighter one purse of gold.

Therefore Chesterton employs images of roominess to explain his experience of Catholicism as something which expands the mind, rather like the way post beams expand a room by holding up the ceiling, and our second objective in this chapter is to organize these images. He enlarges on the metaphor of size in three directions: the Catholic authoritative tradition makes our thought broader, longer, and taller. "The only difficulty about the evident reawakening of Catholicism in modern England, is that conversion calls on a man to stretch his mind, as a man awakening from a sleep may stretch his arms and legs."[9]

The only antidote to narrow, heretical thinking is its antipode, Catholic thinking, so it is not surprising that we continue to find images of width at play when Chesterton defines "Catholic." "Of nearly all the non-Catholic types of our time we can truly say, that any such type must broaden his mind to become a Catholic. He must grow more used than he is at present to the long avenues and the large spaces."[10] Chesterton propounds this thesis in the context of pointing out that being Catholic involves being catholic, i.e., universal, comprehensive in scope, including or concerning all humankind. Being Catholic obliges involvement with the very world which presence in the Roman Church leads the puritan to charge it with having become too worldly a church. The allegation that the Roman Church is pagan, we remember, means that it leaves open the back door to a very long avenue connecting us with pagan antiquity; and that it leaves open the side door to the town square peopled with all sorts of dubious and disreputable people, tramps and pedlars who make up the life of an open marketplace; and that it has too gaudily decorated the door fronting the (Roman) forum.

> Now a great deal has been said by Protestants, naturally enough, and not a little even by Catholics, about the danger of displaying before the world a pomp and triumph that might easily be called worldly. Undoubtedly some harm was done, and some misunderstandings did arise, when the Popes of the Renaissance filled Rome with trophies that might have marked the triumphs of the Caesars. . . . But, taking human nature as a whole, the method is justified; because . . . the Faith belongs to the heights and the open spaces, and the circle of the whole world. . . . That is, it does express the first essential fact that Catholicism is not a narrow thing; that it knows more than the world knows about the potentialities and creative possibilities of the world, and that it will outlast all the worldly and temporary expressions of the same culture.[11]

This Church is rather more like a mobile tabernacle than a fixed edifice, in the sense that Catholicism has pitched its tent in many lands and it has not been untouched or undecorated by any one of them: the inhabitants of these lands have brought with them into that ambulatory temple their cultures and philosophies and arts. Catholicism has also pitched its tent in each historical era. "Becoming a Catholic broadens the mind. . . . For instance, many a man who is not yet a Catholic calls himself a Mediaevelist. But a man who is only a Mediaevalist is very much broadened by becoming a Catholic. . . . As a Mediaevalist I am still proudest of the Gothic; but as a Catholic I am proud of the Baroque."[12]

By such an authoritative tradition we have a longer perspective, too. Making room for so many inhabitants requires an extensible, resilient, and flexible institution which can grow older without growing stiffer. It is by consequence of our mind's unreflective association that we think of old as stiff and creaky, and the idea of ancient conjures up crumbling columns and faded frescoes. "It is only by the analogy of animal bodies that we suppose that old things must be stiff. It is a mere metaphor from bones and arteries. In an intellectual sense old things are flexible. . . . A thing as old as the Catholic Church has an accumulated armoury and treasury to choose from; it can pick and choose among the centuries and brings one age to the rescue of another. It can call in the old world to redress the balance of the new." With this armoury of insights the Church can save "a man from the degrading slavery of being a child of his age."[13] The defense against think‐ ing narrow thoughts is to think a long time, but every age tends to think only about what it sees, and it only sees what is current, which does not last very long at all. The current opinion is always narrow because it is con‐ ditioned by what has gone before. The only way to avoid a "revolt against revolts" and a "reaction against reactions" is to "teach men to stretch their minds and inhabit a larger period of time. . . . [I]t will be more apparent than ever that these jerks of novelty do not create either a progress or an equi‐ librium."[14] Such jerks of novelty, yanking history first port, then starboard, Chesterton records in this quick summary.

> Perhaps there is really no such thing as a Revolution recorded in history. What happened was always a Counter‐Revolution. Men were always re‐ belling against the last rebels; or even repenting of the last rebellion. This could be seen in the most casual contemporary fashions, if the fashionable mind had not fallen into the habit of seeing the very latest revel as rebelling against all ages at once. The Modern Girl with the lipstick and the cock‐ tail is as much a rebel against the Woman's Rights Woman of the '80s, with her stiff stick‐up collars and strict teetotalism, as the latter was a rebel against the Early Victorian lady of the languid waltz tunes and the album full of quotations from Byron; or as the last, again, was a rebel against a Puritan mother to whom the waltz was a wild orgy and Byron the Bol‐ shevist of his age. Trace even the Puritan mother back through history and she represents a rebellion against the Cavalier laxity of the English Church, which was at first a rebel against the Catholic civilisation, which had been a rebel against the Pagan civilisation. Nobody but a lunatic could pretend that these things were a progress; for they obviously go first one way and then the other. But whichever is right, one thing is certainly wrong; and that is the modern habit of looking at them only from the modern end.[15]

Chesterton believes there was, beside "mere fashion or mere fa-
tigue . . . a reasonable plan of the proportions of things"[16] and that the pro-
portionate plan which has the most plausible look to it is the plan of the
Catholic faith because it has purposely and conscientiously sought an
eternal equilibrium which will persist through the vagarious imbalances
of each age. It is not as if only a Catholic can oppose an actual untruth, but
Chesterton does think the Catholic is in a better position to oppose poten-
tial untruths. There may be allies to the Catholic position on this end of the
playing field today, but will they be allies when the attack on human dignity
redirects to the other end of the field?

> Even the High Church Party, even the Anglo-Catholic Party only con-
> fronts a particular heresy called Protestantism upon particular points. It
> defends ritual rightly or even sacramentalism rightly, because these are the
> things the Puritans attacked. If it is not the heresy of an age, at least it is
> only the anti-heresy of an age. But since I have become a Catholic, I have
> become conscious of being in a much vaster arsenal, full of arms against
> countless other potential enemies. The Church, as the Church and not
> merely as ordinary opinion, has something to say to philosophies which
> the merely High Church has never had occasion to think about. If the next
> movement is the very reverse of Protestantism, the Church will have some-
> thing to say about it; or rather has already something to say about it. You
> might unite all High Churchmen on the High Church quarrel, but what
> authority is to unite them when the devil declares his next war on the
> world?[17]

To think really broad thoughts, one must have both history and authority.
History alone will not suffice because it is only a record of the aging process,
and where something has been does not tell you where it will go, or where
it should go. Catholicism is not true because it is old, it is old because its deposit of truth refuses to age. "It is not an old religion; it is a religion that
refuses to grow old."[18] It is not just an old tradition, but an eternal tradition,
and "the great difficulty is whether a man can stretch his mind, or (as the
moderns would say) can broaden his mind, enough to see the need for an
eternal Church."[19]

Every age has its own outlook. Persons who agree with each other
agree on the basis of that outlook, and persons who disagree with each

other disagree on the basis of that outlook. The only way to be truly broadened is to take a longer outlook, one where eternity and history have kissed
and left behind a mark known as the character of that age. That is what
gives certain portions of the Catholic household an alien feel to us. They
embody truths in a way that we find difficult to assimilate through our particular gatehouse. The Church holds in its treasure house truths beyond
our limited outlook.

> That every other single system is narrow and insufficient compared to this
> one; that is not a rhetorical boast; it is a real fact and a real dilemma.
> Where is the Holy Child amid the Stoics and the ancestor-worshippers?
> Where is Our Lady of the Moslems, a woman made for no man and set
> above all angels? Where is St. Michael of the monks of Buddha, rider and
> master of the trumpets, guarding for every soldier the honour of the sword?
> What could St. Thomas Aquinas do with the mythology of Brahminism,
> he who set forth all the science and rationality and even rationalism of
> Christianity? . . . Aquinas could understand the most logical parts of
> Aristotle; it is doubtful if Aristotle could have understood the most mysti-
> cal parts of Aquinas. Even where we can hardly call the Christian greater,
> we are forced to call him larger. But it is so to whatever philosophy or
> heresy or modern movement we may turn. How would Francis the Trou-
> badour have fared among the Calvinists, or for that matter among the
> Utilitarians of the Manchester School? Yet men like Bossuet and Pascal
> could be as stern and logical as any Calvinist or Utilitarian. How would
> St. Joan of Arc, a woman waving on men to war with the sword, have
> fared among the Quakers or the Doukhabors or the Tolstoyan sects of
> pacifists? Yet any number of Catholic saints have spent their lives in
> preaching peace and preventing wars. It is the same with all the modern
> attempts at syncretism. They are never able to make something larger than
> the Creed without leaving something out. I do not mean leaving out some-
> thing divine but something human; the flag or the inn or the boy's tale of
> battle or the hedge at the end of the field.[20]

Thus far Chesterton has claimed that Catholic authoritative tradition
is broader than our narrow minds, and longer than our present minds. He
finally claims that the height of Catholic authority enables human beings to

stand up taller than alternatives which tend to stoop the human being. The size of Catholicism prevents its authority from being dehumanizing.

Chesterton knows that this is not how submission to Catholic authority is commonly perceived. He knows that a modern meaning of "docile" has replaced "willing to be taught" with "obsequiousness." He knows that servanthood is mistaken for servility, and being refractory is thought heroic in principle. He knows that "the man who fears to enter the Church commonly fancies that what he feels is a sort of claustrophobia," even though we have already seen that Chesterton believes this person in fact suffers a sort of agoraphobia. For skeptics, "the typical Catholic act is not going into a great thing like a church, but into a small thing like a confessional box. And to their nightmare fancy a confessional box is a sort of mantrap; and presents in its very appearance some combination of a coffin and a cage."[21] This thought seems to amuse Chesterton, for he returns to it on other occasions. He describes outsiders looking at

> the convert entering with bowed head a sort of small temple which they are convinced is fitted up inside like a prison, if not a torture-chamber. But all they really know about it is that he has passed through a door. They do not know that he has not gone into the inner darkness, but out into the broad daylight. It is he who is, in the beautiful and beatific sense of the word, an outsider. He does not want to go into a larger room, because he does not know of any larger room to go into. He knows of a large number of much smaller rooms, each of which is labelled as being very large; but he is quite sure he would be cramped in any of them.[22]

Catholic heads are not hung in humiliation, they are bowed in humility. "When a Catholic comes from Confession, he does truly, by definition, step out again into that dawn of his own beginning and look with new eyes across the world to a Crystal Palace that is really of crystal. He believes that in that dim corner, and in that brief ritual, God has really remade him in His own image. He is now a new experiment of the Creator. He is as much a new experiment as he was when he was really only five years old. . . . He may be grey and gouty; but he is only five minutes old."[23] These youngsters attain passage through a doorway into a world bigger inside than it looks from the outside. In this small chamber, the free citizens of the cathedral do not hear Mr. Blatchford's voice whispering through the cell bars that the will is already determined; neither do they hear Luther's voice whispering that the will is already depraved nor Calvin's voice that one's salvation is already determined. This box wherein penitence can be performed and absolution bestowed is deliberately entered, and it accommodates the magnitudinous divine-human encounter. "It is almost a good thing that nobody outside should know what gigantic generosity, and even geniality, can be locked up in a box, as the legendary casket held the heart of the giant. It is a satisfaction, and almost a joke, that it is only in a dark corner and a cramped space that any man can discover that mountain of magnanimity."[24]

Catholic tyranny, if that is what those who do not understand want to call it, is less oppressive than Protestant liberty which keeps the authority's hands off the goods by prohibiting the good itself.

> The fact is that Protestant tyranny is totally different from Catholic tyranny; let alone Catholic liberty. It is ineradicably rooted in a total opposite motive and moral philosophy. . . . Protestantism is in its nature prone to what may be called Prohibitionism. . . . I mean that the Protestant tends to prohibit, rather than to curtail or control. . . . When puritans abolish ritualism, it means there shall be no more ritual. When prohibitionists abolished beer, they swore that a whole new generation would grow up and never know the taste of it. . . . Thus there is a fanatical quality, sweeping, final, almost suicidal, in Protestant reforms which there is *not* even in Catholic repressions. . . .
>
> In short, apart from Catholic liberty, Catholic tyranny is either temporary in the sense of a penance or a fast, or temporary in the sense of a state of siege or a proclamation of martial law. But Protestant liberty is far more oppressive than Catholic tyranny. For Protestant liberty is only the unlimited liberty of the rich to destroy an unlimited number of the liberties of the poor.[25]

The moralist will have difficulty understanding asceticism because the moralist, as legalist, fails to understand that while there is one path to salvation there may be many paths to holiness. Some heroic saints may make their way to sanctity through celibacy and retreat to the desert; but that is not required of everyone for their salvation. It is the authoritative creed which assures that even while the solitary life in the desert is admired, political life in the city and married life in the home are affirmed. Any human tradi‚ tion would make more of the heroes who suffered for something than of the human beings who simply benefited by it, Chesterton wrote, but that does not alter the fact that there are more human beings than heroes.

This multiplicity is exactly what an authoritative Church protects. The only other alternative is a religion of mood and feeling.

> If, in the really Dark Ages, there had been a religion of feeling, it would have been a religion of black and suicidal feeling. It was the rigid creed that resisted the rush of suicidal feeling. The critics of asceticism are prob‚ ably right in supposing that many a Western hermit did *feel* rather like an Eastern fakir. But he could not really *think* like an Eastern fakir; because he was an orthodox Catholic. And what kept his thought in touch with healthier and more humanistic thought was simply and solely the Dogma. He could not deny that a good God had created the normal and natural world; he could not say that the devil had made the world; because he was not a Manichee. A thousand enthusiasts for celibacy, in the day of the great rush to the desert or the cloister, might have called marriage a sin, if they had only considered their individual ideals, in the modern manner, and their own immediate feelings about marriage. Fortunately, they had to accept the Authority of the church, which had definitely said that mar‚ riage was not a sin.[26]

Creed and authority and doctrine set up the markers within which a teem‚ ing variety of paths to sanctification may be explored.

Catholic tyranny is also less oppressive than servitude to the state, Chesterton contends, which is why the Church has always remained at about the same distance from the state and its experiments. "It is the Church that excommunicates; but, in that very word, implies that a communion stands open for a restored communicant. It is the State that *exterminates*. . . . Every Catholic enjoys much more freedom in Catholicism than any Lib‚ eral does under Bolshevism or Fascism. . . . For the State has returned with all its ancient terrors out of antiquity; with the Gods of the City thundering from the sky . . . and we have begun to understand in what wide fields and playgrounds of liberty, the Faith that made us free has so long allowed us to wander and to play."[27] Chesterton finds Mr. H. G. Wells and Mr. Bernard Shaw to espouse the more captivating philosophy—and he does not mean enchanting or charming—when they propose repair of social chaos by sweeping social regulations of the kind being championed by the early sup-porters of communism. "It is the very men who say that nothing can be classified, who say that everything must be codified. Thus Mr. Bernard Shaw said that the only golden rule is that there is no golden rule. He prefers an iron rule; as in Russia."[28]

Whence arises this confusion? How did authority come to figure so prominently in the impression the Catholic Church has made upon the modern mind? Chesterton has a theory. It is for the same reason that the monastic life of renunciation and austerity (which does exist in Catholi-cism "as a way of asserting the will against the power of nature, of thanking the Redeemer by partially sharing his sufferings, [and] of making a man ready for anything as a missionary or martyr") also came to figure promi-nently in the picture held by a non-Catholic about Catholicism: "These happen to be rare in the modern industrial society of the West, outside his communion; and it is therefore assumed that they are the whole meaning of that communion. Because it is uncommon for an alderman to fast forty days, or a politician to take a Trappist vow of silence, or a man about town to live a life of strict celibacy, the average outsider is convinced, not only that Catholicism is nothing except asceticism, but that asceticism is nothing but pessimism."[29] The latter statement (that asceticism is pessimistic) is not true and the former statement (that Catholicism is nothing but asceticism) is not accurate. Defining Catholicism as asceticism is like naming the peacock tail blue; there is blue in it. But when the modern critic sees this unusual as-cetic ideal in an authoritative Church, he is apt to say

> "This is the result of Authority; it would be better to have Religion without Authority." But in truth, a wider experience outside Brixton or Brighton would reveal the mistake. It is rare to find a fasting alderman or a Trappist politician, but it is still more rare to see nuns suspended in the air on hooks or spikes; it is unusual for a Catholic Evidence Guild orator in Hyde Park to begin his speech by gashing himself all over with knives; a stranger call-ing at an ordinary presbytery will seldom find the parish priest lying on the

floor with a fire lighted on his chest and scorching him while he utters spiri,
tual ejaculations. . . . In short, a real knowledge of mankind will tell
anybody that Religion is a very terrible thing; that it is truly a raging fire,
and that Authority is often quite as much needed to restrain it as to impose
it. Asceticism, or the war with the appetites, is itself an appetite. It can
never be eliminated from among the strange ambitions of Man. But it can
be kept in some reasonable control; and it is indulged in much saner pro,
portion under Catholic Authority than in Pagan or Puritan anarchy. [30]

Perhaps the reason our day fails to appreciate the service which authority
renders in providing reasonable control and sane proportion is due to the
fact that we are in very little danger of being overcome by religion as by a
raging fire. But the day may come again when authority will have to protect
us from ourselves.

Chesterton's theory is that an outsider necessarily finds the most alien
practices the most striking, and because they are the most striking they
seem the most important, when in point of fact they may be either unimpor,
tant or moderate when balanced within the whole. The theory accounts
for many common mistakes. A Catholic doctrine can only be accurately
understood when comprehended within the community of doctrines, like
Catholic discipline can be comprehended only when it is understood
within the whole practice of the religion. "It may still be noted that the
unconverted world, Puritan or Pagan, but perhaps especially when it is
Puritan, has a very strange notion of the collective unity of Catholic things
or thoughts. Its exponents, even when not in any rabid sense enemies, give
the most curious list of things which they think make up the Catholic
life; an odd assortment of objects, such as candles, rosaries, incense (they are
always intensely impressed with the enormous importance and necessity
of incense), vestments, pointed windows, and then all sorts of essentials
or unessentials thrown in in any sort of order; fasts, relics, penances or the
Pope."[31] It is like hearing the words, but not knowing the grammar which
holds the words together, and confusing adjectives for nouns, prepositions
for verbs. How important any given practice is to the whole can only be
grasped by knowing the whole. Unfortunately, people who "fly into a rage
with the Catholic Church" always use an extraordinary diction in which

"all sorts of incommensurate things are jumbled up together, so that the very order of the words is a joke." Chesterton holds that he "never read an attack on Catholicism without finding this ignorant gabble of terms all topsy-turvy. There is always some such medley of misused words, in which mitres, misereres, nones, albs, croziers, virgins and viaticums tumble over each other without the wildest hope that anybody could possibly know what any of them mean." Thus on one occasion he read a description of the Catholic religion as if the author thought it to consist primarily of rosaries or beads, or crucifixes, or paying for candles or masses. "Apparently the first object of a Catholic is to get a candle. If once he can get hold of a candle, and walk about everywhere clasping his candle, he is all right. But if he cannot get a candle, he has the alternative of purchasing a mass; an instrument that is a sort of substitute for a candle."[32]

On another occasion, Chesterton read a critic's report that in Rome's relation with the Russian Uniats (Eastern Christian churches that are in union with the Roman Catholic Church) Rome tolerates "strange heresies and even bearded and wedded clergy." Chesterton does not go on to tell what strange heresies the author was referring to; perhaps the author did not himself go on to say; but it does not matter because Chesterton's attention is arrested by the emphasis in those eight words. "As somebody tumbling down the stairs bumps upon every step, the writer comes a crash upon every word." Each word is strange enough when juxtaposed with the other, "but by far the funniest and most fantastic thing in all that fantastic sentence is the word 'even'" because it is by that word that one grasps, finally, what this critic must think Catholicism is if he finds it surprising that Rome would "*even*" allow aberrant bearded clergy.

There is in the world, they would tell us, a powerful and persecuting superstition, intoxicated with the impious idea of having a monopoly of divine truth, and therefore cruelly crushing and exterminating everything else as error. It burns thinkers for thinking, discoverers for discovering, philosophers and theologians who differ by a hair's breadth from its dog-mas; it will tolerate no tiny change or shadow of variety even among its friends and followers; it sweeps the whole world with one encyclical cy-clone of uniformity; it would destroy nations and empires for a word, so wedded is it to its fixed idea that its own word is the Word of God. When it is thus sweeping the world, it comes to a remote and rather barbarous region somewhere on the borders of Russia; where it stops suddenly; smiles broadly; and tells the people there that they can have the strang/ est heresies they like. . . . We might well suppose, therefore, that the Church says benevolently to these fortunate Slavs, "By all means worship Baphomet and Beelzebub; say the Lord's Prayer backwards; continue to drink the blood of infants—nay, even," and here her voice falters, till she rallies with an effort of generous resolution, "—yes, even, if you really must, grow a beard."[33]

Chesterton solicits the sympathy of the reader to understand what despair falls upon "the hapless Catholic journalist at such moments." How can he begin to explain the importance of authority, the hierarchy of truths, the fact "that a married clergy is a matter of discipline and not doctrine, that it can therefore be allowed locally without heresy—when all the time the man thinks a beard is as important as a wife and more important than a false religion?"[34]

The title of the essay in which this appears is "What Do They Think?" and one of Chesterton's answers to this self/directed question appears in the essay, "What We Think About." There are critics who do not think, who refuse to think, and so it is easier for them to name all Catholicism by the one feature which they themselves cannot understand, in this case authority. Thus they conclude that Catholics are forbidden to think. Chesterton's rec/ ommended cure: "Now what we have really got to hammer into the heads of all these people, somehow, is that a thinking man can think himself deeper and deeper into Catholicism, but not deeper and deeper into difficulties about Catholicism. We have got to make them see that conversion is the beginning of an active, fruitful, progressive and even adventurous life of the intellect. For *that* is the thing that they cannot at present bring themselves to believe."[35] How it happened that authority seems antithetical to thought is a riddle, when every child grows up knowing that what authorizes thought is a parent's authoritative assurance that reality is a reasonable and trust/ worthy mystery, yet still the impression persists that Catholics have only half a brain because the clergy has shut down the other half. Chesterton himself had held this view of Catholicism until he began comparing what the theosophist said with what the theologian said. Then "[d]readful seeds of doubt began to be sown in my mind. I was almost tempted to question the accuracy of the anti-clerical legend; . . . it seemed to me that the despised curates were rather more intelligent than anybody else; that they, alone in that world of intellectualism, were trying to use their intellects."[36]

How can there be less thought upon becoming a believer when the be-liever arrives at the conviction that life is worth thinking about because it is not absurd, and when revelation assures the believer of a reasonable hope of understanding the world because the same Creator made both mind and matter? How can there be less thought when the believer has so much more to think about and so many more people to think with? "A Catholic has fifty times more feeling of being free than a man caught in the net of the nervous compromises of Anglicanism. . . . He has the range of two thousand years full of twelve-hundred thousand controversies, thrashed out by thinker against thinker, school against school, guild against guild, nation against nation, with no limit except the fundamental logical fact that the things were worth arguing, because they could be ultimately solved and settled."[37] Could this impression be caused by the perpetually placid and eternally tranquil state of the Catholic Church, we ask, tongue-in-cheek? Then per-haps Chesterton could let the non-Catholic in upon a small secret. "[I]f any one doubts that there is such a thing as Catholic liberty, I think it can do no harm to let him realise that there is such a thing as Catholic controversy; I mean controversy between Catholics."[38] Mr. Belloc may voice his opinion on matters as a Catholic, and because he is a Catholic, but this does not mean that other Catholics will agree. "On the contrary, each would say something quite different. It is not that they need agree with him; but that he need not agree with them. . . . Catholics know the two or three transcenden-tal truths on which they do agree; and take rather a pleasure in disagreeing on everything else."[39] Nevertheless, these differences do not rend the house or throw the family into denominational diaspora because of the consanguine understanding that nobody is trying to be an original individual, everybody is trying to express individually what the common fundaments mean. The family is confident that as different theologians with differing theologies draw nearer the beatific unity, they will draw nearer to each other. "[T]he theology of a saint is simply the theism of a saint; or rather the theism of all saints. It is less individual, but it is much more intense. It is concerned with the common origin; but it is hardly an occasion for originality. . . . Anyhow, it is but natural that Augustine and Aquinas, Bonaventure and Duns Scotus, all the doctors and the saints, should draw nearer to each other as they approach the divine unity in things."[40] If, as has been insisted all along, grace perfects nature and does not nullify it, then the Church, as sacrament, does not nullify thought but perfects it. Reason may stand in need of healing every bit as much as the bodies of those who cried out from the roadside as Jesus passed by, but upon being healed reason will not sit still.

> In some muddled way people have confused the natural remarks of con-
> verts, about having found moral peace, with some idea of their having
> found mental rest, in the sense of mental inaction. They might as well
> say that a man who has completely recovered his health, after an attack of
> palsy . . . signalises his healthy state by sitting absolutely still like a stone.
> Recovering his health means recovering his power of moving in the right
> way as distinct from the wrong way; but he will probably move a great
> deal more than before. To become a Catholic is not to leave off thinking,
> but to learn how to think. It is so in exactly the same sense in which to re-
> cover from palsy is not to leave off moving but to learn how to move.[41]

Chesterton knows some will ask: "But even supposing that those doctrines do include those truths, why cannot you take the truths and leave the
doctrines? . . . If you see clearly the kernel of common sense in the nut of
Christian orthodoxy, why cannot you simply take the kernel and leave the
nut?"[42] Furthermore, we might wonder why one cannot take catholic teachings and leave the Roman Catholic Church? After all, Rome is a very tough
nut to crack. The third objective in this chapter, then, is to explain why
Chesterton thinks one must take the Church with the doctrines.

Part of Chesterton's apology for why an authoritative institution is
required in order to house abstract truths has already been presented: a religion of feeling does not hold the same way a religion of creed and doctrine
does; the truths which we take are the ones we recognize but may not be the
ones we need; and the truths which we find attractive may require other, less
attractive truths in order to work.[43] But the determinative reason why one

can neither take truth without doctrine, nor doctrine without the Church, lies in Chesterton's image of vitality. One can tell where a thing has been after it is dead, but one cannot know where a thing is going to go unless it is alive. By investigating the history of doctrine one can discover where Catholicism has been, but from that data one cannot know where the Catholic Church will go. The Church will know the answer as soon as the question is put, but for that a Catholic imagination is required, and an imagination is not contained in books and creeds; to learn it requires a living teacher. Vital doctrines breed and develop and are capable of protecting from specious outlooks only insofar as they dwell in a living Church which is a startling Church. "Any number of philosophies will repeat the platitudes of Christianity. But it is the ancient Church that can again startle the world with the paradoxes of Christianity."[44]

Chesterton describes the Church as an armory and treasure house, which is home to the Catholic imagination and which has never thrown any (good) thing away. Like some of our relatives' homes, this house of faith has a packed attic. "For the Catholic commentary on life has gone on so much longer, it has covered so many different social conditions, has dealt so carefully with countless fine shades of metaphysics or casuistry, that it really has a relation to almost any class of speculation that may arise."[45] Chesterton does not acclaim the Church's treasure vaults because they are full of history; he is not interested in the past like a museum director (or worse yet, a mausoleum director) who lines the halls with dioramas of Catholicism's bygone glory days. The treasure vaults are interesting the way the theory of hydraulics is interesting to someone whose city is burning down: from that historic treasury efficient doctrines can be produced—he means doctrines that can produce something, namely, human happiness. And since no one knows in advance under what conditions our quest for our happiness will have to be taken, the full resources of a living, imaginative Church are needed. It is, he confesses, the reason why he finally became Catholic. "The only way really to meet all the human needs of the future is to pass into the possession of all the Catholic thoughts of the past; and the only way to do that is really to become a Catholic. . . . I was converted by the positive attractions of the things I had not yet got, and not by negative disparagements of such things as I had managed to get already."[46] His move to truth was not from false teaching, but from fractional teachings.

We have heard him say in *The Autobiography* that he believes other philosophies, in fact, each philosophy, contains a truth, so why isn't it adequate to stack them together? For the reason a living body is not a stack of cells but an organism, and the whole becomes more than the sum of its parts. The collective mind looks all directions at once, in addition to looking in a particular direction at the moment. "Now there is no other corporate mind in the world that is thus on the watch to prevent minds from going wrong. . . . And all other sects and schools are inadequate for the purpose. This is not because each of them may not contain a truth, but precisely because each of them does contain a truth; and is content to contain a truth. None of the others really pretends to contain the truth. None of the others, that is, really pretends to be looking out in all directions at once. The Church is not merely armed against the heresies of the past or even of the present, but equally against those of the future."[47] Chesterton ungrudgingly admits that catholic truths have taken root outside the Roman Church. He does not think that only Catholicism contains universal truths; but he does think Catholicism contains only universal truths—i.e., truths which are intended for the whole of humanity and the whole of a human life. His reason for becoming Catholic is not that he thinks truths can only be found here, but because they can all be found here. "When the convert has once seen the world like that . . . [he] is not worried by being told that there is something in Spiritualism or something in Christian Science. He knows there is something in everything. But he is moved by the more impressive fact that he finds everything in something. . . . There is nothing supercilious about his attitude; because he is well aware that he has only scratched the surface of the spiritual estate that is now open to him."[48] There are truths yet to be grown on the Catholic estate, and they will be grown when they are needed, because the Catholic possesses the field as well as the fruits. And the field is more important for the future than the fruits, because while this movement or that trend may share the field's produce, it cannot know what the field is capable of producing next season when the wind will blow from another direction. "The men of the Oxford Movement . . . did discover the need of Catholic things, but they did discover the need of one thing at a time. They took their pick in the fields of Christendom, but they did not possess the fields; and, above all, they did not possess the fallow fields. They could not have all the riches, because they could not have all the reserves of the religion."[49]

In order to grow a doctrine from this estate a state of obedience is required, and this for two reasons. First, obedience in the sense of patience is required because if one continually plucks up the developing doctrine to transplant it, it will be killed. Chesterton was convinced of this even before his conversion.

> A man who is always going back and picking to pieces his own first principles may be having an amusing time but he is not developing as Newman understood development. Newman meant that if you wanted a tree to grow you must plant it finally under some definite spot. It may be (I do not know and I do not care) that Catholic Christianity is just now passing through one of its numberless periods of undue repression and silence. But I do know this, that when the great flowers break forth again, the new epics and the new arts, they will break out on the ancient and living tree. They cannot break out upon the little shrubs that you are always pulling up by the roots to see if they are growing.[50]

Second, obedience in the sense of faithfulness is required because the truth grown on the Catholic estate is an inherited truth. What makes the Catholic Church unique is not that it has a message to proclaim. "Huxley has a message; Haeckel has a message; Bernard Shaw has a message. It is only necessary to ask the logical question, 'From whom?' to raise a thousand things that the writers have never thought of. And it is typical of the confusion, that the same person who says that Haeckel has a message probably goes on to say that he is an entirely original thinker. It may be doubted, in any case, whether the professor desires to be regarded as a messenger boy. But, anyhow, we, none of us, desire a messenger boy who originates his own message."[51] Grant, then, that this attempt at accuracy in conveying the message requires a certain faithfulness, and this faithfulness requires a certain tenacity, a tenacity which the world interprets as stubbornness. "What puzzles the world, and its wise philosophers and fanciful pagan poets, about the priests and people of the Catholic Church is that they still behave as if they were messengers. A messenger does not dream about what his message might be, or argue about what it probably would be; he delivers it as it is. It is not a theory or a fancy but a fact. . . . All that is condemned in Catholic tradition, authority, and dogmatism and the refusal to retract and modify, are but the natural human attributes of a man with a message relat⁄ ing to a fact."[52] If understood correctly, the obstinacy signs a humbleness the Church feels about the amount of control it has over the message. Therefore the Church is serious about receiving, preserving, and passing on the whole message, in its entirety.

At this point we can see Chesterton's sympathy with the democratic life expressed not only in space, but also in time. He makes apology not only for the vulgar Christmas celebration in the street, but for the reception of an⁄ tique customs handed down by our ancestors. Actually, handing on any tradition is a stirring responsibility, part of "the awful and ancestral respon⁄ sibility to which our fathers committed us when they took the wild step of becoming men. I mean the responsibility of affirming the truth of our human tradition and handing it on with a voice of authority, an unshaken voice. That is the one eternal education; to be sure enough that something is true that you dare to tell it to a child."[53] Handing on the faith tradition is a religious species of this very human process. Unless one believes that the Church is reconstituted in every generation by original pentecosts, it is a very necessary process. The Church is the body of Christ, a temple made of human stones, founded at a historical moment and historically maintained by people who have found the tradition true enough to tell it to their children and other sinners. The haughty heretic obtrudes his services, unbidden, and stands at the gateway to the past, sifting out what he considers unbelievable or unacceptable (too religious in the pagan sense or too irreligious in the pu⁄ ritan sense) and excludes all other doctrines or practices he judges unfit for religious aristocracy, and this strikes Chesterton as distinctly undemocratic.

> I have never been able to understand where people got the idea that de⁄ mocracy was in some way opposed to tradition. It is obvious that tradition is only democracy extended through time. It is trusting to a consensus of common human voices rather than to some isolated or arbitrary record.

The man who quotes some German historian against the tradition of the Catholic Church, for instance, is strictly appealing to aristocracy. He is appealing to the superiority of one expert against the awful authority of a mob. . . . Tradition may be defined as an extension of the franchise. Tradition means giving votes to the most obscure of all classes, our ancestors. It is the democracy of the dead. Tradition refuses to submit to the small and arrogant oligarchy of those who merely happen to be walking about. All democrats object to men being disqualified by the accident of birth; tradition objects to their being disqualified by the accident of death. Democracy tells us not to neglect a good man's opinion, even if he is our groom; tradition asks us not to neglect a good man's opinion, even if he is our father. . . . We will have the dead at our councils. The ancient Greeks voted by stones; these shall vote by tombstones. It is all quite regular and official, for most tombstones, like most ballot papers, are marked with a cross.[54]

Tradition means "to hand on," and the word might better reveal itself as a verb: the faith has been "traditioned." And the deposit of faith accrues interest; the Church is made roomier by tradition; the more traditional the Church, the greater its amplitude. This is not to say the message changes, if by that one means it changes into a different message; but the rolling stone established upon Peter does gather moss: the unchanged and unchanging message does agglomerate the truths through which it rolls. As the Church moves through history, the faith deposited in it accumulates and preserves the wisdom of the ages. It becomes the rock of ages, for the Church is "not a movement but a meeting-place; the trysting-place of all the truths in the world."[55] Traditioning does not idolize the past, or fear the future, or cling to the present. The task incumbent on the Church is neither to quick-freeze a bygone era nor bemoan the fate of being cast into a brave new world. The tradition is alive, after all.

Tradition is lived, and doctrines are living things, and therefore the Church is flexible and adaptable to hitherto unknown circumstances and forever young. "The Church had any number of opportunities of dying, and even of being respectfully interred. But the younger generation always began once again to knock at the door; and never louder than when it was knocking at the lid of the coffin, in which it had been prematurely

buried."[56] Chesterton identifies five moments in the history of Western civilization when it appeared as though Catholicism was dead. "[W]ith the
Arian and the Albigensian, with the Human sceptic, after Voltaire and
after Darwin, the Faith has to all appearance gone to the dogs. But in each
of the five cases it was the dog that died." Christianity rose after each death
because "it had a God who knew the way out of the grave." "A dead thing
can go with the stream, but only a living thing can go against it."[57] One
cannot take the doctrine without the Church because doctrines or pieties or
spiritual movements tend to fossilize as soon as they die, and they die as soon
as they are cut off from the living body. One cannot have the teaching without the teacher except as a dead thing.

> The Church in its practical relation to my soul is a living teacher, not a
> dead one. It not only taught me yesterday, but will almost certainly teach
> me tomorrow. Once I saw suddenly the meaning of the shape of the cross;
> some day I may see suddenly the meaning of the shape of the mitre. . . .
> Plato has told you a truth; but Plato is dead. Shakespeare has startled
> you with an image; but Shakespeare will not startle you with any more.
> But imagine what it would be to live with such men still living, to know
> that Plato might break out with an original lecture tomorrow, or that at
> any moment Shakespeare might shatter everything with a single song.
> The person who lives in contact with what he believes to be a living
> Church is a person always expecting to meet Plato and Shakespeare to-
> morrow at breakfast. He is always expecting to see some truth he has not
> seen before. . . .
>
> When your father told you, walking about in the garden, that bees
> stung or that roses smelled sweet, you did not talk of taking the best out of
> his philosophy. When the bees stung you, you did not call it an entertain-
> ing coincidence. When the rose smelt sweet you did not say "My father is
> a rude, barbaric symbol, enshrining the deep delicate truths that flowers
> smell." No; you believed your father, because you found him to be a living
> fountain of facts, a thing that knew more than you; a thing that would tell
> you truth tomorrow as well as today. . . .
>
> I give one instance out of a hundred; I have not myself any instinctive
> kinship with that enthusiasm for physical virginity, which has certainly
> been a note of historic Christianity. . . . It takes all kinds to make a church;

she does not ask me to be celibate. But the fact that I have no appreciation of the celibates, I accept like the fact that I have no ear for music. . . . Celibacy is one flower in my father's garden, of which I have not yet been told the sweet or terrible name. But I may be told it any day.

This, then, is, in conclusion, my reason for accepting the religion and not merely the scattered and secular truths out of the religion. I do it because the thing has not merely told this truth or that truth, but has revealed itself as a truth-telling thing. [58]

The teachings and the teacher are connected; one cannot take one and leave the other. We shall see in our final chapter what Chesterton thinks were the results when sixteenth-century reformers took catholic teachings and left the Catholic Church.

EIGHT

An Out-of-Body Experience

As an apologist, Chesterton believes he has something to say not only to movements outside the Church that are not Christian, but also to inside movements that are. We have seen that he believes there is truth in pagan philosophical systems but became a Catholic because he believes these truths are also contained, and better coordinated, in Catholicism. In similar fashion, he believes there are truths in Protestantism but is convinced that they grow bigger in the Catholic garden because, due to its accumulative size, the Catholic Church can grow truths which would otherwise be stunted by isolation.

> Catholicism is not ritualism; it may in the future be fighting some sort of superstitious and idolatrous exaggeration of ritual. Catholicism is not asceticism; it has again and again in the past repressed fanatical and cruel exaggerations of asceticism. Catholicism is not mere mysticism; it is even now defending human reason against the mere mysticism of the Pragmatists. Thus, when the world went Puritan in the seventeenth century, the Church was charged with pushing charity to the point of sophistry. . . . Now that the world is not going Puritan but Pagan, it is the Church that is everywhere protesting against a Pagan laxity in dress or manners. It is doing what the Puritans wanted done when it is really wanted. In all probability, all that is best in Protestantism will only survive in Catholicism; and in that sense all Catholics will still be Puritans when all Puritans are Pagans.[1]

He makes his point, as usual, with a metaphor. There was in London a building known as the Crystal Palace for its glass and iron construction, and it was built to house great expositions which required room to display row after row of exhibits. Chesterton suggests that we have mistakenly believed that Catholicism could be located by browsing the devout displays of churches and sects and religions of the world, much as he had browsed displays in the Crystal Palace as a youth. When told at one point in the tour that some particular exhibit was the Roman Catholic Church, reactions varied. "Some of us were sorry for it and even fancied it had been rather badly used; most of us regarded it as dirty and disreputable; a few of us even pointed out that many details in the ruin were artistically beautiful or architecturally important," but most of us "preferred to deal at more business-like booths where the showman beat the big drum outside." Chesterton seems to claim that conversion happens, his own included, when the Catholic Church is no longer seen as one of the options. "It does not merely belong to a class of Christian churches. It does not merely belong to a class of human religions." It is no longer experienced as one of the booths, but as the Crystal Palace itself.

> Now conversion consists very largely, on its intellectual side, in the discovery that all that picture of equal creeds inside an indifferent cosmos is quite false. It is not a question of comparing the merits and defects of the Quaker meeting-house set beside the Catholic cathedral. It is the Quaker meeting-house that is inside the Catholic cathedral; it is the Catholic cathedral that covers everything like the vault of the Crystal Palace. . . . In other words, Quakerism is but a temporary form of Quietism which has arisen technically outside the Church as the Quietism of Fenelon appeared technically inside the Church. But both were in themselves temporary and would have, like Fenelon, sooner or later to return to the Church in order to live. The principle of life in all these variations of Protestantism, in so far as it is not a principle of death, consists of what remained in them of Catholic Christendom; and to Catholic Christendom they have always returned to be recharged with vitality.[2]

This is a delicate chapter to write. It cannot be avoided because Chesterton's scrimmage with Protestantism makes up a considerable share of his apologetical corpus and, likewise, his own personality. Yet in a day when ecumenical relationships between Catholics and Protestants have happily progressed, before rehearsing Chesterton's polemic a word of warning is required. This is not because of some shallow truce, by which each party politely agrees to ignore some dogmatic stumbling block, as one would politely refrain from pointing out a food particle stuck in the teeth of one's dinner partner. There are still subjects which Catholics and Protestants have reason to lean across the table and discuss frankly, not least among them whether one day they might assemble around a table of a different kind. Rather, a word of warning is required lest Chesterton's criticisms be transplanted uncritically. One cannot apply the quarrel he had with the liberal Protestantism of his day to our day indiscriminately (any more than his opposition to women's suffrage). Do some who bear the name Protestant still hold positions like those contested by Chesterton? No doubt, yes; no doubt, no. Insofar as the positions he challenged are still adhered to, it could be useful for his opinion to be confronted, but I have taken pains to point out that Chesterton does not attack persons (individual or corporate), he likes to joust with positions, and it would be the responsibility of individuals or groups denominated Protestant to say whether they feel targeted by Chesterton; I cannot decide this. Do some who bear the name Catholic offend by their bulwarking and narrow-mindedness, censoring conversation and failing to exhibit the sort of good will that Chesterton's magnanimous nature showed? No doubt, yes; no doubt, no. I am not commenting upon this, either. The main purpose here will be to understand Chesterton's defense of the Church of Rome in the face of the anti-Catholic polemics which he encountered in his day.

We shall therefore first see what Chesterton thinks remains of the Protestant reform, i.e., what is the condition of those churches which took catholic teachings and left the Catholic Church. Second, we will outline his belief that the Catholic doctrine of the human is more humane than Luther's or Calvin's anthropology. And third, we will aggregate replies he makes to a set of complaints typical of a spiritualistic ecclesiology. Through all of this, we find one more expression of Chesterton's assessment that Catholicism is expansive and capacious.

To begin, it is instructive to recall one of Chesterton's more insightful descriptions of heresy. He said that St. Francis had something in him of what makes the founder of a religion, and that some of the saint's followers were almost ready to treat him so. They were willing to let the Franciscan spirit escape from Christendom, and the pope had to settle whether Chris-

tendom should absorb Francis or Francis Christendom. If the latter had oc-
curred, the result would have been a narrowing effect, because the Church
could include all that was good in the Franciscans but the Franciscans could
not include all that was good in the Church. To understand Chesterton's
attitude toward Protestants, one could replace St. Francis's name with
Luther's or Calvin's. These men, too, had something in them which makes
the founder of a religion, and their followers were prepared to treat them so;
their spirit did escape from Catholicism; and when it did, the most characteristic feature of heresy happened: the mood was set over against the mind.
The mood was indeed originally the good and glorious mood of the doctor
from Wittenberg or the lawyer at Geneva, but it was not the whole mind of
God, or even of the Church. Something built on an individual mood, to
meet an individual need—no matter how keenly felt, and even if true in
part—is never as large as the Crystal Palace which houses it.

In the course of Church history since the Reformation, genuine
Christian potentialities in theology, piety, liturgy, community life, and the
arts have been realized outside Catholicism, undeniably. Something of what
the Church is called to become has attained realization, at least temporarily,
outside of the Catholic body. Protestantism is a Catholic out-of-body experience. But however these truths may be realized outside the subsisting
Catholic body, temporarily, Chesterton claims that sooner or later they
must return or they will die. In fact, he thinks that most of the out-of-body
reform movements of the sixteenth century have either already returned, or
have already died and fossilized. They are no longer recognizable even to
their adherents.

Is Chesterton being defensive about his Church? In the sense of making a defense, yes; in the sense of being oversensitive, he claims not, though
some critics accuse him of being a provocateur when he says, for example,
that the Reformation was the shipwreck of Christendom. Chesterton defends his defense by explaining that when he makes such an allegation it is
only meant in the solid and objective sense that "there certainly was a united
vessel or vehicle and it certainly did break up into different parts." We can
imagine that some people thought it was a rotten ship that was bound to
break up; others believed it was sturdy and seaworthy until the crew became
mutinous; some were gleeful and others rueful about its dilapidation. But

the simple statement that a unified Church disintegrated is not meant to be provocative, and if it is taken that way, then the fault lies not with the apologist but with a certain kind of bigot who "cannot distinguish between provocative statements and plain inevitable statements." If one wants provocative, then here's provocative.

> If I say that the Reformation was a relapse into barbarism, a return to all that was worst in the Dark Ages without anything of what was best in them, an idolatry of dead Hebrew documents full of visions and symbols without any Daniel to interpret the dreams, a stampede of brutal lux-ury and pride with a vulgar howl of hot-gospelling for an excuse, a riot of thieves and looters with a few foaming and gibbering lunatics carried in front of it like live mascots for luck; the return of the Manichee, the dirty ape of the ascetic, conspiring with the devil to destroy the world—if I were to say all this I should think that these remarks about Protes-tantism certainly had a slightly provocative flavour. But if I were to say, with Mr. Belloc, that Protestantism was the shipwreck of Christendom, I should regard it as an ordinary historical statement, like saying that the American War of Independence was a split in the British Empire.[3]

There may be a cutting edge to Chesterton's apology, due to his exact-ness, but he claims that he is simply interested in prying open the Protestant heresies by employing the same Catholic tools he has used to dilate other narrow points of view. To make his point, he utilizes an image that we have already seen is dear to him, the image he used to describe how he feels about coming upon a precious creation. He is gratified to see that since the shipwreck Protestants have often returned to the Roman ruins to salvage precious reserves from the tradition. Indeed, that's the crux of his argu-ment here. "All the movements of all the sects of late have been in the direc-tion of trying to put together again those separate pieces that were pulled apart in the sixteenth century. The main feature of our time has been the fact that one person after another has recovered one piece after another, and added it to the new scheme by borrowing it from the old. There is one suffi-cient proof that there has indeed been a shipwreck. And that is that Robin-son Crusoe has, ever since, been continually going back to get things from the wreck."[4]

One must be concerned not only with the flowering of truth but additionally with where the plant is potted. A cultivated truth, i.e., one grown in intercourse with a practiced cult, becomes more refined than a solitary truth held in the wilderness of rugged individualism. It is not that Catholics have different truths than Protestants, it is that the same truth grows differently in the Catholic garden than in the Protestant wilderness. "At the moment when Religion lost touch with Rome, it changed instantly and internally, from top to bottom, in its very substance and the stuff of which it was made. It changed in substance; it did not necessarily change in form or features or externals. It might do the same things; but it could not be the same way. It might go on saying the same things; but it was not the same thing that was saying them. At the very beginning, indeed, the situation was almost exactly like that. Henry VIII was a Catholic in everything except that he was not a Catholic."[5] Although the particular truth does not change its features when it is no longer bonded with the larger coalition of truths, the end result is substantially different, like a particular atom might not become a different entity by losing its bond with other atoms, but the end molecule is substantially different. Gaseous hydrogen is no longer liquid without the company of another of its kind plus oxygen. So, for example, Chesterton readily acknowledges that the Anglican Prayer Book has "a power like that of great poetry upon the spirit and the heart" but wonders aloud exactly why this is so. The reason, he concludes, is because "it has style; it has tradition; it has religion; it was written by apostate Catholics. It is strong, not in so far as it is the first Protestant book, but in so far as it was the last Catholic book. The most moving passages in the old Anglican Prayer-Book are exactly those that are least like the atmosphere of the Anglicans. They are moving, or indeed thrilling, precisely because they say the things which Protestants have long left off saying; and which only Catholics still say."[6] *Mutatis mutandis*, one could say the theology of Luther and Calvin had style, it had tradition, it had religion. Of course; they were apostate Catholics.

As members of the unreformed Church, Catholics can be original; but as members of a Church that is eternally reforming, reformers are shaped by the form which they discard. The traditional Church can have original thoughts; the reforming Church is scripted by the text it emends. "They are not people who have really created something entirely new. . . . Protestants are Catholics gone wrong; that is what is really meant by saying they are Christians."

> Thus a Calvinist is a Catholic obsessed with the Catholic idea of the sov-ereignty of God. But when he makes it mean that God wishes particular people to be damned, we may say with all restraint that he has become a rather morbid Catholic. In point of fact he is a diseased Catholic; and the disease left to itself would be death or madness. But, as a matter of fact, the disease did not last long, and is itself now practically dead. But every step he takes back towards humanity is a step back towards Catholicism. . . . [E]very step he takes back towards common sense is a step back towards Catholicism. In so far as he was right he was a Catholic; and in so far as he was wrong he has not himself been able to remain a Protestant.[7]

The best eventuality for these out-of-body experiences would be if the lonely extremes could find their way back to the convivial middle. The spell is now practically broken (we mean broken in practice), even within Protes-tantism, because every progressive step since the Reformation has been a step back. "Three hundred years felt with their full weight, really measured out in time and experience, endured as a man actually endures the passage of his days, would prove the whole Protestant story to have been the most prepos-terous and disproportionate detour, or straggling a chapter of accidents, that ever set out in the wrong direction and came back to the same place."[8]

Evidence for this includes the fact that the very issues which pro-voked the Reformers to depart from Rome are issues which heirs of the emi-grants no longer recognize, will no longer honor. Chesterton believes that what was condemned in the Catholic Church was eventually reintro-duced; however, without organic connection to the whole these restored doctrines and practices have lost their ampleness and returned in a de-graded form.

> The Puritans rejected art and symbolism, and the decadents brought them back again, with all the old appeal to sense and an additional appeal to sensuality. The rationalists rejected supernatural healing, and it was brought back by Yankee charlatans who not only proclaimed supernatu-ral healing, but forbade natural healing. Protestant moralists abolished the

confessional and the psychoanalysts have reestablished the confessional, with every one of its alleged dangers and not one of its admitted safe, guards. Having complained that the family was insulted by monasticism, they have lived to see the family broken in pieces by bureaucracy; having objected to fasts being appointed for anybody during any exceptional in, terval, they have survived to see teetotalers and vegetarians trying to impose a fast on everybody for ever.[9]

To take a more serious theological issue, Chesterton observes that the pessimism which Luther held about people's religious capacities, the pes, simism upon which the whole protest was built, is so foreign to today's Protestants that we may say Luther's theology is "a thing that no modern Protestant would be seen dead in a field with. . . . That Protestantism was pessimism; it was nothing but bare insistence on the hopelessness of all human virtue, as an attempt to escape hell. That Lutheranism is now quite unreal."[10] Although there may be repristinators who live their lives locked in the debates of the sixteenth century, most of today's Protestants have so "lost faith in [Protestantism], that they have mostly forgotten what it was." The idea of faith alone, stark and bare, was unreasonable as an ancient battle cry, and the contemporary Protestant is hard pressed to find any good reason to defend it as a shibboleth any longer.

> If almost any modern man be asked whether we save our souls solely through our theology, or whether doing good (to the poor, for instance) will help us on the road to God, he would answer without hesitation that good works are probably more pleasing to God than theology. It would probably come as quite a surprise to him to learn that, for three hundred years, the faith in faith alone was the badge of a Protestant, the faith in good works the rather shameful badge of a disreputable Papist. . . . If [the ordinary Englishman] believes in a God at all, or even if he does not, he would quite certainly prefer a God who has made all men for joy, and de, sires to save them all, to a God who deliberately made some for involuntary sin and immortal misery. But that was the quarrel; and it was the Catholic who held the first and the Protestant who held the second. The modern man not only does not share, he does not even understand, the unnatural aversion of the Puritans to all art and beauty in relation to religion. Yet that was the real Protestant protest; . . . On practically every

essential count on which the Reformation actually put Rome in the dock, Rome has since been acquitted by the jury of the whole world.

It is perfectly true that we can find real wrongs, provoking rebellion, in the Roman Church just before the Reformation. What we cannot find is one of those real wrongs that the Reformation reformed.[11]

Chesterton first began thinking about this when he noticed certain discrepancies internal to the Liberal Protestantism of his day. It did strike him as odd that certain critics "were prepared to pay divine honors to a certain person while doubting whether he was divine," or "took off their hats in his churches while denying that he was present on his altars,"[12] yet these were the very critics who accused Catholicism of being afflicted with a "false sentiment." Any charges of sentiments which are disingenuous seem more aptly applied to the protest movement which no longer maintains the original principles of its protest. For example, even at the time when Chesterton was still in the space between traditions, a certain Lord Hugh Cecil struck him as someone who did not fit into Protestantism for the very surprising reason of being too Protestant.

> I was myself still a thousand miles from being a Catholic; but I think it was the perfect and solid Protestantism of Lord Hugh that fully revealed to me that I was no longer a Protestant. He was, and probably still is, the one real Protestant; for his religion is intensely real. From time to time, he startles the world he lives in by a stark and upstanding defence of the common Christian theology and ethics, in which all Protestants once believed. For the Protestant world in England today is a very curious and subtle thing, which it would not become me to criticise; but this may be said of it without offence, that while it is naturally a little disturbed by a Protestant accepting Catholicism, it is far more terribly disturbed by any Protestant who still preserves Protestantism.[13]

In a sense, Chesterton can almost say that he has never met a true Protestant, because scarcely any contemporary believer still believes the original protests.

Any number of Catholic religious practices, banned by the original Protestant impulse, have been readmitted. The reform impulse was a weave of conclusions, all of one cloth, and the whole would threaten to unravel if any single thread was pulled out. The single and central scheme of salvation worked out by Protestantism came in two forms. One supposed "that God chose some to receive the benefits of redemption and rejected others even in the act of creating them; the other, that men could accept God but only by accepting this theological scheme of salvation, and that their good works had no effect on the result." Either way, this is the "great doctrine of Faith independent of Works, which was so universally recognised as that chief mark and test of Protestantism." From this starting point followed the ideal of instantaneous individualist acceptance of the Atonement as an act of pure faith, and from this, that there were no degrees of sin, and hence no details of penance, since works were not in question. "That is why they needed no Confessor or Sacrament of Penance; because there was nothing *they* could do to diminish sins either hopeless or already abolished and ignored." The dead were not to be prayed for because they were either already instantly be‑atified by faith alone, or lost for lack of it. And that was why there could be no progress of further enlightenment, i.e., no Purgatory, and "*that* was what was meant by being a Protestant; disapproving of prayers for the dead, dis‑approving of progress after death; disapproving of any religion that relied on good works." It was integral to the weave of the great Protestant religion of Western Europe that prayer for the dead was worse than useless.

> Today, as a national and normal thing, it has utterly vanished. Not one man in ninety really disapproves of praying for the dead. . . . Not one man in ninety is either a Calvinist or an upholder of Faith against Works. Not one man in ninety thinks he will go to hell if he does not instantly accept the theological theory of redemption. . . . Not one man in ninety believes the Bible infallible, as real Protestants believed it infallible. Of all that wonderful system of religious thought, thundered against Rome in so many sermons, argued against Rome in so many pamphlets, thrown out scornfully against Rome in so many Exeter Hall meetings and Parliamen‑tary debates, nothing remains.[14]

Chesterton sees two options for the out‑of‑body reform movement if it is not repositioned in the body of Catholic beliefs. It will continue to exist in one of two modes: either positively or negatively. "If Protestantism is a posi‑tive thing, there is no doubt whatever that it is dead. In so far as it really was a set of special spiritual beliefs it is no longer believed. The genuine Protes‑

tant creed is now hardly held by anybody—least of all by the Protestants."[15] It died because it grew old, and the "Reformation grew old amazingly quickly. It was the Counter-Reformation that grew young."[16] But it is not exactly accurate to say nothing whatsoever remains of this positive thing; what remains is fossilized Catholicism. "A fossil is not a dead animal. . . . The whole point of a fossil is that it is the *form* of an animal or organism, from which all its own animal or organic substance has entirely disappeared; but which has kept its shape, because it has been filled up by some totally different substance by some process of distillation or secretion, so that we might almost say, as in the medieval metaphysics, that its substance has vanished and only its accidents remain. This is perhaps the very nearest figure of speech we can find for the truth about the New Religions, which were started only three or four hundred years ago. They are Fossils."[17]

The other form in which the movement can continue to exist outside the body is as a criticism of Catholicism, negative and parasitical. This form of Protestantism derives its identity by censuring whatever is Catholic for the tautological reason of being Catholic. This Protestant identity is maintained by keeping alive the feud with Rome, but it is a ghostly and depleted existence. "For, after all, what sort of a tradition is this, that tells a different story every day or every decade, and is content so long as all the contradictory tales are told against one man or one institution? What sort of holy cause is it to inherit from our ancestors, that we should go on hating something and being consistent only in hatred; being fickle and false in everything else, even in our reason for hating it?" Chesterton was personally unpersuaded to remain Protestant if no more convincing reason could be adduced than continuing the feud. "It was simply a question of whether I should cling to the Protestant feud. And to my enormous astonishment, I found a large number of my fellow Liberals eager to go on with the Protestant feud, though they no longer held the Protestant faith. . . . [T]o find out that you have been slandering somebody about something, to refuse to apologize, and to make up another more plausible story against him, so that you can carry on the spirit of the slander, seemed to me at the start a rather poor way of behaving."[18]

That the Church has required and has benefited from criticism, Chesterton does not deny; that the Church might undergo yet another vigorous critique by theologian, mystic, or magisterium, he would welcome; so how can Dean Inge's definition of Protestantism as "an attempt to check the tendency to corruption and degradation which attacks every institutional religion" be a sufficient definition to distinguish Protestant from Catholic? By this definition, we should have to also call St. Charles Borromeo, St. Dominic, and St. Francis leading Protestants. Has not Dean Inge noticed that since he thinks all religions, as soon as they are institutionalized, begin the ineluctible process of decay, then the Protestant institution will need reforming by now, too? In that case, "Protestants might possibly appear to purge Protestantism; but so did Catholics appear to purge Catholicism. Plainly this definition is perfectly useless as a *distinction* between Protestantism and Catholicism."[19] Protestantism cannot be defined as the effort to curb an institution's tendency toward corruption if Catholics do the same. And when Catholics do so, they at least apply their medicaments to the body to which they belong, while one must wonder about the value of a therapy which separates itself from the very organism it claims to exist to heal. "Not Nestorius, nor Mahomet, nor Calvin, nor Lenin have cured, nor will cure the real evils of Christendom; for the severed hand does not heal the whole body."[20]

Put another way, Chesterton's apologetic can be construed as a copyright argument for rights to a name. If a monarchist and a republican are discussing what is a good king, and if it happens during the discussion that even the republican begins to agree that a king has some good, then one would say that the republican is becoming less what he was and the monarchist more. Chesterton points out case after case in which the subsequent reforms undergone by the churches of the Reformation have made it less Protestant, not more. "Not one man in a hundred of these people would ever have joined his present communion if he had been born outside it. Not one man in a thousand of them would have invented anything like his church formulas if they had not been laid down for him."[21] Therefore, he concludes, those who continue to maintain anti-Catholic positions do so more out of spite than conviction. Perhaps it's all in a name; but a name is everything when identifying consistent positions. "Protestantism is now only a name; but it is a name that can be used to cover any or every 'ism' except Catholicism. It is now a vessel or receptacle into which can be poured all the thousand things that for a thousand reasons react against

Rome; but it can only be full of these things because it is now hollow; because it is itself empty."[22] Of positive Protestantism, only a fossil remains. Of negative Protestantism, only anti-Catholicism remains.

Chesterton thinks Catholicism's obituary has been written prematurely on more than one occasion in European history. The Catholic Church resurrects with regularity because it is not merely an old thing which survives, it is a living thing which thrives. Like Merlin living life backward, Catholicism becomes more vigorous as it ages because doctrine embodied in authority quickens life and the imagination. The thought amuses Chesterton. As his mind surveys the expansive scope of Church history, he can sympathetically juxtapose an ancient pagan's fear of this new religion to a modern Protestant's fear of this even newer religion, for there was in fact a kind of fear of Catholicism as a corrupting agent during Chesterton's day. "The worthy merchant of the middle class, the worthy farmer of the Middle West, when he sends his son to college, does now feel a faint alarm lest the boy should fall among thieves, in the sense of Communists; but he has the same sort of fear lest he should fall among Catholics." However, the very fact that the risk of becoming Catholic can cause an anxious night for a pitiable parent indicates that Catholicism is still a viable option, something capable of living and germinating under favorable circumstances, while other heretical movements are not.

> Now [the merchant] has no fear lest [his children] should fall among Calvinists. He has no fear that his children will become seventeenth-century supralapsarians, however much he may dislike that doctrine. He is not even particularly troubled by the possibility of their adopting the extreme solfidian conceptions once common among some of the more extravagant Methodists. He is not likely to await with terror the telegram that will inform him that his son has become a Fifth-Monarchy man, any more than that he has joined the Albigensians. He does not exactly lie awake at night wondering whether Tom at Oxford has become a Lutheran any more than a Lollard. All these religions he dimly recognises as dead religions; or at any rate as old religions. And he is only frightened of new religions. He is only frightened of those fresh, provocative, paradoxical new notions that fly to the young people's minds. But amongst

these dangerous juvenile attractions he does in practice class the freshness and novelty of Rome.

Now this is rather odd; because Rome is not so very new. . . . When it was originally and really new, no doubt a Roman father often found himself in the same position as the Anglican or Puritan father. He too might find all his children going strange ways and deserting the household gods and the sacred temple of the Capitol. He too might find that one of those children had joined the Christians in their Ecclesia and possibly in their Catacombs. But he would have found that, of his other children, one cared for nothing but the Mysteries of Orpheus, another was inclined to follow Mithras, another was a Neo-Pythagorean who had learned vege-tarianism from the Hindoos, and so on. . . . Only by this time most of the streams have run rather dry. It is seldom necessary for the anxious parent to warn his children against the undesirable society of the Bull of Mithras, or even to wean him from the exclusive contemplation of Orpheus; and though we have vegetarians always with us, they mostly know more about proteids than about Pythagoras. But that other youthful extravagance is still youthful. That other new religion is once again new.[23]

Catholicism does not survive the way Orphism does, in books written by professors of Hellenism, or the way predestination does, in histories of doc-trine written by professors of Calvin. "Whenever Catholicism is driven out as an old thing, it always returns as a new thing. . . . It is not a survival." Imagine, Chesterton suggests, if somewhere someone could be found still practicing the religion of the Druids: it would not look old like the Catholic Church looks ancient, it would look old like an antiquated thing that has survived. "[T]he Druids would look lingering; the Druids would look two thousand years old; in short, the Druids would look like Druids. The Catholic priests do not look in the least like Druids. . . . There has not been a Druidic revolution every two or three hundred years, with young Druids, crowned with fresh mistletoe, dancing in the sun on Salisbury Plain. Stonehenge has not been re-built in every style of architecture from the rude round Norman to the last rococo of the Renaissance."[24] The Catholic tradition is not just old; it is alive.

Only a living tradition can serve people's lives, and so we move to our second point of investigation which considers reasons why Chesterton thought Catholicism to be a more felicitously human religion. Catholicism is the more humane religion, because the more humanitarian. The ground-work for this has already been laid in Chesterton's appreciation of the vul-gar elements of piety. While Protestants seem to treat Christianity as the one great exception to the practice of religion in order to preserve the majesty of God from any encroachment by natural theology, Chesterton treats the Christian cult as the final perfection of the human thirst for the divine. This means that from the very start a different anthropology is at work than that found in Luther or Calvin. There are probably internal differences between these two reformers which insiders would be excited to tell us about, but to an outsider looking in, their disagreement over human depravity looks like two wrestlers circling each other, hunched over, arms groping for a take-down hold, Luther growling, "The divine image stamped on the human soul has been totally destroyed and extirpated, I tell you!" "No," Calvin replies with equal ardor and conviction, "it has only been fearfully disfig-ured, mutilated and deformed." It does not matter which of these two combatants won the contest to abase human nature for the glory of God, be-cause Chesterton contradicts them both.

On the one hand, Chesterton disapproves of the interpretation given by Calvinists to the Catholic idea of the absolute knowledge and power of God "as a rocky irreducible truism so solid that anything could be built on it, however crushing or cruel. They were so confident in their logic, and its one first principle of predestination, that they tortured the intellect and imagination with dreadful deductions about God, that seemed to turn Him into a demon."[25] The result was the reissue of a very old heresy. "The old Manicheans taught that Satan originated the whole work of creation com-monly attributed to God. The new Calvinists taught that God originates the whole work of damnation commonly attributed to Satan. One looked back to the first day when a devil acted like a god, the other looked forward to a last day when a god acted like a devil."[26] We doubt Chesterton was ever seriously tempted by this theology, because the price for it would have been losing the wonder and drama which he had seen in life ever since the man with the golden key introduced him as a child to his fairy godmother, and his fairy godmother introduced him as an adult to the doctrine of con-ditional joy. Life, as Chesterton knows it, is an ascetical drama: every act is a crisis, in the sense of a decision. His friend Bernard Shaw quipped that

"Calvin was quite right in holding that 'if once a man is born it is too late to damn or save him,'" but this sigh of resignation will not escape the Catholic's lips.

> To the Catholic every other daily act is a dramatic dedication to the service of good or evil. To the Calvinist no act can have that sort of solemnity, because the person doing it has been dedicated from eternity, and is merely filling up his time until the crack of doom. The difference is something subtler than plum-puddings or private theatricals; the difference is that to a Christian of my kind this short earthly life is intensely thrilling and precious; to a Calvinist like Mr. Shaw it is confessedly automatic and uninteresting. To me these threescore years and ten are the battle. To the Fabian Calvinist they are only a long procession of the victors in laurels and the vanquished in chains. To me earthly life is the drama; to him it is the epilogue.[27]

On the other hand, Chesterton differs with Luther about human nature, and over a point which results in greater and greater differences between them. The latter believes that sin is due to a bondage of the will, while the former believes that sin proceeds from a will which possesses so much liberty that it must take care not to loose itself from the divine orders. There is always talk of a "New Reformation," but what does this mean? Does it mean to reform the Reformation, or does it mean to repeat the Reformation, as further extending the Reformation? Are we to "look for somebody who will be more Lutheran than Luther?" That would take a good deal of inventiveness, Chesterton ruminates. "I suppose the real doctrine of the great Reformer might possibly be pushed further than he pushed it. It is very difficult to imagine any doctrine that could make man more base, describe human nature as more desperately impotent, blacken the reason and the will of man with a more utterly bottomless and hopeless despair than did the real doctrine of Luther. But it may be that there are depths below the depths and that it is possible to damn the dignity of Adam more completely than Luther damned it. Is that what is meant by a New Reformation?"[28]

Chesterton's cheerful disposition would not fare well in Luther's household. We imagine their increasing incompatibility in this way. Suppose a person received a set of directions to locate a treasure, and suppose these instructions were given something like this: "Forward three paces; six paces left; four paces right"; etc. At first glance, it would appear as though the fortune could be missed in only one of two ways: if the instructions were false (but Luther did not have false instructions, he was a Scripture scholar), or if a person followed the instructions incorrectly (but like the Protestant Prayer Book, Luther made theological moves which had style, had tradition, had religion; he was an apostate Catholic). Then how could Chesterton and Luther come to such different ends? There could be a third way to miss the treasure. It would be if someone was facing the wrong direction at the beginning, before the first step. The romantic of Fleet Street thinks the pessimist of Wittenberg is wrong from the beginning about human nature being depraved, totally. So we picture the two of them standing back to back, like duelists at dawn, one facing the setting sun with a failing hope in a fallen nature, the other facing the rising sun with a surging confidence that our appetite for God is intact though our ascetical discipline is wanting, and as the directions are read aloud, they make their moves in mirror image of each other.

Chesterton depicts the sixteenth-century Protestant reform as a belated revolt by thirteenth-century pessimists. It was Augustinianism raised exponentially. "It was a backwash of the old Augustinian Puritanism against the Aristotelian liberality."[29] The robust Thomism which had baptized Aristotle and harnessed the old philosopher's power for the faith was never completely digested by "the gloomy Christians," the "narrow Augustinians, who would have no science or reason or rational use of secular things." Though this Manichean spirit had been defeated in controversy by Thomas in the thirteenth century, it had accumulated a passion of conviction since then, and "there was an Augustinian monastery in the North where it was near to explosion." The Augustinian pole stressed the idea of "the impotence of man before God, the omniscience of God about the destiny of man, the need for holy fear and the humiliation of intellectual pride," and this pole is a necessary and sometimes noble element in the Christian religion. But it always needs to be balanced by more gentle and generous elements in the faith.

> The difference, like every difference between Catholics, was only a difference of emphasis. . . . But there is emphasis and emphasis; and a time was coming when emphasising the one side was to mean flatly contradicting

the other. . . . For there was one particular monk, in that Augustinian monastery in the German forests, who may be said to have had a single and special talent for emphasis; for emphasis and nothing except emphasis; for emphasis with the quality of an earthquake. He was the son of a slatecutter; a man with a great voice and a certain volume of personality; brooding, sincere, decidedly morbid; and his name was Martin Luther. Neither Augustine nor the Augustinians would have desired to see the day of that vindication of the Augustinian tradition; but in one sense, perhaps, the Augustinian tradition was avenged after all.

It came out of its cell again . . . and cried out with a new and mighty voice for an elemental and emotional religion, and for the destruction of all philosophies. . . . It had one theory that was the destruction of all theories; in fact it had its own theology which was itself the death of theology. Man could say nothing to God, nothing from God, nothing about God, except an almost inarticulate cry for mercy and for the supernatural help of Christ, in a world where all natural things were useless. Reason was useless. Will was useless. Man could not move himself an inch any more than a stone. Man could not trust what was in his head any more than a turnip. Nothing remained in earth or heaven, but the name of Christ lifted in that lonely imprecation; awful as the cry of a beast in pain. . . . So it is with that great Augustinian monk, who avenged all the ascetic Augustinians of the Middle Ages; and whose broad and burly figure has been big enough to block out for four centuries the distant human mountain of Aquinas.[30]

Luther not only blocked subsequent Protestant generations from the warmth of St. Thomas's theology, he also blocked them from the light of natural reason which had been forged in alliance with antiquity. If all natural things are useless for salvation, then what use was that faculty most natural to human beings, reason? The monk at Wittenberg "riveted the mind back to the literal sufficiency of the Hebrew Scriptures," and substituted force of conviction for reason. "Now Luther did begin the modern mood of depending on things not merely intellectual. It is not a question of praise or blame; it matters little whether we say that he was a strong personality, or that he was a bit of a big bully. When he quoted a Scripture text, inserting a word that is not in Scripture, he was content to shout back at all hecklers: 'Tell them that Dr. Martin Luther will have it so!' That is what we now call Personality. A little later it was called Psychology. After that it was called Advertisement or Salesmanship. . . . He destroyed Reason; and substituted Suggestion."[31] In the scholastic kingdom, theology baptized the Philosopher and made peace with reason; in the kingdom of *sola fides*, reason which was not under the rule of faith was called a whore for imperiling revealed grace with works-righteous natural theology. So Siger of Brabant won after all, and the human mind was split into two worlds: a world of faith which hasn't need for reason, and a world of reason which hasn't room for faith. "It was the very life of the Thomist teaching that Reason can be trusted; it was the very life of the Lutheran teaching that Reason is utterly untrustworthy."[32]

Against the backdrop of this sullen distrust of the human capacity for reason and piety and religion, Lutherans find scholasticism and piety and religious cult suspiciously superstitious. If grace is disjunctive to nature, then the less Christian liturgical practices look like pagan religious practices, the more certain we may be of their unadulterated purity; the less Christian theology sounds like pagan philosophy, the more certain we may be that the words are of God and not ourselves. Chesterton, however, is neither startled nor alarmed by affinities between natural religion (humankind's natural appetite for God, organized) and the revealed fulfillment of that appetite. Catholic Christianity confirms what is true, perfects what is fledgling, and keeps at liberty what the Protestant would imprison. "A person with a taste for paradox (if any such shameless creature could exist) might with some plausibility maintain concerning all our expansion since the failure of Luther's frank paganism and its replacement by Calvin's Puritanism, that all this expansion has not been an expansion, but the closing in of a prison, so that less and less beautiful and humane things have been permitted. The Puritans destroyed images; the Rationalists forbade fairy tales. Count Tolstoi practically issued one of his papal encyclicals against music; and I have heard of modern educationists who forbid children to play with tin soldiers."[33] It is factual, not provocative, in Chesterton's opinion, to say that it was the reforming Church which discarded music and icons, vestments and fairy tales, and has since found the wisdom to retract such strident prohibitions. Every step taken back towards humanity is a step towards Catholicism.

Humanity possesses a religious nature. We were earlier reminded by Chesterton that it is a mistake to say that religions of the earth are the same in what they teach and only differ in their rites and forms. He believes the opposite. The religions of the earth differ greatly in what they teach, but they share the common machinery of rites and forms, holy priests and sacred texts, vows of virginity and sworn brotherhoods, venerable altars and hallowed days. Therefore he can state (in fact, slightly overstate) that these features are exactly the features he is proud to possess in Catholicism because they are the most humanitarian features of religion—even if they vex the Protestant.

> As an apologist I am the reverse of apologetic. So far as a man may be proud of a religion rooted in humility, I am very proud of my religion; I am especially proud of those parts of it that are most commonly called superstition. I am proud of being fettered by antiquated dogmas and enslaved by dead creeds (as my journalistic friends repeat with so much pertinacity), for I know very well that it is the heretical creeds that are dead, and that it is only the reasonable dogma that lives long enough to be called antiquated. I am very proud of what people call priestcraft; since even that accidental term of abuse preserves the medieval truth that a priest, like every other man, ought to be a craftsman. I am very proud of what people call Mariolatry; because it introduced into religion in the darkest ages that element of chivalry which is now being belatedly and badly understood in the form of feminism. I am very proud of being orthodox about the mysteries of the Trinity or the Mass; I am proud of believing in the Confessional; I am proud of believing in the Papacy.[34]

Why does Chesterton defend precisely those things which others assail as superstitious? He is going on the counteroffensive against objections typical of spiritualists who are troubled by the worldly quality of the Roman Church. It is our third task to amass some of these aggressive retorts.

An embodied Church is bound to be worldly, because it is practiced by beings who are bound to time and space. Worldliness is a consequence of heaven having descended into the world of matter. "The supreme spiritual power is now operating by the machinery of matter. . . . It blesses even material gifts and keepsakes, as with relics or rosaries. It works through water or oil or bread or wine. Now that sort of mystical materialism may please or displease the Dean [Inge], or anybody else. But I cannot for the life of me understand why the Dean, or anybody else, does not see that the Incarnation is as much a part of that idea as the Mass; and that the Mass is as much a part of that idea as the Incarnation. A Puritan may think it blasphemous that God should become a wafer. A Moslem thinks it blasphemous that God should become a workman in Galilee."[35] Being worldly means being visible; in fact, it requires being visible. Christ did not come to add a philosophy to the queue but to found a Church which would proclaim him in the world; and an embodied, terrestrial, political force which will subsist throughout the historical life of humankind requires visible vestiges. A philosophy does not need a society, but the Church *is* a society. The ancient world had a bellyful of philosophies but it had not one Church. "Very early in its history this thing became visible to the civilisation of antiquity," and from the beginning it appeared as a Church, "with everything that is implied in a Church and much that is disliked in a Church. . . . It had a doctrine; it had a discipline; it had sacraments; it had degrees of initiation; it admitted people and expelled people; it affirmed one dogma with authority and repudiated another with anathemas. If all these things be the marks of Antichrist, the reign of Antichrist followed very rapidly upon Christ."[36] There may be occasions when abuses by the Vicar of Christ need reform, but the way to do it is not to name him the Antichrist and remove the papacy along with the abusive pope.

I am struck by a brief thought, Chestertonian in form. Even the carping by critics about the Catholic Church discloses the Church to be exactly what it claims to be: catholic. Catholicity involves unity, and even persons antipathetic to Catholicism prove its unity by their practice of using a point from anywhere in the history of the Church to censure today's institution. One might expect a Catholic to quote Augustine to endorse or dispute some issue on the current horizon, since the Catholic claims a universality for the Church mystically based in the transcendence of God, but for the critics to cite archaic practices of primitive monasteries, or the papal muscle of Gregory VII, or the Spanish Inquisition to the disfavor of today's institution is a surprise. When the faultfinders use any one of these historical phenomena as a basis for criticizing today's Church they assume the very connection between past and present, and between monk, pope, inquisitor, and philosopher, which the believer professes. So if the modern Catholic suffers guilt by association with the inquisitor and crusader, then the modern Catholic is also blessed by a tie which binds men and women, civilizations, cultures, and strangers across generations, eras, and epochs. What properties connect an American Catholic to a Spanish inquisitor? or a married layperson to the celibate hermit of the desert? or a literary theologian to an illiterate friar? Only that they are all Catholic. That is the only reason why the former are asked to answer for the sins and excesses of the latter. The Reformers selected persons of preceding generations who fit their viewpoint; however, to deny affiliation with past movements because they are disapproved in light of current tendencies denies the very bonds which keep us from becoming ecclesiastical solipsists. We might not now approve of what Uncle Gregory did then, but members of the family are not voted in or out by each succeeding generation. We can only be blessed by the same ties which indict.

When Chesterton defends aspects of the medieval Church, he is not indulging in intellectual regression or nostalgic desire for bygone glory days. But what would we think of someone who looks into the mirror and cannot recognize his or her own countenance? Chesterton's attitude toward our medieval ancestors is another exercise of the capacious catholic character. He does not say that everything in the Middle Ages was good, but he can say that Catholicism can contain everything which was good in the Middle Ages, while the medievalist cannot contain everything which is good in Catholicism.

> Becoming a Catholic broadens the mind. . . . Standing in the centre where all roads meet, a man can look down each of the roads in turn and realise that they come from all points of the heavens. As long as he is still marching along his own road, that is the only road that can be seen, or sometimes even imagined. For instance, many a man who is not yet a Catholic calls himself a Mediaevalist. But a man who is only a Mediaevalist is very much broadened by becoming a Catholic. I am myself a Mediaevalist, in the sense that I think modern life has a great deal to learn

from mediaeval life; that Guilds are a better social system than Capitalism; the friars are far less offensive than philanthropists. But I am a much more reasonable and moderate Mediaevalist than I was when I was only a Mediaevalist. For instance, I felt it necessary to be perpetually pitting Gothic architecture against Greek architecture, because it was necessary to back up Christians against Pagans. But now I am in no such fuss and I know what Coventry Patmore meant when he said calmly that it would have been quite as Catholic to decorate his mantelpiece with the Venus of Milo as with the Virgin. As a Mediaevalist I am still proudest of the Gothic; but as a Catholic I am proud of the Baroque.[37]

It is said by some that the Catholic Church is violent because it has been a source of wars and conflict. Chesterton admits the human habit of fighting for what is precious, and asks us to examine what we find precious enough to fight for. Why is waging war over oil beneath the sand or imaginary boundary lines on a map more excusable than fighting for souls and salvation? Medieval wars and crusades were conducted when the stakes were eternal beatitude; why is an idealistic battle more forgivable than a religious battle? "The mere flinging of the polished pebble of Republican Idealism into the artificial lake of eighteenth century Europe produced a splash that seemed to splash the heavens, and a storm that drowned ten thousand men. What would happen if a star from heaven really fell into the slimy and bloody pool of a hopeless and decaying humanity? Men swept a city with the guillotine, a continent with the saber, because Liberty, Equality, and Fraternity were too precious to be lost. How if Christianity was yet more maddening because it was yet more precious? . . . [Thus] when the learned sceptic says: 'Christianity produced wars and persecutions,' we shall reply: 'Naturally.'"[38]

It is said by some that the Catholic Church is exclusive. This belief "is symbolised in the sort of man who says, 'These ruthless bigots will refuse to bury me in consecrated ground, because I have always refused to be baptised.'" Chesterton wonders why, if such a person "thinks that baptism does not matter, he should think that burial does matter. If it is in no way imprudent for a man to keep himself from a consecrated font, how can it be inhuman for other people to keep him from a consecrated field?" It is as though the revolutionaries insist upon the queen's blessing as they behead her. Why is someone nettled by being excluded from the intimacies of a community he or she thinks is a mockery? "It is surely much nearer to mere superstition to attach importance to what is done to a dead body than to a live baby. I can understand a man thinking both superstitious, or both sacred; but I cannot see why he should grumble that other people do not give him as sanctities what he regards as superstitions."[39] Perhaps what annoys such a person is Catholicism's adamantine (and, to them, antiquated) belief that where something is right, something can be wrong. Chesterton never fully understood what was meant by crediting the Reformation with obtaining a Promethean freedom to different points of view, when the value of possessing different viewpoints was to permit everyone to charge Rome with their favorite reproach. When the reformer boasts that, unlike Rome, Protestants grant many and varied free points of view, "he means that they give freedom to the Universalist to curse Rome for having too much predestination and to the Calvinist to curse her for having too little. He means that in that happy family there is a place for the No Popery man who finds Purgatory too tender-hearted and also for the other No Popery man who finds Hell too harsh. He means that the same description can somehow be made to cover the Tolstoyan who blames priests because they permit patriotism and the Diehard who blames priests because they represent Internationalism."[40]

It is said by some that the Catholic Church is extravagant, wasteful, too mystical. The very Church accused of having too worldly a polity is, on the other hand, denounced for having cathedrals that are too otherworldly. In the letter Chesterton writes to Frances during their engagement where he reckons up the estate he has to offer her, he includes as number six on the list a box of matches, and writes, "Every now and then I strike one of these, because fire is beautiful and burns your fingers. Some people think this a waste of matches: the same people who object to the building of Cathedrals."[41]

It is said by some that the Catholic Church suffers guilt by association with a medieval Church which is guilty of being exactly that: medieval. Very well, let it be as the Renaissance would have it, and let the Middle Ages be called the dark ages, brutal and in need of governance. Why, then, denounce the Church for trying to govern that society?

Seemingly from the dawn of man all nations have had governments; and all nations have been ashamed of them. . . . The religious basis of govern-ment was not so much that people put their trust in princes, as that they did not put their trust in any child of man. It was so with all the ugly in-stitutions which disfigure human history. Torture and slavery were never talked of as good things; they were always talked of as necessary evils. A pagan spoke of one man owning ten slaves just as a modern business man speaks of one merchant sacking ten clerks: "It's very horrible; but how else can society be conducted?" A mediaeval scholastic regarded the possibility of a man being burned to death just as a modern business man regards the possibility of a man being starved to death: "it is a shocking torture; but can you organize a painless world?" It is possible that a future society may find a way of doing without the question by hunger as we have done with-out the question by fire.[42]

Did any interrogator involve himself in the Inquisition with the determined purpose of obfuscating the truth, and making the dark ages darker? Or were these admittedly misdirected methods employed in the hope of finding a way out of the dark? "The creeds and the crusades, the hierarchies and the horrible persecutions were not organized, as is ignorantly said, for the sup-pression of reason. They were organized for the difficult defence of reason. Man, by a blind instinct, knew that if once things were wildly questioned, reason could be questioned first."[43]

It is said by some that the Church opposes reason, and with it, science. But how does it happen that the very Church called an enemy of scholar-ship is also accused of suffering from scholasticism? Perhaps it is due to a general blur about those Middle Ages by a bleary mind which sees every previous century as backward because it is behind us. But by what ana-chronistic reading of history can the Church of any previous century be expected to know what the Church of the succeeding century knows? The proper question would be to examine how the Church judged science in comparison with others in its own century, not in comparison with persons in our own.

Serious historians are abandoning the absurd notion that the medieval Church persecuted all scientists as wizards. It is very nearly the opposite of

the truth. The world sometimes persecuted them as wizards, and sometimes ran after them as wizards; the sort of pursuing that is the reverse of
persecuting. The Church alone regarded them really and solely as scientists. Many an enquiring cleric was charged with mere magic in making
his lenses and mirrors; he was charged by his rude and rustic neighbors;
and would probably have been charged in exactly the same way if they
had been Pagan neighbors or Puritan neighbors or Seventh-Day Adven-
tist neighbors. But even then he stood a better chance when judged by the
Papacy, than if he had been merely lynched by the laity. The Catholic
Pontiff did not denounce Albertus Magnus as a magician. It was the half-
heathen tribes of the north who admired him as a magician.[44]

When the critic impugns the medieval Church for not having lived up to
its ideals, he thereby advocates the very ideals which the Church holds.
"My point is that the world did not tire of the church's ideal, but of its reality. Monasteries were impugned not for the chastity of monks, but for the
unchastity of monks. . . . The Christian ideal has not been tried and found
wanting. It has been found difficult; and left untried."[45]

It is said by some that Catholicism risks blasphemy for honoring Mary.
This is accounted for by the general Protestant confusion of mariology with
mariolatry, and it results in a "mad vigilance that watches for the first
faint signs of the cult of Mary as for the spots of a plague; that apparently
presumes her to be perpetually and secretly encroaching upon the preroga-
tives of Christ."[46] But the fantastic stories told in the Middle Ages of the
Mother of God interceding for the sinner on judgment day do not mean
there is any other way to heaven than by Christ. It is not as if Mary has
an alternate set of keys than Peter (maybe only an additional set) and the
power of the keys has only ever been Christ. Above the binding and loosing power entrusted to the Church on earth stands the Church of heaven,
over which Mary is Queen in communion with the will of Christ. She is
always in communion with the will of Christ, always inseparable from
Christ. Mary does not change Christ's will when she is spiritually filled
by him, as once she was literally filled with him. The human Mother and
the incarnate babe are inseparable ever since she said, "Let it be."

When I was a boy a more Puritan generation objected to a statue upon my
parish church representing the Virgin and Child. After much contro-

versy, they compromised by taking away the Child. One would think that this was even more corrupted with Mariolatry. . . . But the practical difficulty is also a parable. You cannot chip away the statue of a mother from all round that of a new-born child. You cannot suspend the new-born child in mid-air; indeed you cannot really have a statue of a new-born child at all. Similarly, you cannot suspend the idea of a new-born child in the void or think of him without thinking of his mother. You cannot visit the child without visiting the mother. If we are to think of Christ in this aspect at all, the other idea follows as it followed in history. We must either leave Christ out of Christmas, or Christmas out of Christ, or we must admit, if only as we admit it in an old picture, that those holy heads are too near together for the haloes not to mingle and cross.[47]

Finally, it is said by some that Catholicism is detachment from the world, and so Catholics are detached from real life. This position supposes that the most characteristic Catholic act, were one not too cowardly to do it, would be retreating from the world to a cloistered celibacy (monastic or clerical). Chesterton received quite a different impression from his encounter with a certain celibate. In *The Autobiography* he relates the circumstances under which he conceived the Father Brown mysteries, a set of detective stories revolving around a priest whose detective powers are enhanced by a knowledge of human nature accrued over years of hearing confessions. Chesterton was already thinking of a possible storyline, though not yet with a clerical detective, when he shared the plot of vice and crime with Father John O'Connor during a walk. To his surprise, the priest pointed out some incredibilities in the plot line due to a naiveté on Chesterton's part about the perverted practice. "[I]n my own youth I had imagined for myself any amount of iniquity; and it was a curious experience to find that this quiet and pleasant celibate had plumbed those abysses far deeper than I. I had not imagined that the world could hold such horrors."

When the two reached the house, Chesterton watched Father O'Connor chat with some of his other friends, a conversation of a completely different, lighter variety. When it had finished and the priest had left the room, Chesterton overheard one of his peers remark, "All the same, I don't believe his sort of life is the right one. It's all very well to like religious music and so on, when you're all shut up in a sort of cloister and don't know anything about the real evil in the world. But I don't believe that's the right idea. I believe in a fellow coming out into the world, and facing the evil that's in it, and knowing something about the dangers and all that. It's a very beautiful thing to be innocent and ignorant; but I think it's a much finer thing not to be afraid of knowledge." The coincidence of having just been taught something about wickedness by Father O'Connor and then hearing the opinion that the priest's sheltered life made him naive about the ways of the world, in a pitiable sort of way, struck Chesterton as such an irony that he confesses to having nearly laughed out loud. "I was surprised at my own surprise. That the Catholic Church knew more about good than I did was easy to believe. That she knew more about evil than I did seemed incredible."[48] The charge that the priest's knowledge of evil was unrealistic because Catholics are called upon to be innocent and ignorant could be met by the same reply Chesterton gives to his contemporaries who accuse the Victorians of being prudish. The Victorian was accused of trying to preserve innocence by averting his or her eyes from a realistic view of the world. This does not quite have it right. "What disgusted him, and very justly, was not the presence of a clear realism, but the absence of a clear idealism. Strong and genuine religious sentiment has never had any objection to realism; on the contrary, religion was the realistic thing, the brutal thing, the thing that called names."[49]

Chesterton refuses to say with the unrealistic optimist that there is nothing wrong with the world, but he also refuses to say with the unrealistic pessimist that the world is too evil to be enjoyed. The world can be enjoyed ideally, under the rules of conditional joy, and Catholicism preserves the conditions in order to protect the joys.

Epilogue

As Chesterton was not baptized until 1922, it is strictly anachronistic to cite passages from *Orthodoxy*, written in 1908, as if they reveal his Catholicism. But remember Chesterton's own description of sailing off in search of uncharted truth and discovering that when he fancied he stood alone, he was "really in the ridiculous position of being backed up by all Christendom."[1] His brother Cecil observed in the year of *Orthodoxy's* publication that Gilbert was becoming Catholic even if he didn't realize it yet himself, and that Cecil may have been right can be evidenced by considering the kind of Church Gilbert describes there. It is a Church which puzzles its critics for its size, as if the ecclesiastical continent is so large that it stretches round the back side of the globe to simultaneously oppose the eastern shore of some ideologies and the western shore of others.

> As I read and re-read all the non-Christian or anti-Christian accounts of the faith, from Huxley to Bradlaugh, a slow and awful impression grew gradually but graphically upon my mind—the impression that Christianity must be a most extraordinary thing. For not only (as I understood) had Christianity the most flaming vices, but it had apparently a mystical talent for combining vices which seemed inconsistent with each other. It was attacked on all sides and for all contradictory reasons. No sooner had one rationalist demonstrated that it was too far to the east than another demonstrated with equal clearness that it was much too far to the west. No sooner had my indignation died down at its angular and aggressive squareness than I was called up again to notice and condemn its enervating and sensual roundness.[2]

This motif is continued through several pages, as Chesterton enumerates one paradox after another. He was confused by a Church of such size
that it can be attacked by diametrically opposed critics. Christianity was
attacked for being too sad and too happy. "One accusation against Christianity was that it prevented men, by morbid tears and terrors, from seeking
joy and liberty in the bosom of Nature. But another accusation was that it
comforted men with a fictitious providence, and put them in a pink-and-
white nursery. . . . One rationalist had hardly done calling Christianity a
nightmare before another began to call it a fool's paradise. This puzzled me;
the charges seemed inconsistent. Christianity could not at once be the black
mask on a white world, and also the white mask on a black world. The state
of the Christian could not be at once so comfortable that he was a coward to
cling to it, and so uncomfortable that he was a fool to stand it" (290). Then
Christianity was charged with being too mild and too military: it forbade
war and always produced wars. There was something "timid, monkish,
and unmanly about all that is called 'Christian,'" what with turning the
other cheek and all. But when Chesterton read a bit further in the agnostic
manual he found that he was to hate Christianity "not for fighting too little,
but for fighting too much. Christianity, it seemed, was the mother of wars.
Christianity had deluged the world with blood" (291). Then Christianity
was attacked for being an attack on the family, dragging women to the lone-
liness of the cloister away from their children, while from the other side it was
guilty of forcing family and marriage upon us, dooming women to the
drudgery of their homes and children (293). Then it was "reproached with
its naked and hungry habits; with its sackcloth and dried peas. But the next
minute Christianity was being reproached with its pomp and its ritualism;
its shrine of porphyry and its robes of gold. It was abused for being too plain
and for being too coloured" (293).

This was the beginning of Chesterton's discovery that a Christianity
which is truly catholic must claim a comprehensive cosmology. It must
aim for a doctrine so complete and inclusive that any limited view will discover that the Church is more than can fit into that conception's narrow
evaluation. The only remaining question for Chesterton was whether
Christianity is wrong for its expansiveness, or our prejudices wrong for their
exclusiveness?

I wished to be quite fair then, and I wish to be quite fair now; and I did not conclude that the attack on Christianity was all wrong. I only concluded that if Christianity was wrong, it was very wrong indeed. . . . [I]f this mass of mad contradictions really existed, quakerish and bloodthirsty, too gorgeous and too thread/bare, austere, yet pandering preposterously to the lust of the eye, the enemy of women and their foolish refuge, a solemn pessimist and a silly optimist, if this evil existed, then there was in this evil something quite supreme and unique. . . .

And then in a quiet hour a strange thought struck me like a still thunderbolt. There had suddenly come into my mind another explanation. Suppose we heard an unknown man spoken of by many men. Suppose we were puzzled to hear that some men said he was too tall and some too short; some objected to his fatness, some lamented his leanness; some thought him too dark, and some too fair. One explanation (as has been already admitted) would be that he might be an odd shape. But there is another explanation. He might be the right shape. Outrageously tall men might feel him to be short. Very short men might feel him to be tall. Old bucks who are growing stout might consider him insufficiently filled out; old beaux who were growing thin might feel that he expanded beyond the narrow lines of elegance. Perhaps Swedes . . . called him a dark man, while negroes considered him distinctly blonde. Perhaps (in short) this extraordinary thing is really the ordinary thing; at least the normal thing, the centre. Perhaps, after all, it is Christianity that is sane and all its critics that are mad—in various ways.[3]

The Church which would accommodate Chesterton would have to be of sufficient size to integrate human thought with centuries of experience with the Gospel. It would have to be coterminous with the measure of the Crystal Palace itself. Just before his baptism, in a letter to a friend, he wrote "As you may possibly guess, I want to consider my position about the biggest thing of all, whether I am to be inside it or outside it."[4] It was the Church which contained all the world and all its goodness. Chesterton first circumnavigated the world—its joys and beauties and truths—and then he found that the Church not only explained these things, it protected human happiness in the face of all threats. "When a hammer has hit the right nail on the head a hundred times, there comes a time when we think it was not altogether by accident."[5]

Chesterton was not searching for Catholicism when he set out. He admits that if anyone had told him when he first met Father John O'Connor "that ten years afterwards I should be a Mormon Missionary in the Cannibal Islands, I should not have been more surprised than at the suggestion that, fully fifteen years afterwards, I should be making to him my General Confession and being received into the Church that he served."[6] Chesterton had only set out to find the ordinary rules of conditional joy, but at the end he found that his joy was sanctioned by all of Christendom. Does the reader know the optical illusion in which if one looks at black on white one sees a vase, but if one blinks and looks at white on black one sees two faces? Chesterton was sketching a vase to hold the flowers of his philosophy, and when he blinked, he saw the face of a human, ecclesial community (and it had a Roman nose). This Church was capacious enough to hold all of Christendom, and Chesterton, and his entourage. He required a massive Church to provide accommodations for his accompanying trail of guests: Pan and Dionysius, his fairy godmother and her law of conditional joy, the sausage-seller and the greengrocer and all the ritual dancers in the holiday streets, both Thomas and Francis with their dogmatic and jocund personalities, the ordinary family enjoying its sacred hearthfire, magistrates who trace the boundaries of the playground and saints who draw us into the holy games therein.

Chesterton drew another, insignificant, person into his entourage. By way of autobiographical confession I admit that Chesterton was the single most influential person upon my own journey home to the Catholic Church. I hinted earlier that the ultimate criterion for the selection of material would come clear in the epilogue, and this is it. These are the passages, still vivid in my mind, where the Catholic paradoxes were encountered. Chesterton said saints are medicines because they are antidotes, claiming the saint restores the world to sanity by exaggerating what the world neglects. Chesterton was this author's antidote: the one who exaggerated things which had been neglected. It must be apparent to the reader by now that Chesterton is very skilled in exaggeration! He can feel like a walking overstatement to someone who does not need the elixir, but to someone who does, he is an exact dosage. I have not written this for the purpose that it nec-essarily have the same effect on anyone else, only to repay my own debt by honoring a friend.

Chesterton said that there are a thousand doors into Catholicism. On the surface it would not appear that I have entered by a door in any way simi-lar to his. If he did not come to Catholicism from Luther and Laud and pietism, I did. (Perhaps I am his monstrous double; maybe that is why I am charmed by him.) He has been influential because the route to Rome he charted was a passageway from the partial to the replete. "The Church drew me out of Anglicanism, as the very idea of Our Lady drew me long before out of ordinary Protestantism, by being herself, that is, by being beautiful. I was converted by the positive attractions of the things I had not yet got, and not by negative disparagements of such things as I had managed to get already."[7] Chesterton records a personal trek in which he does not surrender any truth he has learned along the way; he does not regret his past. Neither have I reneged on my tradition. I have brought along all good things into the Crystal Palace, without regret and without disparagement, on Chester-ton's word that, due to its size, Catholicism can hold everything good in my tradition and still have room for things which my tradition could not fit. I was drawn by the positive attractions of things I had not yet got.

Chesterton called heresy a truth held so close to the eye that it blocks other truths from sight. It is a truth, right before our noses, that Scripture is the Word of God; but this truth must be integrated with tradition, the mag-isterium, conciliar definitions, and doctrinal development. It is a truth, looking us square in the eye, that we are saved by grace; but this grace must be proportioned to synergy, conversion, meritoriousness, and ascetical spiri-tuality. It is a truth, staring us in the face, that internal piety and faith are crucial lest sacraments be turned into automated mechanisms; but this must be balanced within the whole external structure of a sacramental tradition, a priesthood, the Church's political role, and the historic apostolic succession.

We have mentioned Chesterton's conviction that in its practical re-lation to the soul the Church is a living teacher, not a dead one. It is the reason he gives for accepting the religion and not merely the truths of the re-ligion. "I do it because the thing has not merely told this truth or that truth, but has revealed itself as a truth-telling thing." Cecil may have been right

that when his brother wrote that line in 1908 he was lifting his foot in an-
ticipation of taking the step of conversion, for this is the crucial threshold
over which the convert must pass. One's relationship with a Church
which is a living teacher is quite different than one's relationship with a
Church which is a lifeless catalogue of truths about which one is already
convinced. Not until such a relationship is in place, does one trust the
teacher regarding other matters, even those about which one does not yet see
the point. Chesterton recalls an example. "I had no instinctive kinship
with that enthusiasm for physical virginity, which has certainly been a note
of historic Christianity. . . . It takes all kinds to make a church; she does not
ask me to be celibate. But the fact that I have no appreciation of the celibates, I accept like the fact that I have no ear for music. . . . Celibacy is one
flower in my father's garden, of which I have not yet been told the sweet
or terrible name. But I may be told it any day."[8]

One could try to mimic the garden and replant the flowers inoppor-
tunely pulled out, but if two persons are discussing the value of something
there is a certain honor in calling it by the right name. If a Protestant and a
Catholic are discussing what is a good tradition, and if it happens during
the discussion that they begin to agree that there is some good to having the
whole tradition, then in that agreement one conversation partner is becoming less of what he was, the other more. This was Chesterton's reason for
not finally simply remaining a high-church Protestant, though he is shy of
saying so.

> I am shy of giving one of my deepest reasons because it is hard to put it
> without offence, and I am sure it is the wrong method to offend the waver-
> ing Anglo-Catholic. But I believe one of my strongest motives was mixed
> up with the idea of honour. I feel there is something mean about not
> making complete confession and restitution after a historic error and slan-
> der. It is not the same thing to withdraw the charges against Rome one by
> one, or restore the traditions to Canterbury one by one. Suppose a young
> prig refuses to live with his father or his friend or his wife, because wine is
> drunk in the house or there are Greek statues in the hall. Suppose he goes
> off on his own and develops broader ideas. On the day he drinks his first
> glass of wine, I think it is essential to his honour that he should go back to

his father or his friend and say, "You are right and I was wrong, and we will drink wine together." It is not consonant with his honour that he should set up a house of his own with wine and statues and every parallel particular, and still treat the other as if he were in the wrong. That is mean because it is making the best of both; it is combining the advantages of being right with the advantages of having been wrong. Any analogy is imperfect; but I think you see what I mean.[9]

On the day the author of this book drank his first glass of wine, and saw a liturgical theology of the Mass (including its sacrificial dimensions), and the synergistic relationship between grace and works, and divine love as the key to liturgical asceticism, and the relationship between ordained priesthood and baptismal priesthood, and the importance of ritual, and the purpose of monasticism, and the Queen of Heaven, and the name of a hundred other flowers in the garden, on that day it seemed that he should stop work on his separate abode, with its parallel statutes and liturgies, and set sail for home on Chesterton's yacht. The shore where we landed was the last place either of us had anticipated, and more delightful than either of us could have imagined.

Throughout this work I have presented Chesterton as too doctrinal to be appreciated by the secular relativist, and too charmed by the world to be understood by the doctrinaire cynic of secular life. He presents a stable, developing Catholicism which survives because it is alive and can grow, alongside a firm, rooted Catholicism which survives because it does not move with the moods. When I was a child, my father planted a tree in the backyard and I had what seemed then the very clever idea of pounding a board into that tree each year as it grew taller so that when it was fully grown there would be a ladder to the top. My arboreal miscalculation, of course, is that trees don't grow out of the ground; they grow from the top. If a board is nailed three feet above the ground, it will remain three feet above the ground, yet the tree will continue to grow taller because it grows out the tips of the branches. Now, on the one hand, there are some who seem to think that doc⁄trine can be modified like a step can be moved. But this is not true: neither the Nicene doctrine at the three⁄foot mark, nor the Tridentine board at fif⁄teen feet, nor the most recent step taken by Vatican II, can be moved at our discretion. Chesterton would deter us from reinventing the Church every generation (in our own image, no less) because the tree will never grow if its roots are disturbed by being replanted in every age's new ideology. On the other hand, there are some who seem to think that Catholicism is a sixteen-foot stump, and would stubbornly prune back any sprouts of new growth. This has not been my experience of Chesterton, either.

Chesterton finds that the Petrine Crystal Palace includes everything; or, if it does not yet, it is able to. If one does not see this, then one may have confused the Church with a mood, or an ideal, or a devotion. Catholicism can indeed house many pious moods, it has an array of good ideals, and some deeply religious and salutary devotions dwell there, but the Catholic Church is not identical with any one of these. It is more than the sum of its parts. The Church is a living thing, and as such it can develop and reform itself. Of course, it is one thing to reform and another to re-form. It is one thing for liturgy and dogma to develop as they are traditioned from one generation to the next; it is quite another thing for a generation to repudiate its inherited liturgy and doctrine and piety in order to re-form it according to the reigning mood. And it is yet another thing, also not quite reform, to simply reestablish the past again out of a nostalgic retroversion.

Catholicism does not develop by opposing but by exceeding. The first Catholic reaction to any heresy is to oppose the error, that is true; but this is not the final Catholic reaction to heresy. The question must first be engaged, and during that phase Catholicism may have to speak to the question at hand in the only categories available at the time: the heretic's own jargon. But this is only temporary. The final treatment of heresy will repudiate the suggestion that any truth be ignored. The either/or will be exceeded, and without losing the force of either pole of the paradox. The day will come, it will inexorably come, when Catholicism will not simply oppose what is wrong but preserve what is true in the heresy by planting it within itself. A truth held within Catholicism will be different than a truth held without Catholicism. The Church is sometimes faster and sometimes slower about this, which creates a puzzlement for both those inside and outside Catholicism. To the puzzled insider, the good old days probably always look better. To the puzzled outsider, the Catholic Church probably appears chameleon when it adopts and endorses practices which in an earlier century it had stubbornly insisted on inspecting first. But both miss the fact that the capacious Catholic paradox refuses reduction.

Chesterton has revealed for us a twofold pattern of resistance to reduction, and once we have grasped this pattern we can close, for it is what distinguishes Chesterton's greater approach from two attenuating approaches. The first lessens by reducing in number, and the second by reduction of force. The first was Protestant; the second was pagan.

The tendency to reduce by demanding a choice was a tendency the Protestants suffered. They insisted that a choice be made between positions which only together construct the paradox. As Rome and Luther severed ties, the Wittenberg cutler sharpened and honed his doctrines to a cutting edge: it is what makes him so incisive on some points, able to cut through the balderdash, get to the meat of things and pare down excesses, as a reformer should. But incisions can be divisive, and Luther's effect on classic Catholic combinations was decisively so. He cleaved law and gospel, church and state, scripture and tradition, faith and works, God's work and human cooperation, lay and monk, lay and cleric, revelation and intellection. Now, a reformer of any given century might be persuaded by circumstantial contingencies that a certain side of the paradox needs more emphasis, but it would be a mistake to preclude in advance other configurations of the truth on the basis of that reformer's mood. The Catholic Church is broadminded because it is accumulative; because it keeps many choices in its treasury; because it has sustained the mind of its ancestors and does not disregard their voice. The Church today is not confined to merely repeating yesterday's choices—I do not believe Chesterton is advocating that—but we can learn from our forebears, and the first thing we can learn is that our mood is only the mood of the moment and should not be set against the mind. Tradition is the democracy of the dead. Proportioning one truth to another is a greater accomplishment than displacing one mood by another. "It is constantly assured, especially in our Tolstoyan tendencies, that when the lion lies down with the lamb the lion becomes lamb-like. But that is brutal annexation and imperialism on the part of the lamb. That is simply the lamb absorbing the lion instead of the lion eating the lamb. The real problem is—Can the lion lie down with the lamb and still retain his royal ferocity? That is the problem the Church attempted; that is the miracle she achieved."[10] The miracle is making truths like faith and revelation lie down with truths like works and reason. When Chesterton said we need a Church which is right when we are wrong, he meant we need a Church which preserves the larger mind, and can speak the wisdom of past ages to a particular age because the Catholic sum is larger than any individual's perspective. The acknowledgment of this has, in the past, been called "docility."

The tendency to reduce by amalgamation was the tendency suffered by the pagan. This approach to paradox tried to coordinate the two extremes by finding a golden mean between them, like pink is between red and white. In the first case, Catholicism was unwilling to fractionate truth and force a choice; in this second case, Catholicism is unwilling to add two truths together and divide them into a common denominator. "It is true that the historic Church has at once emphasised celibacy and emphasised the family; has at once (if one may put it so) been fiercely for having children and fiercely for not having children. It has kept them side by side like two strong colours, red and white, like the red and white upon the shield of St. George. It has always had a healthy hatred of pink."[11] Catholic para-dox is not the same as compromise, or finding the golden mean, or being so vague as to be incontestible, or finding the lowest common denominator, or balancing, as paganism wished to do.

> Paganism declared that virtue was in a balance; Christianity declared it was in a conflict; the collision of two passions apparently opposite. Of course they were not really inconsistent; but they were such that it was hard to hold simultaneously. . . . Christianity got over the difficulty of combining furious opposites, by keeping them both, and keeping them both furious. . . . Christianity separated the two ideas and then exagger-ated them both. In one way Man was to be haughtier than he had ever been before; in another way he was to be humbler than he had ever been before. . . . We must be much more angry with theft than before, and yet much kinder to thieves than before. There was room for wrath and love to run wild. And the more I considered Christianity, the more I found that while it had established a rule and order, the chief aim of that order was to give room for good things to run wild.[12]

Catholicism simultaneously affirms pure white celibacy and red-blooded marriages. It does not keep order for the sake of discouraging movement, but it does mark the terms so that when wrath and love run in the extreme, they do not run beyond the rule of God.

The first approach is inadequate to life's complexity because it forces a choice, even if it is a choice between two truths; the second approach is inadequate to life's mystery because it neutralizes a terrible truth by diluting it, even if the countervail used is a correlative truth. The approach which Chesterton outlines for us not only keeps both truths, it keeps both truths at full strength. To be useful to the Church, truths must be catholic and ultimate. No deletion and no dilution. If Chesterton's Catholicism is well-sized, it is because it withstands the diminutional effect of reducing either the number of truths, or the force and fury of the promise of God.

Notes

For the sake of ease and continuity, all quotations unless otherwise noted have been coordinated to refer to the *Collected Works of Chesterton* being published by Ignatius Press, San Francisco. Following are the volumes in which the various titles appear. The year of original publication is given in parentheses.

Volume 1

    Heretics, pp. 39–207 (1905)
    Orthodoxy, pp. 211–366 (1908)
    The Blatchford Controversies, pp. 369–95 (1904)

Volume 2

    St. Francis of Assisi, pp.25–133 (1923)
    The Everlasting Man, pp. 143–407 (1925)
    St. Thomas Aquinas, pp. 419–551 (1933)

Volume 3

    Where All Roads Lead, pp. 27–58 (1922)
    The Catholic Church and Conversion, pp. 61–124 (1927)
    Why I Am a Catholic, pp. 127–32 (1926)
    The Thing: Why I Am a Catholic, pp. 135–335 (1929)
    The Well and the Shallows, pp. 339–533 (1935)

Volume 4

    What's Wrong with the World, pp. 35–224 (1910)
    The Superstition of Divorce, pp. 229–90 (1920)
    Eugenics and Other Evils, pp. 293–418 (1922)

Volume 16

    The Autobiography of G. K. Chesterton (1936)

1. THE AMPLITUDE OF MR. CHESTERTON

1. *The Autobiography of G. K. Chesterton,* p. 85.
2. Ibid., p. 187.
3. Maisie Ward, *Gilbert Keith Chesterton* (New York: Sheed & Ward, 1943), pp. 205–6, quoting Belloc's "On the Place of Gilbert Chesterton in English Letters."
4. *The Catholic Church and Conversion,* p. 106.
5. As cited in Ward, *Chesterton,* pp. 155–56.
6. *The Autobiography of G. K. Chesterton,* pp. 172–73.
7. Ibid., p. 21.
8. Ward, *Chesterton,* p. 8. A sister died very young.
9. *The Autobiography of G. K. Chesterton,* p. 48.
10. Ibid., p. 38.
11. Ibid., p. 36.
12. Ward, *Chesterton,* pp. 25–26.
13. *The Autobiography of G. K. Chesterton,* p. 177.
14. Introduction to vol. 27 of the Collected Works, p. 19.
15. Ward, *Chesterton,* pp. 258–59.
16. *Gilbert Keith Chesterton: A Criticism* (New York: John Lane, 1908), p. 99.
17. John O'Connor, *Father Brown on Chesterton* (London: Frederick Muller, 1937) pp. 85–86.
18. *The Autobiography of G. K. Chesterton,* p. 170. Cecil quips that his brother underwent a complete transformation of his views in regard to the existence of evil. "The cause of G.K.C.'s return to a dogmatic faith was not, as has been the case with others, his discovery of the need for a personal God. In that he had always believed. . . . His epoch-making discovery was his discovery of the need for a personal Devil." *Gilbert Keith Chesterton: A Criticism,* p. 104.
19. *The Well and the Shallows,* p. 353.
20. *Heretics,* p. 39.
21. *Orthodoxy,* p. 213.
22. *What's Wrong with the World,* p. 153.
23. *The Autobiography of G. K. Chesterton,* pp. 164–65. By one account, Chesterton apparently amused himself as well. He used to write his articles in a Fleet Street café and "One day . . . the headwaiter approached Masterman. 'Your friend,' he whispered, admiringly, 'he very clever man. He sit and laugh. And then he write. And then he laugh at what he write.'" Ward, *Chesterton,* p. 157.
24. Ward, *Chesterton,* p. 497.
25. *The Autobiography of G. K. Chesterton,* p. 51.
26. Ward, *Chesterton,* pp. 60, 61.
27. *The Autobiography of G. K. Chesterton,* pp. 214–15.
28. *The Thing: Why I Am a Catholic,* p. 135.

29. *The Well and the Shallows,* pp. 340–41.

30. Ward, *Chesterton,* p. 307.

31. Ibid., pp. 189–90, quoting GKC on Dickens.

32. Ibid., p. 155. She elaborates further at another point. "This is very important to the understanding of Chesterton. With him, profound gravity and exuberant fooling were always intermingled and some of his deepest thoughts are conveyed by a pun. He always claimed to be intensely serious while hating to be solemn and it was a mixture apt to be misunderstood. If gravity and humor are the two lobes of the average man's brain, the average man does not bring them into play simultaneously to anything like the extent that Chesterton did" (pp. 176–77).

33. *The Thing: Why I Am a Catholic,* p. 132.

34. Ibid., p. 127.

35. *The Catholic Church and Conversion,* p. 72.

36. *The Well and the Shallows,* "St. Thomas More," p. 505.

37. *St. Francis of Assisi,* pp. 127–28, 130. Emphasis added.

38. *The Thing: Why I Am a Catholic,* "Why I Am a Catholic," p. 190.

39. Ibid., p. 132.

40. *The Thing: Why I Am a Catholic,* "The Idols of Scotland," p. 317. The passage concludes, "That is what happened to the Calvinistic Scotsman. . . . The Calvinist was a Catholic whose imagination had been in some way caught and overpowered by the one isolated theological truth of the power and knowledge of God; and he offered to it human sacrifice, not only of every human sentiment, but of every other divine quality. Something in that bare idea of all-seeing, all-searching and pitiless power intoxicated and exalted certain men for a certain period. . . . The Scots can look proudly back on their Calvinism. But they cannot look proudly forward to Calvinism. They really know, as well as anybody else, that this isolated religious idea can no longer be kept separate from all the other religious ideas to which it belongs."

41. *The Well and the Shallows,* "A Century of Emancipation," pp. 472–73.

42. "It must be remembered that the modern world has done deep treason to the eternal intellect by believing in the swing of the pendulum. A man must be dead before he swings. It has substituted an idea of fatalistic alternation for the mediaeval freedom of the soul seeking truth. All modern thinkers are reactionaries; for their thought is always a reaction from what went before. When you meet a modern man he is always coming from a place, not going to it. . . . Because a narrow Protestant sect called Materialists declared for a short time that there was no soul, another narrow Protestant sect called Christian Science is now maintaining that there is no body." *What's Wrong with the World,* p. 142.

43. *Where All Roads Lead,* pp. 47, 49. And again, "The Christian Scientist can go on monotonously repeating his one idea and remain a Christian Scientist. But if he ever really goes on to any other ideas, he will be so much the nearer to being a Catholic." *The Catholic Church and Conversion,* p. 105.

44. *Where All Roads Lead,* p. 41.

45. *The Thing: Why I Am a Catholic,* "Is Humanism a Religion?" p. 152.

46. The main exception being Maisie Ward's biography for its personal remarks and unpublished letters.

47. *The Thing: Why I Am a Catholic,* p. 129.

48. *Orthodoxy,* pp. 211, 213.

2. THE FAIRY GODMOTHER PHILOSOPHY

1. "For this reason (we may call it the fairy godmother philosophy) I never could join the young men of my time in feeling what they called the general sentiment of revolt. I should have resisted, let us hope, any rules that were evil. . . . But I did not feel disposed to resist any rule merely because it was mysterious." *Orthodoxy,* p. 260.

2. *The Autobiography of G. K. Chesterton,* p. 97.

3. *Orthodoxy,* p. 212.

4. *The Catholic Church and Conversion,* p. 108.

5. *The Thing: Why I Am a Catholic,* "Is Humanism a Religion?" pp. 149–50. That it was difficult for Chesterton to part with Whitman was once literally enacted as well, humorously enough, at an earlier point in his early life. He explains in a letter to Frances, later his wife, that he has in his possession "A copy of Walt Whitman's poems, once nearly given to Salter, but quite forgotten. It has his name in it still with an affectionate inscription from his sincere friend Gilbert Chesterton. I wonder if he will ever have it." Ward, *Chesterton,* p. 94.

6. *The Autobiography of G. K. Chesterton,* p. 325.

7. He uses an inventory as the basis of a love letter to his fiancée, Frances. "I am looking over the sea and endeavouring to reckon up the estate I have to offer you. As far as I can make out my equipment for starting on such a journey to fairyland consists of the following items." He mentions such apparatus as a Straw Hat, a Walking Stick, the copy of Whitman's poems, and a pocket knife—all perfectly inadequate supplies, of course. The knife, for example, has an element for taking stones out of a horse's hoof. "What a beautiful sensation of security it gives one to reflect that if one should ever have enough money to buy a horse and should happen to buy one and the horse should happen to have a stone in his hoof—that one is ready; one stands prepared, with a de-fiant smile!" But precious nonetheless. Also in his estate is a box of matches. "Every now and then I strike one of these, because fire is beautiful and burns your fingers. Some people think this a waste of matches: the same people who object to the building of Cathedrals." Ward, *Chesterton,* p. 95.

8. *Orthodoxy,* pp. 267–68.

9. From the *Notebooks,* cited in Ward, *Chesterton,* p. 62. One other example:

You say grace before meals
   All right.
But I say grace before the play and the opera,
And grace before the concert and pantomime,
And grace before I open a book,
And grace before sketching, painting,
Swimming, fencing, boxing, walking, playing, dancing;
And grace before I dip the pen in the ink.

10. Ward recollects a friend noticing how Gilbert used to make a mysterious sign in the air as he lit his cigar. That sign, she says, was the sign of the cross. "He saw the Cross signed by God on the trees as their branches spread to right and left: he saw it signed by man as he shaped a paling or a door post. The habit grew upon him of making it constantly: in the air with his match, as he lit his cigar, over a cup of coffee. As he entered a room he would make on the door the sign of our Redemption." Ibid., p. 649.

11. Ibid., pp. 108–9.

12. "What was wonderful about childhood is that anything in it was a wonder. It was not merely a world full of miracles; it was a miraculous world. What gives me this shock is almost anything I really recall; not the things I should think most worth recalling." *The Autobiography of G. K. Chesterton*, p. 45.

13. *St. Thomas Aquinas*, p. 529.

14. *The Autobiography of G. K. Chesterton*, pp. 39 and 55.

15. "To the child the tree and the lamp-post are as natural and as artificial as each other; or rather, neither of them are natural but both supernatural. For both are splen-did and unexplained. The flower with which God crowns the one, and the flame with which Sam the lamplighter crowns the other, are equally of the gold of fairy-tales." *Heretics*, "On Sandals and Simplicity," p. 112.

16. *Orthodoxy*, p. 257.

17. *Heretics*, "Paganism & Mr. Lowes Dickinson," p. 129.

18. *The Thing: Why I Am a Catholic*, "Obstinate Orthodoxy," p. 176.

19. *Heretics*, "Paganism and Mr. Lowes Dickinson," p. 129.

20. *Orthodoxy*, p. 263.

21. *The Autobiography of G. K. Chesterton*, p. 95.

22. From an essay quoted in Ward, *Chesterton*, p. 80.

23. *Orthodoxy*, p. 326. The Greek Orthodox liturgy is said to consist of two movements: anabatic, which is the worshipper's ascent into the heavenly realm, and catabatic, which is the Spirit's descent. The suffix '-batic' means to go: to go up, to go down. We imagine Chesterton amused at the thought of combining the suffix addi-tionally with the prefix 'acro-' meaning aloft. The Holy Spirit makes liturgical acrobats out of humble souls, tumbling, twirling, rolling with the angels above the altar.

24. *Orthodoxy,* pp. 283–84.

25. *The Everlasting Man,* p. 285.

26. *Orthodoxy,* p. 278.

27. Ibid., p. 258.

28. *Heretics,* "Mr. Bernard Shaw," pp. 68–69.

29. *The Autobiography of G. K. Chesterton,* p. 325.

30. "Man has always been looking for that home. . . . But in the bleak and blind⁄ing hail of skepticism to which he has been now so long subjected, he has begun for the first time to be chilled, not merely in his hopes, but in his desires. For the first time in his⁄tory he begins really to doubt the object of his wanderings on the earth. He has always lost his way; but now he has lost his address." *What's Wrong with the World,* p. 77.

31. *Orthodoxy,* pp. 283–84.

32. "I began to examine more exactly the general Christian theology which many execrated and few examined. I soon found that it did in fact correspond to many of these experiences of life; that even its paradoxes corresponded to the paradoxes of life. Long afterwards Father Waggett once said to me. . . . 'Well, anyhow, it must be obvious to anybody that the doctrine of the Fall is the only *cheerful* view of human life.'" *The Autobiography of G. K. Chesterton,* pp. 170–71.

33. *The Thing: Why I Am a Catholic,* "The Outline of the Fall," pp. 311–12.

34. *The Blatchford Controversies,* p. 385.

35. *Orthodoxy,* p. 271.

36. *St. Francis of Assisi,* p. 76.

37. Ibid., p. 77.

38. *Heretics,* "Mr. Bernard Shaw," p. 69.

39. *St. Francis of Assisi,* p. 73.

40. Ibid., p. 27.

41. Ibid., p. 30.

42. *Gilbert K. Chesterton: A Criticism,* p. 21.

43. *The Autobiography of G. K. Chesterton,* p. 53.

44. *Heretics,* "Mr. H. G. Wells and the Giants," p. 71.

45. *Orthodoxy,* p. 261.

46. Ibid., p. 259.

47. Ibid., p. 261.

48. *St. Thomas Aquinas,* p. 424.

49. *Orthodoxy,* p. 271.

50. Ibid.

51. Ibid.

52. *The Everlasting Man,* pp. 354, 356.

53. *St. Thomas Aquinas,* pp. 482–83. And further on, "There was in Plato a sort of idea that people would be better without their bodies; . . . The ultimate phase of this 'Platonic' philosophy was what inflamed poor D. H. Lawrence into talking nonsense,

and he was probably unaware that the Catholic doctrine of marriage would say much of what he said, without talking nonsense" (p. 487).

54. *What's Wrong with the World,* "The Free Family," p. 69.

55. *The Thing: Why I Am a Catholic,* "The Feasts and the Ascetic," pp. 237–38.

56. *The Well and the Shallows,* "The Ascetic at Large," p. 425.

57. *The Everlasting Man,* p. 357.

58. *The Thing: Why I Am a Catholic,* "The Feasts and the Ascetic," pp. 237–38.

59. *St. Thomas Aquinas,* p. 485.

60. Ibid., p. 484.

61. *The Everlasting Man,* pp. 376–77.

62. *St. Thomas Aquinas,* p. 495.

63. *Orthodoxy,* pp. 303–4.

64. *St. Francis of Assisi,* pp. 72–73.

65. *The Blatchford Controversies,* p. 387.

66. *St. Francis of Assisi,* p. 99.

3. THE ORDINARY LIFE

1. *The Thing: Why I Am a Catholic,* "Obstinate Orthodoxy," p. 169.

2. *The Well and the Shallows,* "Reflections on a Rotten Apple," p. 497. In a criti cism particularly focused on trade which exists for profit instead of trade which exists for human life, he writes, "[P]erhaps the shortest statement of it is in the fable of the man who sold razors, and afterwards explained to an indignant customer, with simple dignity, that he had never said the razors would shave. When asked if razors were not made to shave, he replied that they were made to sell" (p. 495).

3. *The Blatchford Controversies,* p. 373.

4. Ibid., p. 395.

5. *What's Wrong with the World,* "The Superstition of Divorce," p. 288.

6. Ibid., "The Fear of the Past," pp. 57–58.

7. "History is not a toboggan slide, but a road to be reconsidered and even re traced." Ibid., "On Female Suffrage," p. 221.

8. Ibid., "The Insane Necessity," p. 104.

9. *The Well and the Shallows,* "The Higher Nihilism," p. 423.

10. *What's Wrong with the World,* "History of Hudge and Gudge," p. 75.

11. Ibid., "A Last Instance," p. 214.

12. Ibid., "The New Hypocrite," p. 51.

13. *Heretics,* "Mr. Bernard Shaw," p. 70.

14. *What's Wrong with the World,* "The Empire of the Insect," p. 204.

15. Ibid., "The Universal Stick," pp. 110–12.

16. Ibid., "The Emancipation of Domesticity," pp. 118–19.

17. *The Autobiography of G. K. Chesterton,* pp. 42, 48.
18. *Heretics,* "Mr. McCabe and a Divine Frivolity," pp. 164–65.
19. Ibid., "Mr. H. G. Wells & the Giants," p. 81.
20. *What's Wrong with the World,* "Conclusion," pp. 216–18.
21. *Eugenics and Other Evils,* "The Lunatic and the Law," p. 322.
22. *Orthodoxy,* p. 250.
23. *The Thing: Why I Am a Catholic,* "The Drift from Domesticity," p. 160.
24. *What's Wrong with the World,* "The Common Vision," p. 97.
25. *St. Thomas Aquinas,* p. 514.
26. *What's Wrong with the World,* "The Enemies of Property," p. 66.
27. *Eugenics and Other Evils,* "The End of the Household Gods," p. 412.
28. *What's Wrong with the World,* "The Free Family," p. 67.
29. *The Thing: Why I Am a Catholic,* "The Drift from Domesticity," pp. 161–63.
30. *What's Wrong with the World,* "The Wildness of Domesticity," p. 72.
31. *Eugenics and Other Evils,* "The Anarchy from Above," p. 310.
32. *The Thing: Why I Am a Catholic,* "Obstinate Orthodoxy," p. 170.
33. *The Well and the Shallows,* "The Return to Religion," p. 397.
34. *What's Wrong With the World,* "The Free Family," p. 69.
35. *The Superstition of Divorce,* p. 288.
36. *The Everlasting Man,* pp. 186–87.

4. PAN AND PETER

1. Ward, *Chesterton,* pp. 99–100.
2. Unpublished essay, quoted in ibid., p. 81.
3. *The Everlasting Man,* pp. 186–87.
4. *The Blatchford Controversies,* p. 374.
5. *St. Thomas Aquinas,* pp. 432–33.
6. *The Catholic Church and Conversion,* p. 108.
7. *The Everlasting Man,* p. 293.
8. *St. Francis of Assisi,* p. 40.
9. *Heretics,* "Paganism & Mr. Lowes Dickinson," p. 122.
10. *Orthodoxy,* p. 364.
11. *The Well and the Shallows,* "A Century of Emancipation," p. 473.
12. Ibid., "Sex and Property," pp. 501–2.
13. *What's Wrong with the World,* "The Empire of the Insect," p. 207.
14. *The Blatchford Controversies,* p. 385.
15. *St. Francis of Assisi,* p. 38.
16. *The Well and the Shallows,* "A Century of Emancipation," p. 473.
17. *Eugenics and Other Evils,* "The Flying Authority," pp. 333–34.

18. *Heretics,* "Paganism & Mr. Lowes Dickinson," p. 127.

19. *The Everlasting Man,* p. 291.

20. *Heretics,* "Paganism & Mr. Lowes Dickinson," p. 131.

21. *St. Francis of Assisi,* p. 44.

22. Ibid., p. 40.

23. *Orthodoxy,* p. 317.

24. Our modern ecological interests may be more naturally drawn to Francis as an icon of harmony with nature, but it is a one-sided picture if it overlooks humanity's dominion over nature. The tendency to see only one facet of the saint, like one plane of the gemstone, is due to an approach to the saints from outside a theological anthropology, with the result that one might find the personality engaging, but probably for a hastily conceived mistake. What Chesterton says regarding the mistake made about St. Thomas is equally true of the mistake made regarding St. Francis: "They will discover his attraction, and somewhat hastily assume that he was like themselves, because he was attractive." *St. Thomas Aquinas,* p. 431.

25. *St. Francis of Assisi,* p. 85.

26. *St. Thomas Aquinas,* p. 492.

27. Ibid., p. 493.

28. *The Everlasting Man,* p. 313.

29. Ibid., p. 306.

30. *St. Thomas Aquinas,* p. 428.

31. *St. Francis of Assisi,* pp. 70–72.

32. Letter to Maurice Baring in Ward, *Chesterton,* pp. 467–68.

33. *The Well and the Shallows,* "The Church and Agoraphobia," p. 452.

34. "Now a child is the very sign and sacrament of personal freedom. He is a fresh free will added to the wills of the world. . . . He is also a much more beautiful, wonderful, amusing and astonishing thing than any of the stale stories or jingling jazz tunes turned out by the machines. When men no longer feel that he is so, they have lost the appreciation of primary things, and therefore all sense of proportion about the world. People who prefer the mechanical pleasures, to such a miracle, are jaded and enslaved. They are preferring the very dregs of life to the first fountains of life." Ibid., "Babies and Distributism," p. 441.

35. *The Autobiography of G. K. Chesterton,* p. 146.

36. *Heretics,* "On Sandals and Simplicity," p. 111.

37. Ibid., "Christmas & the Esthetes," p. 89.

38. "It is best perhaps to take in illustration some daily custom we have all heard despised as vulgar or trite. Take, for the sake of argument, the custom of talking about the weather. . . . Now there are very deep reasons for talking about the weather, reasons that are delicate as well as deep; they lie in layer upon layer of stratified sagacity. First of all it is a gesture of primeval worship. The sky must be invoked; and to begin everything with the weather is sort of a pagan way of beginning everything with prayer. . . .

Then it is an expression of that elementary idea in politeness—equality. For the very word politeness is only the Greek for citizenship. . . . Arising out of this is the third wholesome strain in the custom; I mean that it begins with the body and with our in-evitable bodily brotherhood. All true friendliness begins with fire and food and drink and the recognition of rain or frost." *What's Wrong with the World*, p. 93.

39. *Eugenics and Other Evils*, "The End of the Household Gods," p. 413.

40. *The Well and the Shallows*, "The Church and Agoraphobia," p. 453.

41. *St. Thomas Aquinas*, p. 465.

42. *The Thing: Why I Am a Catholic*, "A Spiritualist Looks Back," p. 271.

43. *Orthodoxy*, p. 333. Again, elsewhere: "There is a sort of notion in the air everywhere that all the religions are equal because all the religious founders were rivals; that they are all fighting for the same starry crown. It is quite false. The claim to that crown, or anything like that crown, is really so rare as to be unique. Mohamet did not make it any more than Micah or Malachi. Confucius did not make it any more than Plato or Marcus Aurelius. Buddha never said he was Bramah. Zoroaster no more claimed to be Ormuz than to be Ahriman." *The Everlasting Man*, p. 334.

44. *Where All Roads Lead*, p. 52.

45. *Orthodoxy*, pp. 350 and 362.

46. A letter to Frances in Ward, *Chesterton*, pp. 111–12.

47. *What's Wrong with the World*, "The Superstition of Divorce," p. 264.

48. *St. Francis of Assisi*, pp. 128–29.

49. *The Everlasting Man*, p. 243.

50. *St. Thomas Aquinas*, pp. 469, 470, 473.

51. Ibid., p. 489.

52. *The Everlasting Man*, p. 288.

53. *The Catholic Church and Conversion*, p. 94.

54. *The Thing: Why I Am a Catholic*, "Is Humanism a Religion?" p. 147.

55. Ibid., "What We Think About," p. 302.

56. *Heretics*, "Paganism & Mr. Lowes Dickinson," p. 124.

57. *The Everlasting Man*, p. 332.

58. *The Catholic Church and Conversion*, p. 97.

59. *The Everlasting Man*, p. 316.

60. Ibid., p. 303.

5. PRACTICALLY PRACTICING RELIGION

1. *The Autobiography of G. K. Chesterton*, pp. 149–50.

2. *What's Wrong with the World*, "The Universal Stick," pp. 110–12.

3. *Heretics*, "The Fallacy of the Young Nation," p. 174.

4. Ibid., "Science & the Savages," pp. 116–17.

5. Ibid., "The Fallacy of the Young Nation," p.175.

6. Ibid., "Science and the Savages," p. 120.

7. Ibid.

8. *The Everlasting Man*, pp. 165–66.

9. Ibid., p. 181.

10. *Orthodoxy*, p. 349.

11. *Heretics*, "Christmas & the Esthetes," p. 87.

12. Ibid., p. 89.

13. *The Autobiography of G. K. Chesterton*, p. 146.

14. *Heretics*, "Omar and the Sacred Vine," pp. 92, 95.

15. Ibid., "Christmas & the Esthetes," p. 88.

16. *The Autobiography of G. K. Chesterton*, p. 97.

17. *Orthodoxy*, p. 220.

18. Ibid., p. 230.

19. *Heretics*, "Mr. McCabe and a Divine Frivolity," pp. 164–65.

20. Ward, *Chesterton*, p. 290.

21. *The Catholic Church and Conversion*, p. 73.

22. Ibid., p. 72.

23. *The Thing: Why I Am a Catholic*, "A Simple Thought," p. 215.

24. Ibid., p. 217.

25. Ibid.

26. *The Well and the Shallows*, "The Religion of Fossils," p. 359.

27. *The Everlasting Man*, p. 242.

28. *St. Thomas Aquinas*, p. 437.

29. *The Thing: Why I Am a Catholic*, "Inge versus Barnes," p. 295. William Ralph Inge (1860–1954) was dean of St. Paul's, London, from 1911 to 1934. He published works ranging over ethics, mysticism, philosophy, and religion and science. A profound thinker, he was deeply influenced by Plotinus.

30. Ibid., "The Hat and the Halo," p. 249.

6. THE KEY IN THE LOCK

1. *What's Wrong with the World*, p. 43.

2. *Heretics*, "Introductory Remarks on the Importance of Orthodoxy," pp. 45, 46.

3. *What's Wrong with the World*, p. 92.

4. *Orthodoxy*, p. 287.

5. Ibid., p. 282.

6. Ibid., p. 287.

7. "We are Christians and Catholics not because we worship a key, but because we have passed a door; and felt the wind that is the trumpet of liberty blow over the land of the living." *The Everlasting Man,* p. 381.

8. Ibid., p. 346.

9. Ibid., p. 347.

10. *Heretics,* "Concluding Remarks on the Importance of Orthodoxy," p. 196.

11. *Where All Roads Lead,* p. 38.

12. *The Thing: Why I Am a Catholic,* "The Optimist as a Suicide," pp. 307–8.

13. *Where All Roads Lead,* p. 37. "Atheism is, I suppose, the supreme example of a simple faith. The man says there is no God; . . . when he has said it, he has said it; and there seems to be no more to be said. The conversation seems likely to languish."

14. *The Thing: Why I Am a Catholic,* "The Usual Article," p. 181.

15. Ibid.

16. From a letter, in Ward, *Chesterton,* pp. 602–3.

17. *Orthodoxy,* p. 305.

18. *The Catholic Church and Conversion,* p. 105.

19. *Heretics,* "Concluding Remarks on the Importance of Orthodoxy," p. 203.

20. *The Thing: Why I Am a Catholic,* "What We Think About," p. 303.

21. Ward, *Chesterton,* quoting GKC but no reference, p. 449.

22. *Where All Roads Lead,* p. 38.

23. *The Thing: Why I Am a Catholic,* "What We Think About," p. 300.

24. *St. Thomas Aquinas,* p. 427.

25. Ibid., pp. 466–67.

26. *The Thing: Why I Am a Catholic,* p. 129.

27. *Orthodoxy,* p. 350.

28. *The Autobiography of G. K. Chesterton,* p. 170.

29. Ibid., pp. 328–29.

30. *The Well and the Shallows,* "The Prayer-Book Problem," p. 373.

31. *Heretics,* "On the Negative Spirit," p. 51.

32. Ibid., "Introductory Remarks on the Importance of Orthodoxy," p. 39.

33. *The Autobiography of G. K. Chesterton,* pp. 169, 171.

34. *The Thing: Why I Am a Catholic,* p. 256.

35. *St. Thomas Aquinas,* p. 425.

36. Ibid., p. 434.

37. *What's Wrong with the World,* "The Superstition of Divorce," p. 231.

38. *St. Thomas Aquinas,* p. 499.

39. Ibid.

40. Ibid., p. 476.

41. *The Thing: Why I Am a Catholic,* "The Roots of Sanity," p. 278.

42. *What's Wrong with the World,* pp. 48, 49.

43. *St. Thomas Aquinas,* pp. 474–75.

44. *Orthodoxy,* p. 287.

45. *St. Thomas Aquinas,* p. 499.

46. *The Well and the Shadows,* p. 339.

47. *St. Thomas Aquinas,* pp. 471, 472.

48. Ibid., pp. 455–56.

49. *Orthodoxy,* p. 317.

50. *The Blatchford Controversies,* p. 384.

51. *St. Thomas Aquinas,* pp. 525–26.

52. Ibid., p. 460.

53. Ibid., p. 508.

7. ROOM TO RUN WILD

1. *The Thing: Why I Am a Catholic,* "The Drift from Domesticity," p. 157.

2. *Orthodoxy,* p. 300.

3. *The Catholic Church and Conversion,* p. 94.

4. *The Autobiography of G. K. Chesterton,* pp. 109–110. Chesterton takes obvious delight in the bustling energy of children's play, play which we call monotonous because repetitive, and unliberating because not unlimited. "Children who are lucky enough to be left alone in the nursery invent not only whole games, but whole dramas and life-stories of their own; they invent secret languages; they create imaginary families; they laboriously conduct family magazines. This is the sort of creative spirit that we want in the modern world." *The Thing: Why I Am a Catholic,* "The Spirit of Christmas," p. 333.

5. *Orthodoxy,* p. 243.

6. Ibid.

7. *What's Wrong with the World,* p. 65.

8. *Orthodoxy,* p. 237.

9. *The Well and the Shallows,* "The Last Turn," p. 430.

10. Ibid., "The Church and Agoraphobia," p. 452. Also, "Most men would return to the old ways in faith and morals if they could broaden their minds enough to do so." *The Thing: Why I Am a Catholic,* "A Simple Thought," p. 215.

11. *The Well and the Shallows,* "The Church and Agoraphobia," p. 452.

12. *The Catholic Church and Conversion,* p. 94.

13. Ibid., pp. 110–11.

14. *The Well and the Shallows,* "The Last Turn," p. 433.

15. *St. Thomas Aquinas,* pp. 462–63.

16. *The Well and the Shallows,* "The Last Turn," p. 433.

17. Letter to Maurice Baring, in Ward, *Chesterton,* p. 458.

18. *Where All Roads Lead,* p. 29.

19. *The Well and the Shallows,* "The Last Turn," p. 433.
20. *The Everlasting Man,* p. 310.
21. *The Well and the Shallows,* "The Church and Agoraphobia," p. 451.
22. *The Catholic Church and Conversion,* "The World Inside Out," p. 107.
23. *The Autobiography of G. K. Chesterton,* pp. 319–20.
24. *The Catholic Church and Conversion,* "The Real Obstacles," p. 87.
25. *The Well and the Shallows,* "Why Protestants Prohibit," p. 525.
26. *St. Thomas Aquinas,* p. 487.
27. *The Well and the Shallows,* "The Return of Caesar," pp. 511, 512.
28. *St. Thomas Aquinas,* p. 535.
29. Ibid., p. 482.
30. Ibid., p. 483.
31. *The Well and the Shallows,* "Mary and the Convert," p. 462.
32. Ibid., "Levity—or Levitation," p. 409.
33. *The Thing: Why I Am a Catholic,* "What Do They Think?" p. 192.
34. Ibid.
35. Ibid., "What We Think About," p. 299.
36. *The Autobiography of G. K. Chesterton,* p. 154.
37. *The Well and the Shallows,* "The Prayer-Book Problem," p. 373.
38. Ibid., "An Explanation," p. 521.
39. *The Thing: Why I Am a Catholic,* "On Courage and Independence," p. 265.
40. *St. Thomas Aquinas,* pp. 507, 508.
41. *The Catholic Church and Conversion,* p. 106.
42. *Orthodoxy,* p. 347.
43. "Alone of all creeds [Christianity] is convincing where it is not attractive. . . . The unpopular parts of Christianity turn out when examined to be the very props of the people." *Orthodoxy,* p. 362.
44. *St. Francis of Assisi,* p. 106.
45. *The Well and the Shallows,* "A Century of Emancipation," p. 474.
46. *Where All Roads Lead,* p. 39.
47. *The Thing: Why I Am a Catholic,* p. 130.
48. *The Catholic Church and Conversion,* p. 105.
49. *Where All Roads Lead,* p. 40.
50. From an essay in the *Nation,* in Ward, *Chesterton,* p. 196.
51. *Where All Roads Lead,* pp. 42–43.
52. *The Everlasting Man,* p. 399.
53. *What's Wrong with the World,* p. 167.
54. *Orthodoxy,* p. 251.
55. *The Thing: Why I Am a Catholic,* p. 132.
56. *Where All Roads Lead,* p. 34.

57. *The Everlasting Man,* pp. 387, 382, 388.

58. *Orthodoxy,* pp. 359–61.

8. AN OUT-OF-BODY EXPERIENCE

1. *The Thing: Why I Am a Catholic,* p. 131.

2. *The Catholic Church and Conversion,* p. 101. Fenelon was the archbishop of Cambrai in the eighteenth century and championed quietism in France.

3. *The Thing: Why I Am a Catholic,* "The Idols of Scotland," p. 315.

4. Ibid., p. 317.

5. *The Well and the Shallows,* "The Surrender upon Sex," p. 367.

6. Ibid., "The Prayer-Book Problem," p. 373.

7. *The Catholic Church and Conversion,* p. 103.

8. *The Well and the Shallows,* "The Last Turn," p. 432.

9. *Where All Roads Lead,* p. 46.

10. *St. Thomas Aquinas,* p. 549.

11. *The Thing: Why I Am a Catholic,* "Why I Am a Catholic," pp. 185–86.

12. Ibid., "The Hat and the Halo," p. 248.

13. *The Autobiography of G. K. Chesterton,* p. 249. Lord Hugh Cecil was a prominent Conservative politician and High Churchman (1869–1956).

14. *The Well and the Shallows,* "A Century of Emancipation," pp. 468–69.

15. *The Thing: Why I Am a Catholic,* "Why I Am a Catholic," pp. 185–86.

16. *Where All Roads Lead,* p. 33.

17. *The Well and the Shallows,* "The Religion of Fossils," p. 358.

18. *The Thing: Why I Am a Catholic,* "Why I Am a Catholic," pp. 187–88.

19. Ibid., "Protestantism: A Problem Novel," pp. 211–13.

20. Ward, *Chesterton,* p. 618, quoting the final chapter in Chesterton's book on Chaucer.

21. *The Catholic Church and Conversion,* p. 68.

22. *The Well and the Shallows,* "A Century of Emancipation," pp. 468–69.

23. *The Catholic Church and Conversion,* pp. 65–66. Supralapsarianism is a variety of Calvinist predestinarianism. Solfidianism is the doctrine of justification by faith alone, excluding good works. The fifth-monarchy men were Puritan radicals in the seventeenth century who believed Christ would return to establish his reign on earth.

24. *Where All Roads Lead,* pp. 35–36.

25. *The Thing: Why I Am a Catholic,* "Is Humanism a Religion?" pp. 152–53.

26. *St. Thomas Aquinas,* p. 485.

27. *What's Wrong with the World,* p. 153.

28. *The Well and the Shallows,* "The New Luther," pp. 437–38.

29. *St. Thomas Aquinas,* p. 420.
30. Ibid., pp. 547–49.
31. Ibid., p. 550.
32. Ibid., p. 431.
33. *What's Wrong with the World,* p. 168.
34. *The Autobiography of G. K. Chesterton,* p. 85.
35. *The Thing: Why I Am a Catholic,* "The Protestant Superstitions," pp. 258–59.
36. *The Everlasting Man,* p. 349.
37. *The Catholic Church and Conversion,* p. 93.
38. *The Blatchford Controversies,* p. 378.
39. *The Superstition of Divorce,* p. 271.
40. *The Catholic Church and Conversion,* p. 85.
41. Ward, *Chesterton,* p. 95.
42. *What's Wrong with the World,* p. 135.
43. *Orthodoxy,* p. 237.
44. *St. Thomas Aquinas,* p. 455.
45. *What's Wrong with the World,* pp. 60–61.
46. *The Well and the Shallows,* "Mary and the Convert," p. 461.
47. *The Everlasting Man,* p. 303.
48. *The Autobiography of G. K. Chesterton,* pp. 317–19.
49. *Heretics,* "On the Negative Spirit," p. 49.

EPILOGUE

1. *Orthodoxy,* p. 214.
2. Ibid., p. 289.
3. Ibid., pp. 294–95.
4. Ward, *Chesterton,* p. 452.
5. *The Thing: Why I Am a Catholic,* "Why I Am a Catholic," p. 190.
6. *The Autobiography of G. K. Chesterton,* p. 316.
7. *Where All Roads Lead,* p. 39.
8. *Orthodoxy,* pp. 361–62.
9. Letter cited in Ward, *Chesterton,* pp. 457–58.
10. *Orthodoxy,* p. 303.
11. Ibid., pp. 301–2.
12. Ibid., pp. 297–300.

Index